US Education in a World of Migration

Given the protracted, varied, and geographically expansive changes in migration over time, it is difficult to establish an overarching theory that adequately analyzes the school experiences of immigrant youth in the United States. This volume extends the scholarly work on these experiences by exploring how immigrants carve out new identities, construct meanings, and negotiate spaces for themselves within social structures created or mediated by education policy and practice. It highlights immigrants that position themselves within global movements while experiencing the everyday effects of federal, state, and local education policy, a phenomenon referred to as glocal (global-local) or localized global phenomena.

Chapter authors acknowledge and honor the agency that immigrants wield, and combine social theories and qualitative methods to empirically document the ways in which immigrants take active roles in enacting education policy. Surveying immigrants from China, Bangladesh, India, Haiti, Japan, Colombia, and Liberia, this volume offers a broad spectrum of immigrant experiences that problematize policy narratives that narrowly define notions of "immigrant," "citizenship," and "student."

Jill Koyama is Assistant Professor in Educational Policy Studies and Practice at the University of Arizona. Her publications include her 2010 book, *Making Failure Pay: For-Profit Tutoring, High-Stakes Testing, and Public Schools* and articles in *Anthropology and Education Quarterly, British Journal of Sociology of Education, Journal of Education Policy, and Educational Researcher.*

Mathangi Subramanian is a writer, educator, and activist. A former Fulbright Scholar, her work has appeared in academic and mainstream publications including Gender and Education, Current Issues in Comparative Education, The Hindu Sunday Magazine, and the anthology *Click!: The Moment We Knew We Were Feminists.* Her book, *Bullying; The Ultimate Teen Guide*, will be published in 2014.

Routledge Research in Education Policy and Politics

The Routledge Research in Education Policy and Politics series aims to enhance our understanding of key challenges and facilitate on-going academic debate within the influential and growing field of Education Policy and Politics.

Books in the series include:

1 **Teacher Education through Active Engagement**
Raising the professional voice
Edited by Lori Beckett

2 **Health Education**
Critical perspectives
Edited by Katie Fitzpatrick and Richard Tinning

3 **US Education in a World of Migration**
Implications for Policy and Practice
Edited by Jill Koyama and Mathangi Subramanian

US Education in a World of Migration
Implications for Policy and Practice

Edited by Jill Koyama and Mathangi Subramanian

Routledge
Taylor & Francis Group

NEW YORK AND LONDON

First published 2014
by Routledge
711 Third Avenue, New York, NY 10017, USA

and by Routledge
2 Park Square, Milton Park, Abingdon, Oxfordshire OX14 4RN

First issued in paperback 2016

*Routledge is an imprint of the Taylor & Francis Group,
an informa business*

Library of Congress Cataloging-in-Publication Data
US education in a world of migration : implications for policy and practice /
    [16 authors] ; edited by Jill Koyama, Mathangi Subramanian.
        pages cm — (Routledge research in education policy and politics)
    Includes bibliographical references and index.
    1. Immigrants—Education—United States.   2. Education and
globalization—United States.   3. Education and state—United States.
I. Koyama, Jill Peterson, editor of compilation.   II. Subramanian,
Mathangi, 1980– editor of compilation.
    LC3731.U72 2014
    371.8290973—dc23
    2013037521

Typeset in Sabon
by IBT Global.

ISBN 13: 978-1-138-28671-9 (pbk)
ISBN 13: 978-0-415-73429-5 (hbk)

Dedicated to
Bamini Subramanian and Ramiah Subramanian
and
Bluma Melamed and Nachman Melamed
with respect and gratitude for their migration

Contents

Figures

Tables

Acknowledgments

This book would have been impossible without the support of our friends and colleagues. We would like to thank Lesley Bartlett and Ameena Ghaffar-Kucher for connecting us with this opportunity. We greatly appreciate Lauren Verity and Stacy Noto, our tireless editorial team at Routledge, for their flexibility and support. Thanks to the blind reviewers who provided us with invaluable feedback and offered important insights on our initial proposal. Thank you to Ellen Melamed for her thorough and thoughtful copyediting. Most of all, we thank our contributors, whose careful scholarship and intellectual curiosity, as well as dedication, patience, and responsiveness to the editorial and publication processes, have made this an important body of work.

Royalties from this publication will be donated to Journey's End Refugee Services (JERS), an organization committed to providing a variety of consistent and high-quality services and supports to refugees as they enter the US and become community members in Buffalo, New York.

1 Introduction

Locating Immigrants in US Education Contexts

Jill Koyama and Mathangi Subramanian

As they move across borders, blurring established edges and engaging new and unfamiliar contexts, immigrants are repeatedly made, unmade, and remade. Sometimes, and with varying degrees of difficulty, they engineer these changes through their own agency; other times, they are constructed by structures and institutions that have comparatively greater power in the contexts they inhabit. Policies defining categories of citizenship, the purpose of education, and the rights and privileges associated with permanent and impermanent residency circumscribe all of the spaces immigrants inhabit—including the physical, educational, discursive, and symbolic. Yet these borders, intended to impede immigrants, result in innovations as well as constraints, and in creative strategies transnational subjects use to ensure that their voices, bodies, and selves find homes in the margins and beyond.

Tracing, framing, and analyzing the unprecedented, diverse, and varied movement of people—an estimated 214 million people migrated transnationally in 2010 (World Bank 2011)—in what is often described as an era of modernity or globalization, poses particular challenges to existing frameworks that aim to capture the ways in which immigrants strategically navigate overlapping and, at times, incompatible worlds. To understand how immigrants conceptualize and engage with the contexts they inhabit, we must move beyond binaries—such as local/global, micro/macro, and Western/non-Western—and, instead, reveal the hybridities, pluralities, and flexibilities of migration, in which experiences of displacement and difference unfold independently. Yet, as immigrants engage "with the potentialities and possibilities their connected world offers, [t]heir interest is not in the hybridity, resistance or even reappropriation, but rather in creating new connections, new meanings, [and] novel forms of relation" (Moore 2011, 9). In this volume, we frame the experiences of immigrants as part of the creation of new spaces of identification, of belonging, and of global imagination, specifically in educational settings (Chen and Koyama 2012; Dolby and Rizvi 2007; Roy and Ong 2011). We bring together empirical studies that situate immigrants' self-making and lived possibilities, as well as their new imaginations of sociality and novel forms of belonging, in educational spaces within linked global processes. Additionally, the research in this collection troubles common assumptions about the immigrant experience that inherently limits our understanding of educational trajectories: that the end goal of all immigrants is citizenship; that a lack of citizenship is an insurmountable barrier to access; and that large institutions prohibit the formation of spaces for the varying educational needs and desires of immigrant students and their allies.

While increasing attention has been directed to within-state migrations, transnational movements, and regional circulations, including South-South migration (Bartlett and Ghaffar-Kucher 2013), the US remains the primary receiving country for immigrants. An estimated one million immigrants relocate to the US annually, and, according to the US Census Bureau's American Community Survey (2010), forty million Americans or (13% of the US population) are immigrants. Today, nearly a quarter of all school-aged children in the US have at least one immigrant parent (Terrazas and Batalova 2009); 25% of these youth are foreign born (Gibson and Koyama 2011). Immigrants can be found participating throughout the US education system, which extends beyond K–12 contexts to college and adult vocational settings, and includes practitioners as well as students. Unlike earlier generations, many are from non-European nations.

The studies in this volume focus on the experiences of these immigrants as they shape and are shaped by—even if temporarily—US educational spheres, carving out new identities, meanings, and spaces for themselves within existing social structures. As part of the transnational flows of people who find their way to the US, the immigrants introduced in the following chapters actively participate in the production and enactment of American culture, in particular by calling our attention to their schooling experiences (including both teaching and learning), their influences in higher education, and their impact on educational policy in the US.

Our approach focuses less on what Bourdieu (1998) refers to as *habitus* in order to include a greater consideration of *inhabitus*, or the everyday interactions with the places, processes, and policies migrants inhabit and encounter (Varenne and McDermott 1998). In this volume, immigrants not only locate themselves within global movements, but also experience the everyday "stillness" of being in a US context. They affect and are affected by *glocal* (global-local) or localized global phenomena. For us, that explicitly includes education policy. We are interested in exploring how policy both constrains and enables immigrants, as well as how immigrants become local informal policymakers through their everyday appropriation of or sensemaking with respect to their relationships with policy and the contexts within which they interact with policy—that is, the places they inhabit.

We examine the intersections of migration and policy in the US in order to qualitatively document the ways in which policy, as a productive, performed, ongoing practice, includes immigrants in and excludes them from categories, such as "citizen," in American society. Following Anyon

(2005), we define education policy broadly to include those international, federal, state, and regional policies that restrict opportunities, create/perpetuate/maintain societal inequities, and in Anyon's words "create environments that overwhelm the potential of educational policy to create systemic, sustained improvements in the schools" (66). Documenting how immigrants engage with education policy draws attention to the everyday enactment of policy, but also highlights the agency of the immigrants, who often "refuse to know their place" (Clarke 2005, 460). As noted by Shore and Wright (2011): "Policy finds expression through sequences of events; it creates new social and semantic spaces, new sets of relations, new political subjects and new webs of meaning" (1). Policy aims to fragment, manage, order, and control the literal and metaphorical movements of immigrants (Kugelberg 2011; Peró 2007, 2011), and yet we see that its power is far from absolute.

In this volume, the contributors use qualitative methods to examine the multiplicities, complexities, and nuances of immigrants and education across a wide range of spaces, both within educational institutions and on the margins. While some focus on K–12 schooling, the volume is unique in that it includes research that extends through higher education, adult education, and work programs. Recasting the US education system to explicitly include nonformal schooling for children and adults, as well as university settings, the volume moves away from much of the scholarship on immigrants and education in the US that focuses on how youth do or do not become incorporated into formal settings. Rather, it follows the tradition of scholars that recognize that education occurs in far more contexts than classroom settings, and that educational outcomes are determined by more than schooling (Varenne 2007).

No volume on immigration and education is complete without an examination of the multiplicities of citizenship—from the official and institutionalized conceptions of citizenship that are codified in policy to the enacted forms of belonging and participation. Citizenship has become a contested construct, increasingly detached from territories and nation-states, and yet still powerful in its ability to categorize. We resist the temptation here to talk about "global citizens," as discussed by Myers and Zaman (2009), and instead take to heart the precautions these authors articulate, including recognizing that although global citizenship connotes a positive image of engagement across the world, it is too vague, lacks grounding, and overestimates its reach. Instead, we prefer "transnational citizenship," which Myers and Zaman (2009) use to denote the more tangible ways in which immigrants enact forms of citizenship across national boundaries (Fox 2005). In this framing, citizenship focuses on the nuances of border-crossing statuses and recognizes the ongoing political linkages immigrants often maintain to their countries of origin even while establishing connections in their new countries. In this volume, the authors also explicitly and implicitly employ the notion of "cultural citizenship," a term Ong (1996) uses to refer to "the cultural practices and beliefs produced out of negotiating the often ambivalent and contested relations with the state and its hegemonic forms that establish the criteria of belonging within a national population and territory" (738). It is, in her description, a "dual process of self-making and being-made within webs of power," of being simultaneously constructed and able to construct (ibid). The term is useful in analyzing issues faced by immigrants like the ones discussed in this volume, who navigate policies with various degrees of power, and who find innovative ways to situate themselves within this contested environment.

Consequently, the chapters in this volume move away from earlier understandings of migration as a unilateral movement from one context (usually a bounded nation-state) to the US. Instead, they are situated within more recent scholarship that frames the movement of immigrants as circulation and citizenship as flexible. As Sassen (2000) has argued, "international migrations are not autonomous processes" (66). When globalization is taken into consideration, migration is no longer seen as permanent, linear, or exclusively governed by one-sided action by individual states. In the literature on the global knowledge economy, for instance, what was once examined as a "brain drain" is increasingly described as part of a multifaceted movement of academics and knowledges. Similarly, the work on identity and belonging has moved away from duality and even states of being "betwixt and between" to more critical analyses of participating in multiple "scapes" and "spheres" simultaneously. These evolving bodies of literature undergird the themes highlighted in this volume to demonstrate how movement (migration, circulation), even when temporal, encompasses both the trajectory of travel and the participation in a current location. Immigrants are located and interpreted both through historical lenses and through their current social worlds.

In this volume, Carhill-Poza, Chikkatur, Q. Chen, and other contributors demonstrate how policy processes position immigrants within the historical (legislative) dimensions of the US while immigrants simultaneously bring themselves into new configurations and emerging arrangements made possible by their participation in American life. The chapter by Smalls, for example, situates the schooling experiences of transnational African students within the persistent issues of racism in schools, whereas A. Chen's chapter on undocumented immigrants in higher education draws us directly into the current debate surrounding the DREAM Act. So, too, in this volume do we see immigrants challenging and talking back to policy, selectively *appropriating* elements of it into their everyday situations (Sutton and Levinson 2001). Subramanian's chapter demonstrates how immigrant women can deliberately use storytelling—and counterstorytelling, in particular—to challenge their exclusion from policy conversations within limiting institutionalized structures. These immigrants engage in what Koyama and Varenne

(2012) have termed "productive policy play," in which they "selectively follow, negotiate, and appropriate cultural instructions and rules" (157) across diverse and multiple settings of teaching and learning in order to create change.

As the experiences of migration have changed over time, becoming more protracted, varied, and geographically expansive (Waters and Jiménez 2005), the educational experiences of immigrants have also morphed. Because substantial, up-to-date reviews of the scholarship on educational experiences of immigrants in the US are available (e.g., Portés and Rumbaut 2001; Gibson and Koyama 2011), we don't offer another here. Instead, because the contributors to this volume draw from their empirical work to offer new perspectives that challenge former theoretical and empirical assumptions, we move forward by framing migration experiences with "worldly" views—in which theories are not abstractions, but rather "part of the social world, human life, and, of course, the historical moments in which they are located and interpreted" (Said 1983, 4). This framing emerges from a transnational perspective aimed at better understanding global flows.

ORGANIZATION AND FRAMING

In this volume, we seek to understand the ways in which immigrants engage in what Das Gupta (2006) calls space-making, or the process by which transnational migrants make spaces for themselves within, between, and outside of existing policies, practices, assumptions, and expectations. Whereas Das Gupta's (2006) work focuses solely on the work of progressive South Asian American activists in the 2000s, we are concerned with diverse actors who may not have an explicit agenda beyond advocating for their students, their families, or, as is almost always the case, themselves. The chapters in this collection explore how immigrants and their allies construct assumptions about place, mobility, identity, and educational outcomes, and use these to navigate unsuitable spaces and build new, more adequate spaces for their needs.

Following the key principles of Gupta's work, we organize the chapters under three interrelated headings—identity-staking, place-taking, and space-making—but we also find Tsing's (2005) conceptualization of "friction" useful in discussing the contrasts, contestations, and productivity that emerge when immigrants make space or encounter different contexts, forge new connections, and initiate exchanges. To replace the perspective that globalization invariably signifies a clash of cultures, Tsing uses the notion of friction as a metaphor for the diverse, and sometimes abrasively conflicting, social linkages that increasingly make up our global world. Her concept of the "zone of awkward engagement" (x)—in her research, the rainforests of Indonesia—informs our thinking about the educational contexts of education in which immigrants stake identities, take places, and make spaces.

Identity-Staking

Immigrant youth navigate policies, and the systems and institutions that they produce, at the intersection of multiple aspects of their identities. They are constrained and enabled by the policies and constructed and identified by others, and they also rework and negotiate identities. Thus, we situate identity-staking as an ongoing negotiation, a navigation replete with contestations and conflicts, between being constructed and constructing. Scholars such as Chowdhury (2011), Ladson-Billings and Tate (1995), Nagar (2006), Valenzuela (1999), and Yosso (2006) have argued for embracing the concept of intersectionality as a lens for analyzing how immigrants form identities and how the world reads them. Intersectionality recognizes that all of us have multiple aspects of our identities that make us powerful, and other aspects that subject us to oppression within particular constructions and contexts. It is only through acknowledging how race, class, gender, faith, sexuality, age, and immigration status (among other factors) interact that we can fully understand the lives of immigrant youth, educators, and allies in our current system.

While intersectionality has become an increasingly popular lens for scholars, policymakers rarely acknowledge differences within and between populations derived from identities (Chowdhury 2011; Ginwright, Cammarota, and Noguera 2005; Nagar 2006; Stone 2002). Chowdhury (2011) and Nagar (2006), for example, describe how transnational feminist movements in the Global South advocate for policies that address the needs of the elite women who speak for all women without taking into account class status, religion, or caste, patterns that are repeated in the US across differences in race, class, and sexual orientation among women. Likewise, Ginwright, Cammarota, and Noguera (2005) document how young people are excluded from conversations about policies that affect them, and that policymakers ignore race, class, and gender when seeking to address low income among young people of color. In order to create sound policy, policymakers must understand who immigrant youth are, and how their intersecting identities mediate their access to power.

In Chapter 2, Smalls unpacks the racialized experiences of African immigrant youth, demonstrating how schools inadequately address students' experiences of intersectionality, and focusing on race or immigration status without considering the intersection of both. In her examination of cultural belonging in the US, she complicates issues of race and static notions of identity by specifically, and in detail, unpacking the politics of race-making and cultural belonging among African transnational high school students. Smalls disentangles the tensions and contestations between African-born youth and African American students to reveal that their actions are grounded within sociohistorical phenomena and noxious constructions of African personhood. By manipulating the social meaning of communicative practices, the participants resituate and remake themselves on interpersonal, local, regional, national, and global scales. In Smalls's words, they "smash the racial category 'black' to pieces and reconfigure it" (27). Through sociolinguistic analysis, Smalls argues that educational policies must create space for and encourage personal and collective reworkings of race not only to challenge pernicious racial misattributions and inequities, but also to further prevent conflicts between African newcomers and African Americans in US schools.

In Chapter 3, Chikkatur also interrogates race in a K–12 setting, focusing on Asian American students and the model minority myth, and how these racial expectations play out in a school. Drawing on two years of ethnographic research conducted in a large, comprehensive urban US high school, she examines the dominant narrative in which America is situated as the land of educational and economic opportunities. She focuses on the discourse of opportunities among immigrant students, their US-born peers, and their US-born teachers, revealing how the discourse becomes bound to notions of immigrant students' superiority to their American counterparts, especially those who are identified by the teachers as unmotivated. Chikkatur disaggregates the narratives to demonstrate how the teachers rely on stereotypical and homogenous perceptions of immigrants and Asian Americans that do not take into account transnational trends, educational inequities, or cultural frictions. She repositions these notions to illuminate the nuances of race and racism inherent in the narratives. Building on her analysis, she highlights changes that could be made in school policies to disrupt and, eventually, critically unravel such pernicious discourses.

Carhill-Poza, in Chapter 4, examines the linguistic implications of segregation in US high schools. She reveals the ways in which policies designed to support language development instead create boundaries for access to educational opportunities and the development of peer relations critical to identity development and learning English. Although the organization and structure of schools and classrooms institutionally marginalized the participants in her study, some were, as Carhill-Poza's work demonstrates, able to overcome the unintended negative consequences of programmatic groupings and labeling based on students' command of English, as assessed by the school system. Her work suggests a critical need for critiquing and reforming the assumptions about second-language acquisition that undergird current education policy for adolescents.

Muñoz-García's work continues the examination of multiplicity and hybridity in students' identities, and their impact on their education, but shifts the focus to graduate students from Chile and Colombia. In Chapter 5, she discusses how universities restrict students' abilities to reflect on their class status rather than on their country of origin, native language, or ethnicity. She problematizes the discourses about Latin American students that aim to homogenize them and demonstrates how students from the Andes Mountains rework class while abroad in the US. Muñoz-García's work demonstrates that there are spaces within universities where students and educators can come together to examine their privilege, an exercise that is an important step on the path to institutional change.

Q. Chen, in Chapter 6, the last chapter in this section, keeps the investigative lens on those in academe, this time focusing on educators rather than on students. She discusses how professors of Chinese origin carve out spaces for themselves within US universities that allow them to continue to live as flexible citizens, strategically taking advantage of policies that allow them the ability to transcend the restrictions of borders and nationhood. Chen's piece questions identities associated with citizenship, particularly in light of literature that questions static notions of home and belonging (Collier and Ong 2005; Dolby and Rizvi 2007). Despite what is commonly assumed in public discourse—that American citizenship is the ultimate goal for immigrants—the participants in Chen's study use citizenship as a tool rather than as a goal. As privileged immigrants, they are able to be flexible in their citizenship and national identifications.

The chapters in this section elucidate how intersectionality affects the ways in which immigrant students and educators navigate landscapes created by policies and institutions that fail to recognize multiple aspects of individuals' identities. Each critiques the practices codified by institutionalized authority to make sense of them in specific, and often homogenizing, ways. They reveal strategic and innovative ways that immigrants find places for themselves by challenging narrow identity definitions. Intimately linked to identity-staking is the notion of place-taking, to which we now turn.

Place-Taking

Das Gupta (2006) defines place-taking as the practice of restricting, constraining, or eliminating spaces for multiple identities and political activism in the name of authenticity or assimilation. In this vein, some scholars, including Fine (2007) and Valenzuela (1999), document the ways in which mainstream schooling engages in place-taking by devaluing the home cultures of immigrant youth, forcing them to adapt mainstream, white, middle-class values and practices in order to succeed in schools. Likewise, Collier and Ong (2005) and Dolby and Rizvi (2007) analyze how restrictive concepts of nationhood and citizenship inadequately capture the lives and concomitant educational expectations of immigrant young people and adults. But place-taking is not purely assimilationist in nature: in fact, Das Gupta (2006) and Maira (2002) document how some immigrants use the false notion of authenticity and cultural purity to determine what knowledge, skills, and behaviors ought to be acceptable within their own ethnic communities. As a result, in-group norms can play a place-taking role by restricting gender expression, sexuality, and even educational expectations.

When immigrants encounter these place-taking practices, they enter zones of awkward engagement, that is, spaces in which they engage in resistance and, unfortunately, frequently also face the consequences of systematic and institutionalized oppression.

Place-taking practices are not limited to educational institutions. In fact, the authors in this section focus on how a wide range of laws and policies intersects within the classroom. The chapters examine how policies governing citizenship, employment, and national security interlock to obstruct access to education. Taken together, they remind us of Anyon's (2005) claim that to achieve true equity in the education system, we must address oppressions built into multiple systems, not just schools. Further, the authors in this section illustrate how webs of inequitable and repressive policies affect more than just students. In these chapters, parents, teachers, and administrators play pivotal roles in enforcing place-taking policies and practices or are themselves circumscribed by policies designed to restrict their movements, opportunities, and aspirations.

This section begins with several chapters that identify and critically analyze place-taking practices enacted through federal, state, local, and school-level policies. In Chapter 7, the first of this section, Wicks-Asbun and Torres turn our attention beyond high school to issues of access to higher education. They document the ways in which a combination of education and immigration policies restricts the options for undocumented youth who seek to pursue higher education, thereby curbing their aspirations, a pattern that manifests itself as a lack of achievement. They probe socio-spatial perspectives to examine the academic aspirations of Latino students in rural eastern North Carolina who have become part of what can be considered the "new Latino diaspora" (Wortham, Murillo, and Hamann 2002), characterized by immigrants and children of Latinos moving into less-urban areas in the middle and southern states of the US. They offer a theoretical model in which transnational dimensions cut across multiple spheres and demonstrate the interplay at and fluidity of the borders that define these spheres—and influence the youths' academic aspirations and attainment. These spheres, or zones of awkward engagement, if you will, are not equal in their influence. Wicks-Asbun and Torres find that factors in the microsphere and mesosphere, such as parental encouragement, positively influence the aspirations; factors associated with the exosphere and macrosphere—in particular, state and federal policies that limit educational opportunities—have negative influences, and thus create gaps between aspiration and attainment. The lack of access to college scholarships and the failure of the DREAM Act to pass during the time of the study, as well as immigration policies which encourage the detainment and deportation of undocumented immigrants in the community, clearly diminish the youths' long-term educational goals.

Fuentes's study, in the next chapter, provides a complement to the work of Wicks-Asbun and Torres by examining policy and practices in an adult community-based English as a second language (CESL) program that similarly fails to meet the needs of students. In fact, the CESL program's aim of assimilating immigrants into US society creates friction with the adult students' transnational identities and multilingual needs. Framing the experiences of three adult females who are enrolled in a CESL program at a major public university in the rural southeast with the concept of "flexible citizenship," Fuentes discusses what could be gained in an adult ESL program that is attentive to global movements and transnational linkages.

Thomas, in Chapter 9, interrogates how immigration and higher education policies impact the educational opportunities and experiences of another group of immigrant students, Indian students with F-1 visas. She argues that the concurrent marketization and internationalization of higher education and more stringent national security measures dramatically affect the ability of the Indian students to survive economically in a higher education setting. In her ethnographic study, set in a public university in New York, she considers the strains that internationalization places on international programs in the post-9/11 era. She reveals how the Indian students make sense of the social, economic, and legal circumstances attached to their statuses as F-1 students, and also how they are positioned in specific raced and classed ways at the university. Thomas's piece demonstrates the lack of institutional capacity to address the needs of young people whose documentation status severely restricts their rights and ability to advocate for themselves.

Kamara and Monkman, in the final chapter of the section, demonstrate how teachers from abroad are also impacted by international and national policy. They describe how policies designed to attract foreign teachers to fill shortages have inadequately supported immigrant educators, thereby creating a group of professionals who—along with their families—lack immigration status. They bring to the fore the often understudied international labor market of teachers. Qualitatively examining the experiences of teachers from African countries recruited to work in one of the US's largest school districts, they reveal the instability of their employment by detailing their struggles to effectively understand and participate in the US school system, their precarious immigration status, and their hope that being employed as a teacher might enhance the path to US citizenship and economic security. However, the teachers experienced unpredictable circumstances resulting from both federal immigration regulations and district policies.

Taken together, these chapters demonstrate how federal, state, and local education and immigration policy and practice restrict the lives of immigrant students and educators throughout their lives, and point to the need for comprehensive immigration reform and educational policies that truly promote equity. They provide poignant examples of the lives of students and teachers, and their activities, being predetermined by bounded categories and geographical sites established through policies. They also demonstrate the ways in which the established authority and legitimacy of ideas and practices impact the educational experiences of immigrants. Whereas this section focuses on borders, constraints, and contestations, the next section offers examples of immigrant learners and allies actively refusing to accept these place-taking practices.

Space-Making

Despite the fact that place-taking strategies are often enacted by individuals with privilege and power both within and outside ethnic communities, immigrants are adept at carving out spaces for themselves using space-making strategies. Das Gupta (2006) documents how South Asian American political organizing led to greater awareness about issues that place-takers had silenced, including the prevalence of domestic violence and the existence of politically active lesbian, gay, bisexual, transgender, and queer individuals within the South Asian American community. Likewise, as documented in a volume edited by Noguera, Cammarota, and Ginwright (2006), marginalized young people (both immigrants and native-born Americans) have found ways to resist policies that restrict their abilities to access education because of their economic status, aspects of their identities, or their age. Immigrants innovate on the personal and public level, carving out spaces that meet the needs of their flexible citizenship status, mobile lifestyles, and educational and economic goals. In this section, we celebrate and explore both immigrants and their allies, and the ways in which they make spaces for themselves and others like them.

In Chapter 11, a study of Japanese language schools, Doerr and Lee provide our first example of a space-making policy. In their four-year ethnographic study of minority heritage language education, they demonstrate how a federal policy that identifies Japanese as a critical language and the US College Board's subsequent adoption of Japanese as an Advanced Placement subject for high schools encourage middle-school children to continue their participation in a weekend Japanese language school. The authors reveal how this policy has motivated K–12 students to develop and/or maintain fluency in Japanese, thereby preserving ties with their homeland and valuing, rather than degrading, their own bilingual status. Further, in this chapter, Doerr and Lee show how policy can work to create and support spaces of belonging for those who might otherwise be situated as outsiders in educational settings. The authors argue that the changing motivations for continuing to learn Japanese corresponded, in part, to the policy changes that elevated the Japanese language, and thus, by extension, gave it greater value on college applications.

In Chapter 12, Bangura offers an analysis of the ways in which young African women labeled "students with interrupted formal education" (SIFE) engage in early marriage as a strategy for maintaining independence and accessing educational opportunities. She demonstrates how schools devalue or ignore these practices, and how young women engage in them strategically even without support. Tracing the life and school trajectories of adolescent African female immigrants, she reveals schools as negotiated spaces. She investigates the ways in which the young women's decisions to marry while in high school challenge the conventional US understandings of studenthood, complicate perceptions of education as an antidote to female submission, and create challenges for adult staff who may consider early marriage a symptom of an oppressive culture rather than a potentially liberating practice. From a feminist perspective, Bangura details the complexities of compromises that are made by the young women as they negotiate the contentious edges of US and African cultures, in addition to borders that define schooling. She argues that the education policies and school practices, which reflect the larger societal values, do not accommodate or appreciate the African females' refusal to accept either schooling or marriage as a singular path. However, through the stories of the young women, Bangura provides glimpses into the fluidity of the dichotomy, troubling the notion that female immigrants of color from the Global South lack agency in their educational decisions, and that traditional practices such as early marriage can be easily classified as helpful or detrimental to a young woman's ability to thrive.

Subramanian's research, presented in Chapter 13, documents how storytelling is an avenue for young immigrant women to both immediately influence policy and build the skills necessary to continue to be politically effective, all while disrupting norms of increased testing and standardization in schools and after-school programs. Drawing upon data from her larger mixed methods study of South Asian American young women between the ages of eighteen and nineteen, Subramanian demonstrates, through the counterstories crafted by the study participants in a community-based program, that there is more than one entry point for learning and change. These women produce and respond to digital stories that question the dominant narrative and that imagine alternative realities for themselves and their communities. They acquire the skills and social capital that are foundational for engaging in successful advocacy. Their experiences provide several recommendations for reform, including a call to educators to embrace the nationwide adoption of common core standards that focus on nonfiction writing and literacy across content areas as an opportunity to design lessons that encourage young people to tell stories based on personal experience that disrupt dominant narratives, which can in turn be a stepping stone to developing political awareness and advocacy skills.

Looking beyond students in the final chapter of this section, A. Chen documents how a group of administrators at a large public university forged a politically risky alliance to successfully support undocumented youth in their pursuit of higher education. She reminds us that allies can be found even in the most repressive institutions, and that educators are key players in the struggle for educational equity and comprehensive immigration reform. She takes up the concern for undocumented students in higher education by examining the ways in which discrimination grounded in racism and xenophobia infiltrates educational policy and institutional practices. The reluctance of institutions of higher education to support undocumented students as full participants reflects both the sharp boundaries of citizenship and all of the rights awarded to those who have it and denied to those who do not. She argues that such exclusionary regulations in colleges and universities legitimize laws that deny undocumented students financial aid, contribute to xenophobia on campus, and further support broader laws that criminalize associating with undocumented immigrants. In this chapter, Chen documents how one California university interprets and complies with federal and state mandates, and also how in response to the resulting restrictions, a group of allies challenges the mandates by covertly supporting students in innovative ways.

The four chapters in this section provide glimpses into the ways in which immigrants and their allies can work back on, or against, institutional policies and practices to create spaces conducive to their academic, personal, and political growth. They also lead us to question the ways in which educational institutions and policies exclude or marginalize programs and practices that might have an academic-social-political objective, rather than a quantifiable achievement. Finally, the scholarship in this section prompts us to reconsider those spaces of learning not necessarily recognized as venues for schooling as important sites of learning and teaching.

CONCLUDING THOUGHTS

We are in the midst of an era increasingly marked by the extraordinarily rapid movement of people, services, ideas, and material goods—and this movement extends across multiple spheres, including, but not limited to, cultural, economic, and political structures worldwide. The contributors to this volume, of course, are certainly not the first to notice this fluidity, and many scholars (e.g., Fahey and Kenway 2010; Rizvi and Lingard 2009) have discussed the effects of what has been euphemistically referred to as "globalization" on education and education policy. At the extreme, Robinson (2010) argues that "mobility is being mobilized (and fetishized) by policymakers . . . as an essential experience for all learners and teachers" (646). Global mechanisms or technologies, such as competitive transnational markets and comparative international assessments, have directly affected education and the edges that bound it; moreover, education and other governed systems shape the lives of those who desire or need to penetrate or traverse these edges.

Throughout this volume, we frame the construction of immigrants by their movement and their stillness; we examine them through discussions about the places they've left, the places they currently inhabit, the places they dare not go, the places where they imaginatively belong, and the places to which they hope to return. We concern ourselves with both continuities and discontinuities in immigrants' experiences as they negotiate multiple educational contexts. Movement, flow, circulation, and stillness are central to our understanding of immigrants. As revealed in each chapter, immigrants are always of several places, actual, perceived, and creatively cobbled together, at once. This is where their stories reside, and it is where our exploration and understanding of immigration, education, and policy begin.

REFERENCES

Anyon, Jean. 2005. "What 'Counts' as Educational Policy: Notes toward a New Paradigm." *Harvard Educational Review* 75 (1): 65–88.

Bartlett, Lesley, and Ameena Ghaffar-Kucher, eds. 2013. *Refugees, Immigrants and Education in the Global South: Lives in Motion.* New York: Routledge.

Bourdieu, Pierre. 1998. *Practical Reason.* Stanford, CA: Stanford University Press.

Chen, Qiongqiong, and Jill P. Koyama. 2012. "Reconceptualising Diasporic Intellectual Networks: Mobile Scholars in Transnational Space." *Globalisation, Societies, and Education* 10 (4): 1–16. doi:10.1080/14767724.2012.690305.

Chowdhury, Elhora. 2011. *Transnationalism Reversed.* Albany, NY: SUNY Press.

Clarke, John. 2005. "New Labour's Citizens: Activated, Empowered, Responsibilized, Abandoned?" *Critical Social Policy* 25 (4): 447–463.

Collier, Stephen. J., and Aihwa Ong. 2005. *Global Assemblages: Technology, Politics and Ethics as Anthropological Problems.* Malden, MA: Blackwell, 2005.

Das Gupta, Monisha. *Unruly Immigrants: Rights, Activism, and South Asian Politics in the United States.* Durham, NC: Duke University Press.

Dolby, Nadine, and Fazal Rizvi. 2007. "Introduction." In *Youth Moves: Identities and Education in Global Perspective*, edited by Nadine Dolby and Fazal Rizvi, 1–14. New York: Routledge.

Fahey, Johannah, and Jane Kenway. 2009. *Brain Drain or Mind-Shift? Reconsidering Policies on Researcher Mobility.* Melbourne, Australia: Monash Institute for the Study of Global Movements.

———. 2010. "Thinking in a 'Wordly' Way: Mobility, Knowledge, Power and Geography." *Discourse: Studies in the Cultural Politics of Education*, 31 (5): 627–640.

Fox, Jonathan. 2005. "Unpacking 'Transnational Citizenship.'" *Annual Review of Political Science* 8: 171–201.

Gibson, Margaret A., and Jill Koyama. 2011. "Immigrants and Education." In *A Companion to Anthropology of Education*, edited by B. A. U. Levinson and M. Pollock, 391–407. New York: Wiley-Blackwell.

Ginwright, Shawn, Julio Cammarota, and Pedro Noguera. 2005. "Youth, Social Justice, and Communities: Toward a Theory of Urban Youth Policy." *Social Justice* 32 (3): 24–40.

Koyama, Jill, and Herve Varenne. 2012. "Assembling and Dissembling: Productive Policy Play." *Educational Researcher* 41 (5): 157–162.

Kugelberg, Clarissa. 2011. "Integration Policy and Ethnic Minority Associations." In *Policy Worlds: Anthropology and the Analysis of Contemporary Power*, edited by Cris Shore, Susan Wright, and Davide Peró, 264–281. Oxford: Berghahn Books.

Ladson-Billings, Gloria, and William F. Tate. 1995. "Toward a Critical Race Theory of Education." In *Critical Race Theory in Education: All God's Children Got a Song*, edited by Adrienne Dixson and Celia Rousseau, 11–30. New York: Routledge, 1995.

Moore, Henrietta L. 2011. *Still Life: Hopes, Desires and Satisfactions*. Malden, MA: Polity Press.

Myers, John P., and Husam A. Zaman. 2009. "Negotiating the Global and the National: Immigrant and Dominant-Culture Adolescents' Vocabularies of Citizenship in a Transnational World." *Teachers College Record* 111 (11): 2589–2625.

Nagar, Richa. 2006. *Playing with Fire: Feminist Thought and Activism through Seven Lives in India*. Minneapolis: University of Minnesota Press, 2006.

Ong, Aihwa. 1996. "Cultural Citizenship as Subject-Making: Immigrants Negotiate Racial and Cultural Boundaries in the United States." *Currently Anthropology* 37 (5): 737–762.

Peró, Davide. 2007. "Migrants and the Politics of Governance in Barcelona." *Social Anthropology* 15 (3): 271–286.

———. 2011. "Migrants' Practices of Citizenship and Policy Change." In *Policy Worlds: Anthropology and the Analysis of Contemporary Power*, edited by Cris Shore, Susan Wright, and Davide Peró, 244–263. Oxford: Berghahn Books.

Portes, Alejandro, and Rubén Rumbaut. 2011. *Legacies: The Story of the Immigrant Second Generation*. Berkeley: University of California Press.

Roy, Ananya, and Aihwa Ong. 2011. *Worlding Cities: Asian Experiments and the Art of Being Global*. Hoboken, NJ: Wiley-Blackwell.

Said, Edward. 1983. *The World, the Text, and the Critic*. Cambridge, MA: Harvard University Press.

Sassen, Saskia. 2000. "Immigration in a Global Age: A New Policy Landscape." *Annals of the American Academy of Political and Social Science* 570: 65–77.

Shore, Cris, and Susan Wright. 2011. "Conceptualizing Policy: Technologies of Governance and the Politics of Visibility." In *Policy Worlds: Anthropology and the Analysis of Contemporary Power*, edited by Cris Shore, Susan Wright, and Davide Peró, 1–25. Oxford: Berghahn Books.

Stone, Deborah. 2002. *Policy Paradox: The Art of Political Decision Making*. Rev. ed. New York: Norton and Company.

Sutton, Margaret, and Bradley A. U. Levinson, eds. 2001. *Policy as Practice: Toward a Comparative Sociocultural Analysis of Educational Policy*. Westport, CT: Ablex Publishing.

Terrazas, Aaron, and Jeanne Batalova. 2009. "Frequently Requested Statistics on Immigrants and Immigration in the United States." Accessed March 2, 2011. http://www.migrationinformation.org/USFocus/display.cfm?ID=747#1.

Tsing, Anna L. 2005. *Friction: An Ethnography of Global Connection*. Princeton, NJ: Princeton University Press.

US Census Bureau. 2010. "American Community Survey." Accessed September 18, 2012. http://www.census.gov/acs/www/.

Valenzuela, Angela. 1999. *Subtractive Schooling: US-Mexican Youth and the Politics of Caring*. Albany, NY: SUNY Press.

Varenne, Herve. 2007. "General Introduction: Alternative Anthropological Perspectives on Education Framework." *Teachers College Record*. 109 (7): 1539–1544.

Varenne, Herve, and Ray McDermott. 1998. *Successful Failure: The School America Builds*. Boulder, CO: Westview.

Waters, Mary C., and Tomas R. Jimenez. 2005. Assessing immigrant assimilation: New empirical and theoretical challenges. *Annual Review of Sociology* 31: 105–125.

World Bank. 2011. *Migration and Remittances Factbook 2011*. 2nd ed. Washington, DC: World Bank.

Wortham, Stanton, Enrique Murillo, and Edmund T. Hamann. 2002. *Education in the New Latino Diaspora: Policy and Politics of Identity*. Westport, CT: Ablex Publishing.

Yosso, Tara. 2006. *Critical Race Counterstories along the Chicana/Chicano Educational Pipeline*. New York: Routledge.

Part I
Identity-Staking

2 The Proverbial Monkey on Our Backs
Exploring the Politics of Belonging among Transnational African High School Students in the US

Krystal A. Smalls

"It just hard to . . . to get a way of get along in this school or in the country . . . in general . . . cause whatever you do, you still gets in trouble. So I don' know," lamented Anthony, a lanky and laid-back seventeen-year-old from Liberia. In many ways his ongoing troubles with school administrators, teachers, local authorities, and American peers of various backgrounds were representative of other African newcomers' experiences at Central High School, a large suburban school located just outside Philadelphia.

Throughout the four years I spent at Central, I would often hear of the troubles African-born students were experiencing—especially in their relationships with African Americans (which, for the purposes of this chapter, I define as, black-identified US citizens who are descendents of enslaved Africans). In some cases, these troubles resulted in physical violence between the groups or in punitive actions by schools and local polities against the newcomer students. During my first year at the school, more than a few students and teachers recounted one particular incident that seemed to characterize the intensity of conflict between the "African" and "black" students. The incident involved a young Liberian newcomer being "jumped" (physically attacked) by a group of African American young men after school. One afternoon, while students were volunteering to participate in a storytelling and interview project one of my advisors and I were conducting in an English as a second language (ESL) classroom, Anthony revealed that he would interview the young man who had been the victim of this infamous attack.

Harkening back to Du Bois's (1898) and others' discussions of "the Negro" as an inexorable problem in twentieth-century America, this chapter considers how Anthony's words signal the ways he and his African transnational peers occupy a similarly troubling space in both US society and the transnational African/black diaspora today. Throughout the chapter I revisit my conversations with Anthony and other students from western Africa—some of which emerged during the aforementioned storytelling project and others during observations at Central High over four years. Specifically, I examine the words and actions of Timothy, Anthony, and two young women named Adima and Poady to unpack some of the ways they navigated and responded to discourses and policies in and out of school that effectively dehumanized them or that rendered them invisible. I pay closest attention to the ways a particular kind of discursive violence seemed to play a part in how they situated themselves in the world: violence inflicted by discourses from peers and media that linked lower primates and African personhood (monkeys, in particular). In addition to inflicting injuries that are endemic in modernity's production of race—via romantic *and* unromantic primitivisms— "monkey discourses" have historically been used to dehumanize the black body in general. However, in the narratives and interactions discussed here, we see that they are often deployed by African Americans to differentiate (and subjugate) the African body specifically. This work marks how a growing African presence in the US may trouble young African Americans by forcing them to engage in an agonizing subjective project: re-conceptualizing themselves in relation to whiteness via rhetorics of white supremacy.

At various points, each young person nimbly addresses the ways their shared birth country, Liberia, has been (mis)imagined and (mis)represented in a range of discourses about Africa and Africans that span "mass media" and local discourses and that invoke primitive "chronotopes" (Bakhtin 1981) and primatial personhood. We begin to sense how these imaginings of Liberia, Africa, Africans, and different kinds of blackness make locating oneself along the rocky social terrains of North America a precarious feat. Moreover, these young people's words and actions help us grasp the ways they and their black-identified peers work together and against one another to negotiate racialized conditions of cultural belonging. Like other newcomers, black African transnationals must weave themselves into our knotty cultural fabric while inhabiting bodies that get saddled with local histories of blackness. The US's long history of criminalizing young black and brown people via race-based policing and media representations, along with the recent murders of Amadou Diallo, Trayvon Martin, and Rekia Boyd, reminds us that living in a black or brown body can be quite treacherous in the US regardless of one's citizenship status, ethnicity, class, or gender. These sensitive and layered issues call into question the efficacy of educational policies that lump heterogeneous "immigrant" students together, or that lump black immigrants and US-born black students together, and that effectively underestimate the material significance, and complex nature, of blackness as a racial category in the US.

This chapter, like that of Chikkatur (this volume), explores students' narratives about cultural belonging in the US, and positions these narratives in conversation with students' daily activities as well as broader sociohistorical phenomena. I suggest that participants were responding to noxious constructions of African personhood by fashioning new ways of understanding Africa and Africans. I argue that by manipulating the social meanings of communicative practices from culturally diverse sources (e.g., hair weaves and Mohawks, cries of "O.M.G.!" and Lil Wayne quotes, *hijabs* and crisp Adidas) to express different aspects of their identities, they ultimately used vast "communicative repertoires" (Rymes 2010) to resituate themselves and others on multiple scales (e.g., interpersonal, local, regional, national, global) and co-construct emergent models of black personhood with their friends and antagonists. The following pages illustrate the complexities of "identity-staking" among Liberian transnational and African American young people as they repeatedly smash the racial category "black" to pieces and reconfigure it to fashion internal, or subordinate, racial categories— categories that reflect their intersectionality by effectively creating differ- ent *kinds* of blacknesses and black personhood while maintaining certain historic meanings.

The policy implications of this project are far-reaching, but I focus on those that pertain to racial identification and antiracism education. Most education policy that addresses race unintentionally reifies static notions of identities and bounded, unmoving categories of race. Central High students' interactions and comments indicate that just as individuals' national, ethnic, and cultural "identities" are dynamic and contingent, so too are racial identities as they function in our daily lives. Moreover, studies like the one presented here show us how issues of race and racism can easily become shrouded by more comfortable conversations about other kinds of difference, allowing us to evade dialogue that directly addresses race and racism in schools and society. Educational policies that create more space for (or that even go so far as to encourage) per- sonal and collective reworkings of race not only help make formal edu- cation more accessible for all students (for whom racialized imaginings are inescapable), but also move us closer to unhinging race from biology in the broader social imaginary. Moreover, discursive "space-making" policies that implement programs through which students and teachers flesh out different collective and individual meanings of race provide opportunities to address (and prevent) many of the verbal and physical conflicts that transpire between students from different backgrounds in schools throughout North America. Guided sessions that help students and teachers examine metadiscourse about race (i.e., talk about race) in popular and local spheres allow for a collective unpacking of the ways we make meaning of race. Through reflective dialogue spaces, students and teachers learn that talk about language often serves as a proxy for expressing ideas about race, especially in this moment of neoliberalism and "racial paranoia" (Jackson 2008). For example, Carhill-Poza (this volume) explains that the ways English language learning is concep- tualized and talked about frequently reveal ideologies about different kinds of speakers, and hence different kinds of people. A guided dia- logue about these categories of learners might reveal that these kinds of people ("Spanish speakers" and "normal people" (Carhill-Poza, this volume) are racialized in unique ways and sometimes map onto existing racial categories.

FRAME: RACE AND BELONGING

In this historical moment, characterized by phenomena scholars describe as "transnationalism," "translocalism," "globalization," or "glocalization" (cf. Copeland-Carson 2004; Alim 2009; Appadurai 1996; Ong 1999; Roudometof 2005; and others) we have become keenly aware of increasingly intense processes that create multidirectional, multilayered, constant, and rapid movements of (and connections between) ideas, practices, and bodies. Correlated with new technologies of production, communication, and transportation, these processes also yield new technologies for self- and other-making. And it is pertinent to this discussion that these new technologies enable the negotiations (as reworkings) of blackness between young people with vastly different personal experiences who come from places with vastly different sociocultural histories.

Because the US's racial history and racial present infect the everyday lives of most individuals, for some African newcomers, cultural belonging becomes almost contingent on racial belonging (cf. Ong 1996), one of the messiest social projects in human history. For some, full "cultural citizenship"[1] (via belonging) and the symbolic capital garnered from certain aspects of American blacknesses (e.g., coolness, toughness, resilience) may make the toils of racially locating oneself in the US worthwhile, and for others, alternative citizenships may render racialized cultural belonging irrelevant or efforts toward it too costly. These alternative citizenships, or "transnational connections" (Chen, this volume) could take the form of "flexible citizenship," that is, a truly transnational subjectivity refereed by familial governmentalities (Ong 1999, 118) which may manifest as a deterritorialized, racialized, or ethnicized sense of belonging (Chikkatur, this volume). For yet others, a kind of nostalgic citizenship may manifest as a veritable rejection of "the West" via what Ong called the "roots phenomenon" (189), or via what Appadurai considered the inevitable nostalgia of modernity (1996). This chapter suggests that where a person chooses to direct his/her efforts in this continuum of citizenship (with full political and cultural belonging at one end and strictly home-based citizenship at the other) is largely informed by the very old and very global logics of racialization and anti-black racism (cf. Pierre 2004). In other words, racial logics, no matter how broad or abstract, help condition how one imagines oneself in the world. With a history of barbarity that is so uncomfortably close in time and space (e.g., lynching, Jim Crow, the Atlantic slave trade) yet so passionately disregarded, anti-black racism plays tricks on most black *and* nonblack peoples enculturated after the invention of race—tricks that are exemplified by pigmentocracies around the world. However, it wreaks special havoc on those with ostensibly black bodies and seems to underpin the ways some black-identified people stratify themselves, as my research suggests.

Attending to these phenomena engenders more nuanced understandings of how young people like Timothy, Anthony, Adima, and Poady are experiencing belonging in US schools (even years after migration) so that we can develop policies and practices that effectively address their particular circumstances. To do this, we must look beyond generic demographic data on West African transnationals, and even beyond raw first-person narratives, to consider information that can only be spotted through an ethnographic lens: the tones, textures, and gestures that punctuate their narratives; the immediate interactions in which their stories emerge; the chains of related interactions in which they form links; and the broader sociopolitical and historical circumstances that help condition their meanings. The complexities of race-making in the US also suggest that we must peer into broad geopolitical frameworks or notions of citizenship to make out the microlevel ways different peoples experience belonging in the US in their daily interactions.

Immediately following the liberation of many African colonies in the 1950s, 60s, and 70s, large numbers of black Africans have migrated from their home countries to different parts of the world. In the last two decades, however, the US has experienced the largest migration of black African peoples since the end of the Atlantic slave trade (Okpewho and Nzegwu 2009; Takyi 2002). Roughly 1.5 million individuals are documented to have relocated to the US since the 1980s, with nearly half arriving since 2000 (McCabe 2011). And while their national and cultural identifications may be manifold and itinerant—constantly moving between different conceptual spaces (as many of their bodies move around in physical space), the conditions of possibility for many African newcomers' racial identification may feel quite narrow and fixed in the US. For those with particular phenotypical features, the inescapability of "blackness" in the context of the US's race history grips these individuals soon after landing.

Awad Ibrahim's (1999, 2010) extensive research on African transnational young people in Canada lays bare key intersections of race, language, and identity and explores these connections from the vantage point of the "marginalized." By doing so, this research makes the subject-formation processes of African-born students like Timothy and Adima the analytical focal point, rather than emphasizing (re)productions of hegemony and treating racialization exclusively as a top-down process. In particular, his work explores how and why many African newcomers to Canada (mostly from eastern Africa) often construct and perform a decidedly *black* subjectivity and social identity through language practices that he says were primarily accessed through black stylized English (1999, 2010) and hip-hop. He explains that these young people's subjective and performative labor is animated by a "desire to belong to a location, a politics, a memory, a history, and hence, a representation" (2010, 89) and suggests that while being raced as black by dominant white Canadian society informed the conditions of their self-making projects, their linguistic choices effectively constitute agency and demonstrate a local "politics of desire" (1999) around subject formation (i.e., they made decisions about what kind of black they wanted to be based on available models of personhood and related language varieties). Ibrahim's findings, which remind of us De Certeau's (1984) account of conditioned agency (vis-à-vis "strategies" and "tactics"), are critical to this analysis because in many ways, Anthony, Timothy, Adima, and Poady, despite feeling raced as black, also displayed such agency by employing communicative practices related to different models of US blackness as they situated themselves on this side of the Atlantic not unlike the young people discussed in Carhill-Poza's chapter (this volume), whose uses of Spanish and English were associated with various notions of personhood and sociality. I also suggest that my participants, and perhaps Ibrahim's subjects as well, may have gone beyond choosing among available models of personhood and may have begun co-constructing new models of transnational black (or possibly diasporic) personhood that are becoming more recognizable among their North American peers.

This work of constructing new models of African personhood appears to be in direct reaction to the discursive and physical violences that characterize many African transnationals' relationships with African American peers. Practically, this implies that in order to mediate nonviolent interactions between these groups, teachers, administrators, and students will need to engage in intensive instruction on and conversations about race and the stealthy workings of racism. While policies that focus explicitly on nonviolence and peace education programs can be invaluable in certain contexts, I think that for matters of racial and intra-racial tension, which tend to manifest as discursive violence first and foremost, interventions that don't specifically address violence (or conflict) but instead focus on creating "dialogue spaces" in which tensions and misunderstandings can be responsibly aired and addressed are a more effective route. For example, Carhill-Poza (this volume) describes a productive classroom discussion that began when the teacher posed a question about Latinos being called "Indians" during the early part of European colonization. While the author offered this glimpse into the classroom to demonstrate how language learners can be positioned as experts to help reshape the ways English language learners are imagined and treated, the example also serves as a great illustration of how a provocative question can be a springboard for critical reflection and can create space for airing tensions that students have experienced or observed in their lives. With a facilitator well versed in Latin American social and political history, Latin American cultures, and racial history in the Americas, the ensuing conversation could have become a "dialogue space" that provided opportunities for students and teachers to learn about themselves, about one another, and about processes of racism and ethnicism. This notion of dialogue spaces will be revisited later in the chapter.

METHODS/METHODOLOGY

This ethnographic inquiry contributes to a growing body of scholarship concerned with African transnational students' social and academic experiences (in addition to work by Ibrahim [1999, 2010], Rong and Brown [2001]; Traoré [2004]; and others) and considers how they draw from new technologies of self- and other-making. I accomplish this by utilizing basic methods from anthropological ethnography (e.g., participant observation and "thick" field notes, ethnographic interviews). Participant-observation occurred over four years in ESL classrooms, lunchrooms, and hallways at Central High, and interviews with thirteen students were conducted periodically throughout. To analyze the data, I conducted discourse analysis (recursively coding transcripts for emergent themes, attending to the form, content, and organization of verbal interactions, etc.; Blommaert 2005), as well as some aspects of critical discourse analysis (CDA; i.e., interpreting every interaction as embedded in larger structures/processes with sociopolitical histories).

To untangle the interactional work and cultural work I saw (and sometimes experienced) in these conversations, I turn to linguistic anthropology and consider concepts like "interdiscursivity" and "indexicality" (Silverstein 2003) as helpful ways of understanding how meaning making transpires. In most discursive acts, the chains of events that create *inter*-*discursive* meanings (i.e., meanings made across discourses—which can be conversations, books, films, letters, Facebook statuses, commercials, etc.) are embedded within individual acts and typically stretch beyond the participants' lifetimes (Agha 2007). "Indexicality" generally refers to the ways a linguistic form or other communicative sign serves as a marker of some kind of social meaning. In other words, a word, phrase, facial expression, hairstyle, or handshake may mark someone's class, or gender, or coolness, depending on whether or not these associations are shared among the parties involved. In the age of globalization, interdiscursivity (and intertextuality) can carry meanings from one encounter to another—across time and space—at lightning speed. As a result, it becomes a rather formidable task to conceptualize the full scope of the kinds of information (or relationships) a young person who engages with various digital media, TV, film, and radio is able to access, and therefore it is equally difficult to concretely interpret which embedded meanings are knowingly being invoked in any given moment. In other words, globalization exposes "context" as an infinite and indeterminate notion when employed in media and cultural studies that address indexicality.

I chose to focus on race, ethnicity, and personhood because they immediately came to the fore during one of my first visits to Central High. I was sitting across from Adima when I heard her ask, "I've lived here since I was twelve. Am I American or am I African?" Not sure whom she was addressing, because I was momentarily focused on the film the substitute teacher was showing the class, I glanced over at her in the dimly lit room and found that she was looking directly at me. Moved by the fact that she had posed such a profound question to me so early in our relationship, I responded that it was up to her, and added that she never had to choose as far as I was concerned. That question, and the stories that Adima and her peers would share with me, animated the next few years of research I conducted with western African (mainly Liberian) transnational young people. The fact that Adima posed the question to me, an African American woman, and that she went on to demonstrate numerous alignments with me through hip-hop music and styles, hair, heritage, and language, has encouraged me to consider the "intersubjective" work (Jackson 1998) that transpires between the researcher and the researched (Muñoz-García, this volume). In this case, my position as an African American contributed to the meaning making set off by her provocative question. In that way, she was not only asking about national citizenship (as "African" is clearly not a category of national citizenship, but a regional and/or cultural distinction), but also about a kind of belonging that was informed by race. Over the next few years, I would also hear Adima and other African transnational students refer exclusively to African Americans as "black"[2] or "American" (unless I used "African American"), and refer routinely to white Americans as "white people." Unlike dominant discourses that equate whiteness with American identity, their default "American" is often the black American in our conversations, making whiteness the clear Other. For these reasons, it seemed to me that Adima was querying both the discreteness and the accuracy of these categories. Her later musings on the term "African American" indicate that this question may have been her way of problematizing the options for naming available to her—as she was an African-born person who was making a life in America and therefore a "true" African American.

DISCURSIVE VIOLENCE: MEDIATING AFRICA

One of the most common narratives[3] I encountered in the four years I spent at Central High is that of the "ignorant" and "mean"[4] African American peer who participates in dehumanizing depictions, posed as questions or secondhand reports, of Africa and African peoples. Like the focal students in Traoré's (2004) study of African "immigrant" students in a Philadelphia high school, comments that associated primitiveness with Africa and African personhood clearly informed the ways eighteen-year-old Timothy, nineteen-year-old Anthony, seventeen-year-old

Adima, and her eighteen-year-old half sister, Poady, were experiencing their immediate social worlds, and how they were understanding themselves in relationship to their peers. Accordingly, any concepts that were easily correlated with primitiveness (e.g., primate similitude, close relationships with plants and animals, different hygienic practices, low intelligence, low linguistic development) were also cited as sources of anxiety, frustration, hurt, or anger by the African transnational students in my study.

This "primitive African" figure of personhood was noted in conversations with seven of the eight African transnational students I spoke with in my first year at Central High, and by many others since. Like Anthony, Timothy, Adima, and Poady, these students described questions and assumptions about their ways of life in Africa that did not leave room to question the linkage between mass-mediated, deficit-oriented constructions of Africa and African personhood. The following excerpt speaks to this:

1 A: . . . it's black (.) Americans (.) (an) you know. Like one time me and some other boy
2   got in a argument in class cuz he gon talk about (.) things like AIDS man. My
3   teacher said some<u>thi</u>ng (.) and (-) discuss-

4 P: -HE SAY AIDS come from green African monkeys=

5 A: =°and then he said (-) all- that Afr-° that some man from Africa brought AIDS

6 P: ((*inaudible*))
7 A: you know (.4) have sex with the monkey and stuff >so I ask him was=like<
8   <u>WHERE</u> <u>WHEN</u> OR HOW DID YOU HEAR that? Cuz <u>I</u> wanna know. I wanna
9   hear about it too. And we got in a <u>big</u> argument (.) like huge argument I got sent
10   down to- (.4) It just piss me off (d-) when I [hear people talk- - - - -]

11 P: [YEAH CUZ IT'S SO IT'S SO I-](.2)
12   IT'S SO IGNORANT BECAUSE THEY DON'T KNOW NOTHING ABOUT
13   AFRICA cause the whi- (.) like people send people go to Africa:: and take the <u>worst</u>
14   picture a Africa and they bring it here in America and they think we (still -) jungle
15   (.) we fight with- we fight with (.2) monkeys. And that's like so embarrassing
16   because you're like saying right that you know you from Africa=

17 A: =((*inaudible*))

18 P: =and they're like saying stuff like that it's so embarrassing to you cuz you like (.)
19   <u>that</u>'s your culture and they're talking about it=be=like 'do ya'll sleep in the
20   <u>TREES</u>? do ya'll- do ya'll wear clothes?' I mean how do you not wear clothes
21   when you-

22 A: =that's the question some boy ask me was that 'oh in Africa do ya'll jump from tree
23   to tree?' (.4) I was like what kind of ignorant question is that- do ya'll jump from-

24   do you jump from tree to tree in America? And then he was like 'no.' cuz (.) the way
25   people you know show Africa that's what d- that's what they think [(- - -)]

26 P: [THAt's not in]
27   <u>our</u> part of Africa- that's a different part of Africa. If- if- you go in my country you
28   gon like it- we have <u>beach</u>, we have good weather, we have good music- it's- it's
29   just like- it's a good place to be- it's just like people got to go there to believe it.
30   YOU SEE LIKE A DIFFERENT PART OF AFRICA than people don't wear
31   clothes they think that that's where we're from- no- we're from in the city we have-
32   we're from the <u>BIg</u> city we have fun there we have party, we have everything, we
33   have clubs, we have ma:lls, we have shopping centers we have everything so:

(Adima and Poady, in conversation with author, February 2009)

While no methodology allows us to actually know a participant's subjectivity, the explicit metapragmatic discourse that Adima and Poady shared in the excerpt above can shed light on how they perceived the US social imaginary and its protagonists, as well as illuminate how they may have been conceptualizing and (re)constructing themselves in relation to these people and ideas (i.e., differentiating themselves from African Americans—"*It's black Americans, you know*" [line 1]—as well as from other Africans—"*That's not in our part of Africa!*" [lines 26–27]). As we see in this exchange, Adima and Poady repeatedly noted references to a "primitive African" model of personhood in various kinds of discourse. Additionally, in lines 11–14, there is some indication that Poady may hold dominant white American culture accountable for circulating these conflated images, not the African American young people who voice them ("*cause the whi- like people send people to go to Africa,*" etc. [line 13]). A later conversation with Adima indicated that she did indeed consider her African American peers the victims of propaganda about Africa mediated by an undefined "they." Anthony and Timothy shared similarly disturbing accounts of Africa and Africans and also cited televised representations and the absence of contemporary Africa from school curricula as the source of misinformation among both peers and teachers.

In the following excerpt, we see further evidence of the complex ways African American and African transnational students relate to one another. Here, Timothy explains why he doesn't waste time trying to educate his African American peers about Liberia or share his personal experiences before moving to the US.

Timothy: They don't know nothing, man. They don't know nothing about me, they just judge people without knowing them. (.4) I ain't got time to sit down here an' explain my life (problem) with dem
Krystal: =I know I know
Timothy: They- they(h)- ((*laughing*)) don't even wanna know, they don't care, they ignorant. All they talk about 'Africa:n: (.) y- in Africa you cl-' They're so dumb. Like they claims Africa is like one country. How- ?

Anthony: ((*laughing in background*))
Timothy: They say you fight baboon. Fight monkeys.

(Timothy, in conversation with author, May 2009)

In this next excerpt, Poady shares an incident in which she was insulted by a female classmate (whom she identified as black American). Her interlocutor's comment was much more insulting than simply linking Africa or African personhood to primates, which, as we saw in the earlier excerpt, certainly "pissed" them off and was considered "embarrassing." Here, an African American peer was actually likening Poady's physical body to a nonhuman animal—and a monkey, at that.

1 Poady: In my class some girl be calling me- she's- she=be=like I look like a monkey (.2) I
2   was [like <u>really</u>↑?]
3 Adima: [(((*giggling*))]
4 Poady: (REALLY) I LOOK LIKE A MONKEY? Say that outside to me and you gon see
5   what↓
6 Adima: ((*giggling*))
7 Poady: They're so <u>mean</u> I just don't get it. If you wanna be mean to me (.2) say it outside of
8   school and you're gon to find out if I'm African or [a <u>monkey</u>]
9 Adima: [<u>vi</u>(h)olent(h)] ((*giggling*))

(Adima and Poady, in conversation with author, February 2009)

All of these evaluations of "mean," "ignorant," and "embarrassing" comments and questions represented comparable metapragmatic (i.e., about behavior) assessments by other transnational African students at Central High and seem to constitute a reliable metadiscursive (i.e., about discourse) frame for understanding some of their interactions with African American and other US-born peers.

For teachers and administrators to begin understanding how monkey discourses (which link primates and African persons) may be functioning in these emotionally violent interactions taking place in many classrooms and hallways, we must go beyond the students' own metapragmatic accounts and attempt to peel back and historicize some of the discursive layers that make up the co-text and context of the exchanges they describe. In particular, discourses about monkeys and black personhood have a long and winding history—and help demonstrate the peculiarity of anti-black racism. While most members of the Global South must contend with various manifestations of social Darwinism that render their cultural practices and structures "primitive," it is worth noting that the post-Enlightenment racial logics that invented biological race effectively posited blackness as the very antithesis of whiteness (playing off of a long-standing black-white dichotomy that demonized darkness). This ancient ideological project, bolstered by science and imperialism, concretely exceptionalized black personhood as a different kind of humanity closer to the lower primates than any other (cf. Wynter 2003). This dehumanization of black personhood may also have spurred a kind of global frenzy for people to locate themselves as far away from the black end of the race spectrum as possible, a tendency manifested in color caste systems from South Asia to South America, and possibly in the interactional work accomplished by African American youths calling their African-born peers "monkeys."

As part of Fanon's (1967) project to "help the Black man free himself of the arsenal of complexes that has been developed by the colonial environment" he explains the notion of African primitiveness as being historically linked to evolution models that position the African as "the link between monkey and man" (30). His assertion that such notions bear upon many black peoples' "psyches" and daily interactions has to be taken up carefully, as it can easily lead to pathologization. Still, the sensibility he encourages can illuminate how these discourses about monkeys and African and black personhood may have impacted both the young transnational students' and the young African American students' (who, on some level, understood themselves to be descendents of African people) self-making and social-identification processes. In other words, considering the weight of monkey analogies can help us comprehend how these students were forming their raced "intersubjectivities" (from Michael Jackson's notion of a socially constituted, dialogic self [1998]) in the imperceptible detritus of colonialism and slavery. Any participant in, or student of, the African diaspora or the "Black Atlantic" (Gilroy 1993) is certainly familiar with discourses, ranging from scholarly publications to colloquialisms, that liken blackness to primitiveness (enlisting monkeys in particular), variations of which have been circulating in the US since the birth of the nation. I would imagine that the specter of "porch monkeys," "jungle bunnies," "yard apes," and "urban jungles" still haunts contemporary US racial relations and, quite possibly, the African American collective unconscious as well, especially when we consider their contemporary verbal counterparts like "chimp out" (cf. www.urbandictionary.com). The plethora of digitally altered images depicting President and Michelle Obama as monkeys and the stream of insults posted to YouTube videos likening Venus and Serena Williams to gorillas are just a few powerful examples of the endurance of these dehumanizing discourses.

I have not spoken directly with any African American students at Central High who would admit to making monkey comments, but it seems reasonable that these dehumanizing discourses could certainly feed anxieties about blackness among black young people of every ilk, especially those whose enculturation processes were steeped in encounters with anti-black racism (via either firsthand interpersonal encounters, mass-mediated representations of blackness, or secondhand oral histories). Even in the absence of recognizable "aversive racisms," such anxieties may also be reinforced by the overabundance of verbal and visual discourses in the US, Caribbean, and postcolonial Africa that tangentially normalize and/or valorize white personhood,[5] and at the same time, erase or exceptionalize positive models of black personhood, as Ibrahim's work proposes (1999, 2010). Such experiences may surreptitiously engender words and practices that some young black people, irrespective of ethnicity, believe will distance them from the models of personhood associated with primitiveness, and may encourage the evocations of class-based constructions of modernity to parse kinds of African personhood (i.e., things like the size of a person's home in Africa, his/her consumption habits before and after migration, or his/her parents' occupations in Africa are communicated).

The fact that every act of dehumanizing discursive violence reported by these students was uttered by another black student (either African American, Caribbean American, or African transnational), and that I overheard no fewer than three African transnational students use the same rhetoric at some point (sometimes as a possible tool of emotional violence and sometimes, more indirectly, as a tool of solidarity), speaks to this kind of haunting and its resulting "diasporic hegemonies" (Thomas and Campt 2006). These complex uses of anti-black racist rhetoric also warrant an extensive and nuanced investigation that goes beyond rudimentary conclusions of "self-hatred." I cautiously suggest that a kind of reconfiguring of race and anti-black racism (which constructs different types of black persons) may be at play, both for the American students (who try to position their African peers at the furthest, primatial end of the human spectrum they've been taught, and themselves somewhere closer to whiteness and modernity) and for the African students (who try to position African Americans as culturally and morally bereft and as somewhat inauthentic or tarnished Africans).

Anthony's and Timothy's narratives about various kinds of violence committed by African American peers differed in disturbing ways from Adima's and Poady's stories because the former went beyond discursive violence and included many accounts of physical violence with peers as well as clashes with school and local authorities that they characterized as a kind of legal or political violence. Overall, the types of barriers to belonging encountered and reported by these four students suggest that both the *kinds* of experiences one has and the *ways* certain experiences affect one's subject formation are gendered phenomena. Whereas the female students I talked to typically cited verbal assaults against their person (and femininity) as their main social troubles,[6] the male students emphasized physical intimidation, physical violence, and institutional and legal policies as their main struggles. However, Anthony's words (which opened this chapter) and Adima's account of being disciplined when responding to a comment she found insulting demonstrate how many young African transnationals of any gender often feel as if they're always "getting into trouble," whether it's interacting with African Americans peers, their mostly white teachers and administrators, "walking while black," "driving while black," "shopping while black," or a number of other daily activities.

DIASPORIC DIFFERENCE AND BELONGING

The tensions that I've thematized thus far should clearly indicate that the young people in this analysis resisted and openly rejected certain forms and practices associated with American blackness and were not shy about explaining why. In one part of his narrative, Timothy explained why he only hung out with other African students after school:

> That's why I hang out with my own people. It's not like . . . I'm racist. Cause we understand each other. I'm not racist, I can be "wassup, wassup, hi" but out of school, we not hangin out. Cu- I don't know what you do after school. Cause <u>we</u> do the same thing, we play soccer together. That's what we do back home. (Timothy, in conversation with author, May 2009)

Timothy's choice of terminology ("racism") to describe differentiations that we tend to think of as ethnic (based on his mention of his "own people" who do the same things they did back home [in Liberia or West Africa, I presume]) may indicate how he and his black peers were constructing different black "human kinds" (Hacking 1995) by creating new racialized subcategories for "Africans" and "Americans." His American peers who invoked monkey discourses, and primitivism in general, seemed to be doing the same kind of work, but to different ends. It is always possible, too, that Timothy may have purposely been using the term to describe generally discriminatory behavior related to difference, or that he may not have understood the technical meaning of "race." Or, he may have understood it fully and been talking about his boundary-keeping relative to white and other nonblack peers as well as non-African black peers.

Intermingled with his many assessments of difference between African American and African transnational students, in this same exchange, Timothy also expressed genuine confusion about perceived differences between the groups and about the resulting tensions, and suggested that shared origins and a kind of inescapable belonging existed:

> It's like African Americans and like the Africans from Africa, they just . . . they just been havin problem. They <u>thinks</u> they better than the African because they from Africa. And I don't get it. You black. It doesn't matter if you was born in America. If you check back you're- you ARE from Africa . . . so I don't care what anybody tell me. You can be . . . whatever you think you are, once you black you from Africa, that's what I- I know. (Timothy, in conversation with author, May 2009)

Interestingly, moments earlier in the conversation, Timothy shared that he "doesn't really discriminate or anything" and that he has a lot of "different friends." My time at Central High confirmed that Timothy did indeed have a lot of different friends, many of them African American classmates and football teammates. However, as we see demonstrated in these few statements, Timothy consistently toggled between expressions of identification *with* and *against* African Americans, and other statements indicated similar toggling in his relationships with other African transnationals. These oscillating statements corroborate more recent conceptualizations of how diaspora functions in people's daily lives (cf. Clarke 2010; Copeland-Carson 2004; Diawara 1998; Edwards 2003; Gilroy 1993; Hall 1996; Rahier 2010; Scott 1991). Many contemporary scholars have contributed an understanding of diaspora as a dynamic and contentious space of difference *and* belonging, a complex phenomenon that seems to be at play in relationships between African transnational and African American young people in and around Philadelphia.[7] This nuanced understanding of diaspora as an ongoing process allows for the African transnational students' pathologization of African Americans and the African Americans' insistence on a uniquely African primitivism to coexist with their many shared interests as well as with notions of shared origins and futures.

From this rendering, diaspora becomes a space in which blackness must be interminably negotiated on every level. In this space, old-school notions of "authentic" blackness don't really hold up, and in many ways, what will constitute "real" (or valid and valued) blackness is up for reconfiguration. John Jackson's "racial sincerity" (2005) may be a more helpful way to conceptualize and describe what is being mediated in these "racioscapes" (i.e., spaces where black people from different parts of the world come into intimate, everyday contact and diasporic belonging and difference come to a head; Jackson 2006). With "racial sincerity" we see that for these young people, "real" blackness will not necessarily hinge on who's more "authentically" black or African in body or mind, but may include hip-hop, punk rock, highlife, or forms from other popular culture genres as criteria.

With the specter of monkey discourses looming overhead, alongside other debris of colonialism, the Atlantic slave trade, Jim Crow, US imperialism, and a host of other racist phenomena, the stakes in forming and occupying valuable and sincere blacknesses become high for young people who inhabit ostensibly black bodies. In these diasporic spaces, we see that racialized becoming, or subject formation, is not only political and material, but also deeply sentimental. The affective nature of figuring out if one is sincerely black, or if one wants to be black at all, while toiling over what it even means to be black (with people from very different cultural backgrounds) cannot be underestimated as a critical component of cultural belonging for African transnational students in the US.

CONCLUSION: RACE AND DIASPORA AT SCHOOL

When we take into account the very delicate and racialized resituating that many young people from Africa must engage in when they move to the US, policies that attempt to help newcomers adjust to "American culture" (whose American culture?) by simply teaching them "English" (which English?) or by teaching them the bare bones of navigating major institutions clearly miss the mark. Even ESL policies that attempt to acknowledge language as a cultural practice and that teach things like greeting etiquette or how to interview for a job do not take into account the ways individuals like Adima, Poady, Timothy, and Anthony are negotiating not only adulthood, transnational cultural/political citizenship, and a number of language varieties, but also dynamic and manifold meanings of blackness in different parts of the world.

Interventions made by major critical race theorists and educationalists, including Derrick Bell, Gloria Ladson-Billings, Daniel Solórzano, and Gregory Tate, have more than demonstrated the need for national, state, district, or at least school-level implementations of a required race curriculum that helps students, teachers, administrators, and families understand sociopolitical constructions of race, as well as systemic inequality vis-à-vis racism. Along with extensive training for preservice teachers around issues of race, class, gender, and culture, any efforts toward a nationally standardized "core curriculum" should include comprehensive and nuanced race curricula. These interventions are the necessary next steps for addressing the plethora of issues that bubble up in classrooms and communities from a widespread and underlying lack of understanding of race and racism, as was indicated in Adima's frustration over a poorly facilitated discussion about Africa, AIDS, and monkeys which resulted in her being disciplined.

In order to attend to some of the complex phenomena I attempted to illuminate in this chapter, however, we need to develop situated and nuanced curricular materials and pedagogical practices that go beyond most critical approaches (and that don't fossilize cultures and races). For example, a core race curriculum that draws from recent anthropological theory should foster better understandings of race-making and race-living from various perspectives. In particular, the biological (mis)constructions of race, the history of sociopolitical constructions of race in the US, and contemporary formations of systemic racism should serve as overarching objectives in this curriculum (cf. the Public Broadcasting Service's film series *Race: The Power of an Illusion* [Adelman et al. 2003]). Relevant audiovisual and digital resources, in tandem with collaboratively designed curricula (that include input from anthropologists, education researchers, teachers, political activists, and others), are imperative for effectively teaching how race is a sociohistorical construction that is "real" in lived experience, and for beginning to explore how and why it has been reconstructed and contested in different places by different people in different historical moments.

In particular, the development of such curricula would allow for a collective exploration into the ways black-identified African transnational students experience race in the US. As I've witnessed in Adima and Anthony's English for English language learners (ELLs) class, well-facilitated classroom dialogue opens up valuable space for beginning to address the ins and outs of cultural belonging as it relates to race. The ELL teacher who opened his class to my colleagues and me for four years faithfully created multimodal assignments and introduced classroom discussions that provided relatively safe spaces for students to talk about race and belonging if they chose. Supported by my colleagues and myself, this teacher was able to gradually develop this approach so that race (along with gender, class, and religion) was strategically integrated into lessons in a productive, thorough, and sensitive manner.

Policies that implement this kind of collaborative work should focus on promoting carefully designed "dialogue spaces" led by educators trained (via preservice or professional development programs) to facilitate such dialogues. That is to say, these dialogues should be led by individuals who are familiar with broad sociohistorical politics around race and class as well as more intimate politics of desire at play in their particular students' lives, and who know how to facilitate large discussions and activities around sensitive matters. Policies that (1) fund the development of a "basic" race curriculum (which can be localized for individual districts and schools), (2) advocate for this kind of race curriculum in any national core curriculum that is passed, and (3) implement dialogue spaces with trained facilitators could certainly provide the vital first steps toward more responsible treatments of race in educational spaces. More importantly, such policies could contribute to better understandings of the troubling tasks of making and living race undertaken every day by African transnational students like Anthony, Poady, Adima, and Timothy.

NOTES

1. This use of "cultural citizenship" is closer to Ong's (1996) notion of the concept, as a kind of "subjectification," than it is to Rosaldo's (1994) notion. However, the subject formation with which I am most concerned is less informed by "the political" and occurs along more ontogenetic and interpersonal scales.
2. I use the term "black" as shorthand for "black-identified."
3. Excerpts from transcripts use Standard American English punctuation and marks, along with conventions from the Jefferson Notation System.
4. "Mean" and "ignorant" are terms used by participants.
5. By "white personhood" I mean any model of personhood widely recognizable (i.e., collectively constructed within a social domain) as "white."
6. It should be noted that Adima and one of the other young women I worked with had been involved in numerous physical altercations as well—with both African American and other African transnational female students.
7. Afro-Caribbean young people are also integral in these relationships and occupy their own complicated role in Afro-diasporic spaces.

REFERENCES

Adelman, Larry, Jean Cheng, Christine Herbes-Sommers, Tracy Heather Strain, Llewellyn Smith, Natatcha Estebanez, Claudio Ragazzi, and CCH Pounder. 2003. *Race: The Power of an Illusion*. San Francisco: California Newsreel.

36   *Krystal A. Smalls*

Agha, Asif. 2007. *Language and Social Relations.* New York: Cambridge University Press.

Alim, H. Samy. 2009. "Introduction." In *Global Linguistic Flows: Hip Hop Cultures, Youth Identities, and the Politics of Language,* edited by H. Samy Alim, Awad Ibrahim, and Alastair Pennycook,1–22. London and New York: Routledge.

Appadurai, Arjun. 1996. *Modernity at Large: Cultural Dimensions of Globalization.* Minneapolis: University of Minnesota Press.

Bakhtin, Mikhail. 1981. "Discourse in the Novel." Translated by Caryl Emerson and Michael Holquist. In *The Dialogic Imagination: Four Essays,* edited by Michael Holquist, 259–422. Austin: University of Texas Press.

Blommaert, Jan. 2005. *Discourse: A Critical Introduction.* Cambridge: Cambridge University Press.

Clarke, Kamari M. 2010. "New Spheres of Transnational Formations: Mobilizations of Humanitarian Diasporas." *Transforming Anthropology* 18: 48–65.

Copeland-Carson, Jacqueline. 2004. *Creating Africa in America: Translocal Identity in an Emerging World City.* Philadelphia: University of Pennsylvania Press.

De Certeau, Michel. 1984. *The Practice of Everyday Life.* Translated by Steven Rendall. Berkeley: University of California Press.

Diawara, Manthia. 1998. *In Search of Africa.* Cambridge, MA: Harvard University Press.

Du Bois, W. E. B. 1898. "The Study of the Negro Problems." *The Annals of the American Academy of Political and Social Science* 11: 1–23.

———. 1903. *The Souls of Black Folk: Essays and Sketches.* Chicago: A.C. McClurg.

Edwards, Brent Hayes. 2001. "Uses of Diaspora." *Social Text* 19 (1): 45–73.

Fanon, Franz. 1967. *Black Skin, White Masks.* Translated by Charles Lam Markmann. New York: Grove Press.

Gilroy, Paul. 1993. *The Black Atlantic: Modernity and Double-Consciousness.* Cambridge, MA: Harvard.

Hacking, Ian. 1995. "The Looping Effect of Human Kinds." In *Causal Cognition: An Interdisciplinary Approach,* edited by Dan Sperber, David Premack, and Ann James Premack, 351–383. New York: Oxford University Press.

Hall, Stuart. 1996."Race, Articulation, and Societies Structured in Dominance." In *Black British Cultural Studies: A Reader,* edited by Houston A. Baker, Manthia Diawara, and Ruth H. Lindeborg, 16–60. Chicago: University of Chicago Press.

Ibrahim, Awad. 1999. "Becoming Black: Rap and Hip-Hop, Race, Gender, Identity, and the Politics of ESL Learning." *TESOL Quarterly* 33 (3): 349–369.

———. 2010. "'Hey, Whadap Homeboy?' Identification, Desire & Becoming Black: Hip-Hop, Performativity, and the Politics of Becoming Black." In *Taboo: Essays on Culture and Education,* edited by Shirley Steinberg and Lindsay Cornish, 117–137. New York: Peter Lang.

Jackson, John L. 2005. *Real Black: Adventures in Racial Sincerity.* Chicago: University of Chicago Press.

———. 2006. "Gentrification, Globalization, and Georaciality." In *Globalization and Race: Transformations in the Cultural Production of Blackness,* edited by Kamari Clarke and Deborah A. Thomas, 188–205. Durham, NC: Duke University Press.

Jackson, Michael. 1998. *Minima Ethnographica: Intersubjectivity and the Anthropological Project.* Chicago: University of Chicago Press.

McCabe, Kristin. 2011. "African Immigrants in the United States." Migration Information Source. Accessed May 15, 2012. http://www.migrationinformation.org/USfocus/display.cfm?id=847.

Okpewho, Isidore, and Nkiru Nzegwu, eds. 2009. *The New African Diaspora.* Bloomington: Indiana University Press.

Ong, Aihwa. 1996. "Cultural Citizenship as Subject-Making. Immigrants Negotiate Racial and Cultural Boundaries in the United States." *Current Anthropology* 37(5): 737–762.

———. 1999. *Flexible Citizenship: The Cultural Logics of Transnationality*. Durham: Duke University Press.

Pierre, Jemima. 2004. "Black Immigrants in the United States and the 'Cultural Narratives' of Ethnicity." *Identities: Global Studies in Culture and Power* 11 (2): 141–170.

Rahier, Jean. 2010. "The Diversity of Diasporic Subjectivities: Different and Separate Ontologies? A Response to Kamari Clarke's 'New Spheres of Transnational Formations: Mobilizations of Humanitarian Diasporas.'" *Transforming Anthropology* 18: 66–69.

Rampton, Ben. 2005. *Crossing: Language & Ethnicity among Adolescents*. 2nd ed. Manchester: St. Jerome Press.

Rong, Xue Lan, and Frank Brown. 2001. "The Effects of Immigrant Generation and Ethnicity on Educational Attainment among Young African and Caribbean Blacks in the United States." *Harvard Educational Review* 71 (3): 536–565.

Rosaldo, Renato. 1994. "Cultural Citizenship and Educational Democracy." *Cultural Anthropology* 9 (3): 402–11.

Roudometof, Victor. 2005. "Transnationalism, Cosmopolitanism and Glocalization." *Current Sociology* 53 (1): 113–135.

Rymes, Betsy. 2010. "Classroom Discourse Analysis: A Focus on Communicative Repertoires." In *Sociolinguistics and Language Education*, edited by Nancy Hornberger and Sandra McKay, 528–546. Bristol: Multilingual Matters.

Scott, David. 1991. "That Event, This Memory: Notes on the Anthropology of African Diasporas in the New World." *Diaspora: A Journal of Transnational Studies* 1 (3): 261–284.

Silverstein, Michael. 2003. "Indexical Order and the Dialectics of Sociolinguistic Life." *Language & Communication* 23 (3–4): 193–229.

Smalls, Krystal. 2010. "Flipping the Script: (Re)constructing Personhood through Hip Hop Languaging in a U.S. High School." *Working Papers in Educational Linguistics* 25 (2): 35–54.

Takyi, Baffour K. 2002. "The Making of the Second Diaspora: On the Recent African Immigrant Community in the United States of America." *The Western Journal of Black Studies* 26 (1): 32–43.

Thomas, Deborah, and Tina Campt. 2006. "Diasporic Hegemonies: Slavery, Memory, and Genealogies of Diaspora." *Transforming Anthropology* 14: 163–172.

Traoré, Rosemary L. 2004. "Colonialism Continued: African Students in an Urban High School in America." *Journal of Black Studies* 34 (3): 348–369.

Wynter, Sylvia. 2003. "Unsettling the Coloniality of Being/Power/Truth/Freedom: Towards the Human, After Man, Its Overrepresentation." *The New Centennial Review* 3 (3): 257–338.

3 Narrating the Nation and Challenging Discourses

Anita Chikkatur

Public schools in racially diverse countries often operate as sites where immigrant youth learn about the social landscapes of their new homes from and alongside their native-born peers. Historically, American public schools have been viewed as key institutions where youth are socialized into the nation (Levinson, Foley, and Holland 1996; Tyack and Cuban 1995) as well as into the nation's racialized structures (Lee 2005; Olsen 1997). Schools are places where racial and other social identities and politics are learned and negotiated. On the other hand, the changing demographics of immigrants to the US—that is, a shift in immigrants' countries of origin since the passage of the 1965 Hart-Cellar Act—have had a great impact on American public schools (Jacobsen, Frankenberg, and Lenhoff 2012). Consequently, educational institutions are important locations to examine when seeking to understand the effects of migration on immigrant youth and on their receiving societies.

This chapter draws on data from a two-year ethnographic study at a large, comprehensive urban high school in the US. The larger ethnography examined new manifestations of identity, positioned at the intersection of racial structures, new patterns of immigration, and American nationhood, as expressed at one school by students and teachers in interactions with each other, the curriculum, and the researcher. This chapter will focus on the dominant narrative among immigrant students, their US-born peers, and their US-born teachers that positioned America as the land of educational and economic opportunities. This discourse about opportunities was coupled with a narrative of how immigrant students were better students than their American peers. Immigrant students drew on this narrative to leverage the privilege of the "good immigrant" status, much as the participants in Muñoz-García's study (this volume) attempted to use their class status to counter the racism they faced in the US.

Teachers made comparisons between motivated immigrant students and unmotivated US-born (mostly African American) students that relied on stereotypical and static views of immigrant cultures (Lee 2005; Louie 2004). They reinforced subtle yet powerful anti-African American discourses that ignored historical and contemporary structural barriers to educational achievement and economic mobility (Brayboy, Castagno, and Maughan 2007; Ladson-Billings 2006) as well as differences in how groups have been incorporated into the racial landscape of the nation (Roediger 2005; Tuan 1998). Teachers also obscured how immigration policies shaped the class profile of contemporary Asian and other immigrants (Prashad 2000; Visweswaran 1997). The views of immigrant and US-born students who were critical of the promise of the American dream were often ignored or dismissed in an effort to focus on the positive aspects of the US.

Given that public schools are a space cohabited by immigrant students and their US-born peers, schools should do more to provide students with the skills and knowledge needed to evaluate critically the benefits and disadvantages of entering the mainstream and espousing white, middle-class values and to participate in the mainstream within the context of this critique (Carter 2005; Delpit 2006; Fine 1991). Rather than reinforcing the meritocracy myth that obscures the role that race and class structures play in shaping educational and life opportunities, schools can instead become sites for social change. They can help students develop "an understanding of their lives that brought into focus structural rather than individual causes" for mobility (Bettie 2003, 203). As Smalls (this volume) posits, policies that create spaces where students can "rework" race, class, gender, and other social identities are necessary. This more critical approach to racial structures and identities has the potential to allow *all* students, both immigrant and US-born, to understand better *both* the promise and the limitations of American educational institutions and economic structures. It could give immigrant students and their US-born peers the space and the support to articulate identities "tied to social change politics that could not be run through the mill of assimilation, accommodation, acculturation, and cultural pluralism" (Das Gupta 2006, 21). Policy makers and educators need to broaden their ideas about citizenship and belonging, as many immigrants are already doing (Q. Chen, this volume). It may also lead students to be more aware and critical of anti–African American discourses and to understand the historical and continuing significance of racialized identities on life opportunities and on individuals' ability to benefit from educational credentials. It may enable immigrant students to imagine and develop identities as "Americans" in a way that does not minimize the social and material significance of blackness, in particular, in the lives of all US residents.

RESEARCH METHODS AND CONTEXT

This chapter draws on data I collected between October 2005 and June 2007 at a large comprehensive public high school that I call Garfield, located in an urban area in the eastern US that I call Douglasstown. I used ethnographic methods—participant observation, interviews, and documentary collection—to collect data. Data sources included fieldnotes from over eighteen months of observations at Garfield, thirty-six student and four teacher interviews, 120 demographic survey responses, curricular material, student work, and district and school documents.

During a pilot study conducted from October 2005 to May 2006, I collected data through weekly participant observation in three classes at Garfield, two taught by Karen Levy and one taught by Renee Parker; informal discussions with teachers and students in these classes; and a life-history interview with Mrs. Levy.[1] Mrs. Levy was a US-born white teacher with thirty years of teaching experience in the school district. At the time of the study, she was working toward obtaining a certificate in teaching English for speakers of other languages (ESOL). Ms. Parker, a US-born white teacher with an Italian immigrant mother, was the coordinator of Garfield's ESOL program and had over fifteen years of teaching experience. She had a master's degree in teaching English to speakers of other languages (TESOL). Mrs. Levy and Ms. Parker became two of the three focal teachers for the second year of the study.

From September 2006 to June 2007, the second year, I was a participant observer biweekly in three classes: a tenth-grade African American History course (taught by Ms. Kuperberg, who became the third focal teacher in the study), an intermediate-level ESOL class (Ms. Parker), and a twelfth-grade English class (Mrs. Levy). All three classes had a diverse group of students with regard to self-ascribed racial identities, place of birth, and immigrant status. During this year, I also observed a variety of nonacademic spaces and contexts, including the English Department office (Mrs. Levy was the department chair), the lunchroom, the prom, sporting events, and a multicultural fair. Semistructured interviews with thirty-six students[2] from the three main classes I observed, representing a cross-section of the student body, allowed me to explore their perspectives on being and becoming "American." Nineteen of the students I interviewed were born in the US and the rest (seventeen) were born outside of the US.

CHANGING DEMOGRAPHIC CONTEXT

During the 2006–2007 school year, the second year of my study, the school's 3,600 students were approximately 35% African American, 30% white, 18% Asian, and 16% Latino.[3] This racial composition had changed considerably since 2001, when the student body at Garfield was approximately 27% African American, 51% white, 11% Asian, and 12% Latino. These changing demographics reflect national trends in public school enrollment. The percentage of nonwhite children enrolled in K–12 public schools in the US increased from 22.2% in 1972 to 38.7% in 2001 and then to 43.1% in 2006 (Planty et al. 2008). This increase is largely due to rising numbers of Hispanic students and, to a lesser degree, of Asian students. While no official information was available about Garfield's immigrant student population, approximately 10% of the students were designated as needing ESOL services. At the time of the study, approximately 10% of the nation's students were classified as English language learners (Payán & Nettles n.d.). The students in Garfield's ESOL classes migrated from Albania, Brazil, China, Colombia, Haiti, Pakistan, and Russia, among other places.

The increase in the numbers of Asian and Latino students at Garfield reflected the changes in Douglasstown's demographics as well as the tendency of urban schools to enroll more racial minority students than would be predicted from the overall racial demographics of the urban area. According to data obtained from the American Community Survey website in July 2006, 45.8% of Douglasstown residents were African American, 45.8% were white, 10.4% were Hispanic/Latino, and 5.4% were Asian. While it has not been a major destination for immigrants over the past two decades, there was a 30% increase in the foreign-born population between 1990 and 2000. In 2006, 39% of Douglasstown's foreign-born population migrated from Asia; 28% from Latin America and the Caribbean; 23% from Europe; and 8% from Africa. In contrast, 82% of immigrants to Douglasstown in 1970 came from Europe.

The shift in the region of origin of Douglasstown's immigrants reflects national trends that have resulted largely from changes in US immigration laws in the 1960s. The 1965 Hart-Cellar Immigration Act eliminated national origin quotas, which led to the arrival of immigrants from Asia, Latin America, and the Caribbean in unprecedented numbers.[4] This act decreed that "immigrants . . . were to be admitted on a first-come, first-serve basis by preference categories for adult family members, professionals and artists, needed skilled and unskilled laborers, and refugees" (Takaki 1989, 419). Post-1965 immigration is different in many important ways than immigration during other periods in US history with similarly high rates of immigration. First, a majority of the post-1965 immigrants have hailed from Asia, Latin America, and the Caribbean, whereas the earlier immigrants were mainly from Europe, as reflected in the data on Douglasstown's immigrants. Second, the changes in immigration laws since the early twentieth century have made terms such as "illegal immigrant" and "undocumented alien" commonplace, whereas such notions did not exist during the previous period of high immigration. Before the passage of the 1924 Johnson-Reed Immigration Act, immigration to the US was largely unrestricted (Ngai 2004). Third, the economic conditions encountered by the immigrants in the US have undergone important transformations. The importance of a high school diploma and a college degree has increased tremendously since the early twentieth century. Unlike the children of immigrants of that era, today's immigrants and their children have to contend with a labor market that, as Holdaway and Alba (2009) note, "offers many fewer stable, well-paying positions . . . [and more] poorer paying and less stable service sector" jobs (598). This large-scale economic restructuring has resulted in the hyperconcentration of poverty among racial minorities living in urban areas, where immigrant families, especially those with limited socioeconomic means, often live (Wacquant 2007; Wilson 2009). In a similar vein, the socioeconomic class backgrounds and educational attainment levels of the post-1965 immigrants themselves are also more diverse, which impacts their paths of adjustment to life in the US. For example, while children of immigrants are almost as likely as children of US-born parents to have highly educated parents, they are also much more likely than their US-born peers to have parents who have not graduated from high school (Hernandez, Denton, and Macartney 2009).

In addition to differences in the economic conditions of the receiving society and the diversity of immigrants' socioeconomic backgrounds, the persistent significance of racialized identities continues to complicate the process of adjusting to life in the US for post-1965 immigrants, many of whom are not racially identified as white or black. Whereas earlier models of assimilation, based on the experiences of European immigrants, posited a straight-line assimilative path to the mainstream, the phenotypes of the majority of the post-1965 immigrants make their assimilative processes different from those of immigrants marked as "white" in a society where skin color and other physical features still confer symbolic capital (Lewis 2003) on those who are seen as white. As Smalls (this volume) notes, the racial category of blackness continues to have a significant impact on the lives and experiences of people who are identified by society as "black."

Race has been central to constructing citizenship throughout American history. The current reality of America being dominated politically, socially, and economically by white citizens is a result of the decimation and destruction of the indigenous inhabitants of the geographical area that is now the US and the long history of unequal citizenship rights and privileges awarded to Americans, mainly along racial, gendered, and class lines (Das Gupta 2006; Glenn 2002). The idea of the US being a "White country" was given "ideological and physical effect" by laws that directly shaped the kinds of people who inhabited the country (Haney-López 1996, 18). Immigration laws restricted entry into the country and antimiscegenation laws shaped the marital choices of people who were already in the country. Such a deliberate fashioning of the nation "has provided the basis for contemporary claims regarding the 'European' nature of the US, where 'European' serves as a not-so-subtle synonym for White" (Haney-López 1996, 18). As Zolberg (2006) and others have also pointed out, transforming the US into a white country required not only legislative acts or discursive maneuvers, but also physical violence and brutal repression.

According to Portes and Zhou (1993), in contrast to the path of assimilation available to European immigrants, the process of assimilation has become segmented for children of immigrants from Asia, Latin America, and the Caribbean, in part because of the continued significance and persistence of racism. One path of adjustment to life "replicates the time-honored growing acculturation and parallel integration into the white middle-class" (Portes and Zhou 1993, 82), whereas a second possibility involves a selective accommodation to the mainstream, thereby achieving a certain level of economic success, while retaining key elements of the immigrant community's values and culture (Gibson 1988; Portes and Zhou 1993). This path is seen as shielding immigrant youth from the third route, which "leads straight in the opposite direction to permanent poverty and assimilation into the underclass" (82). According to Portes and Zhou (1993), immigrant and second-generation children take this third route when they adopt "an adversarial stance toward the white mainstream" (81) that the authors posit is commonplace among urban, racial minority youth.

Studies have questioned the prevalence of "oppositional" attitudes among racial minority youth (Spencer et al. 2001) as well as the association between oppositional attitudes toward mainstream institutions and low academic achievement (Carter 2005). Researchers have noted that the cultural practices of racial minority youth are often strongly related to their negotiations of their racial and ethnic identities, rather than indicating a particular attitude toward education or schools, as is often assumed by teachers and researchers (Carter 2005; Valenzuela 1999).

At Garfield, teachers often viewed student achievement as stemming from "good" cultural practices (which they often associated with white, middle-class cultures or "traditional" immigrant cultures) and attributed student failure to attitudes stemming from "corrupt" forms of Americanness (which they often associated with African American youth cultures). Framing minority student underachievement as a result of culture or student attitudes obscures the role that structural factors, including systemic racism, play in the continued marginalization of US-born *and* immigrant youth of color in public schools (Brayboy, Castagno, and Maughan 2007; Fine 1991; Lee 2005). While second-generation immigrant children might end up occupying a lower economic stratum than their parents, it is questionable to draw a causal line from oppositional identities to such downward mobility or even to academic underachievement.

AMERICA AS THE LAND OF OPPORTUNITY

At Garfield, many students, both immigrant and US-born, talked uncritically about America as a land of educational and economic opportunities, glossing over continuing forms of racial and class marginalization that impact the distribution of such opportunities. Among the thirty-six students I interviewed, twenty-two talked about educational and career opportunities as a defining feature of America. As John, a student who moved to the US from India when he was five, put it, "If you go to every country and ask [people], 'If you were offered a full time visa or citizenship to the United States to live here forever, would you take it?' I guarantee that 99% of the time, they would leave, pack up their stuff and come to this country, knowing what it has to offer. [Anita: And what does it have to offer?] Education . . . this country, the stuff it offers is crazy" (Interview, April 2007). Abigail, a US-born student, told me that her parents moved from Haiti because "the US has more opportunities maybe. There's a lot going on in Haiti. Work and everything, it's really hard. Education really isn't all that good. They just came here for opportunities" (Interview, April 2007). Ramona, a US-born white student, echoed the views of these children of immigrants when she told me, "I think being American means you just have a lot of opportunities not that you should take advantage of [that] but [you should] try to use opportunities wisely" (Interview, April 2007). Similarly, when Ms. Parker asked the students in her ESOL class what they liked the most about the US, nine out of the twenty-eight responses cited educational and job opportunities. In response to a question about why their families decided to move to the US, fifteen out of the twenty-eight students responded that the US offered them more educational, economic, and career opportunities.

This predominant narrative of America as the land of opportunity and implied ideas about the meritocratic nature of American education and society relied on cultural explanations of student achievement and failure. Most teachers I came to know at Garfield were supportive of their immigrant students. Indeed, teachers' discourse on immigrants tended to idealize immigrant students, parents, families, and communities. Immigrant students were often praised for behavior that conformed to the mostly white, middle-class standards that dominate in US public schools today (Carter 2005; Delpit 2006; Lareau 2000; Lee 2005). As Perry (2001) notes, these standards include "rationalism, individualism [and] personal responsibility" (81). Teachers often viewed positive student attitudes toward education as a key marker of praiseworthy behavior. They often expressed their belief that their immigrant students put more value and emphasis on education than their American counterparts.

During one class session, Ms. Parker was talking with her ESOL class about the students who had received academic awards during convocation. Jie, an immigrant from China, proudly announced that her sister won three awards. When Ms. Parker asked how long her sister had been in the country, Jie replied that she had been here only for a year. Ms. Parker told the class that Jie's sister's accomplishment showed that "if you work hard, you can do well." She added that, at convocation, there were numerous students with hard-to-pronounce names, "which means that they were probably born in another country." She told the students that research has shown that it is not that people born in other countries are any smarter, but that their cultures value education more and that they work harder. "American students are lazier, isn't that what you're all always telling me?" she asked the students. "Education is a top priority in your countries but in the US, it's not that much of a priority" (Fieldnotes, June 2007).

Yet, what I heard from students at the school disputed this view. While it was mostly immigrant students who spoke of the educational opportunities available to them in the US and perceived themselves (and were perceived by others) as valuing education more than their American peers, almost all of the immigrant *and* the US-born students I interviewed stated that they and their parents valued education. Rashida, a tenth-grade US-born student who identified as black and Puerto Rican, provided a typical answer to my question about families' views on education: her parents told her that school's "important and that I need to take school seriously" (Interview, May 2007). Additionally, both groups of students expressed the belief that educational credentials would make available to them numerous job and economic opportunities. Almost every student wanted to complete at least some years of college and viewed that as a valuable and necessary future step to achieve their career and life goals.

Some of the immigrant students I interviewed did express the belief that immigrant students were better students than American ones. Sasha, a twelfth grader born in Pakistan, said that one difference between students from "Pakistan, India, Bangladesh" and students from America was that American students "don't take it serious" (Interview, April 2007). Danielle, a ninth-grade student who had moved from Haiti, said, "This I'm not going to get it from American. I'll be the same thing. I respect my teachers," implying that American students do *not* respect their teachers (Interview, May 2007). At the high school, immigrant students were positioned, not only by teachers but also by some immigrant students themselves, as being ideal, hardworking students in contrast to their American peers.

Immigrant students' commitment to educational achievement was viewed as stemming from "their cultures," which were often viewed as static and un-American. As Ms. Parker, the ESOL teacher, explained in the class discussion that immigrant students tended to do well in school because they come from cultures that, unlike "American" culture, value education. Such "cultural" explanations for differences in academic achievement, although positive in their evaluations of some students' cultures and families, naturalize and essentialize "culture" (Louie 2004). These explanations tend to assume "that the high averages have something to do with the immigrant's genetics or culture (in the sense of a noun, as static) rather than something to do with the process of selection by the U.S. state" (Prashad 2000, 6). Given the preference given to highly skilled workers in the 1965 immigrant laws, the Asian diaspora to the US has been characterized by a high number of educationally advantaged and class-advantaged immigrants. Such "designing" of the immigrant population becomes obscured when culture becomes the explanation for immigrant success (Visweswaran 1997).

Additionally, the teachers' homogenizing views about immigrant cultures tend "to highlight an 'us' and 'them' way of reinforcing hegemonic ideas regarding race and American-ness" (Lee 2005, 48). Immigrant students' cultures were viewed as being entirely different from American culture and this view overlooked the possibility of cultural changes that might have occurred as a result of the migration process (Lee 2005). For example, immigrant parents might emphasize education as a way to succeed in their new home, regardless of their view of education before migration. As Louie (2004) found in her study of Chinese immigrant parents, children of immigrants might be urged to do well in school not because parents uncritically imagine America to be an open and meritocratic society where education always pays off, but rather because they see high levels of education as necessary to overcome the racist barriers their children might face in America.

While teachers tended to express appreciation for their immigrant students' cultures, the boundaries of acceptable behavior for immigrant students were subtly policed. This became clear during the discussion in Ms. Parker's class about which students were getting graduation honors. Andre, a student who was born in Paris to Haitian immigrant parents, said that he thought immigrants' educational attainment was not about culture "but certain people are just smarter." He talked about a student from China in his Math class who understood everything after just one explanation from the teacher. Salimah, a student from Pakistan, noted that there was another student in that class who was also from China but was not very good at math. Ms. Parker responded that she did not want to get into the debate but added, "If you work hard and persevere, you'll be able to do it. Andre, you're really smart. You're one of the smartest students in this class, but you're . . . [Andre says: lazy]. You have a great vocabulary and your writing skills are good but you just don't put in the effort. You're not even listening to me now." At this point, another student, Hector, said that he had heard that being a "good" student was about listening to the teacher, and Ms. Parker confirmed that it was (Fieldnotes, June 2007). In this class discussion, what defined a "good" student was listening to the teacher and following directions, rather than intellectual engagement or curiosity, for example. As Lee (2005) notes, "'Good' students do not challenge the school culture or authority" (29). Nor do "good" students challenge the narrative of the US as a meritocratic society where educational attainment and the right attitude and effort are all one needs to achieve economic success.

At Garfield, then, teachers did not view immigrant students' adoption of white, middle-class values—such as the idea that a combination of opportunity and hard work guaranteed educational and economic success—as a negative outcome of assimilation into America. Nor did they view their students' "traditional" immigrant cultures as oppositional to such values. In contrast, immigrant students' adoption of African American practices and attitudes was viewed as troubling. Teachers tended to evaluate negatively what they perceived to be African American youth culture because aspects of this culture were seen as contrary to white, middle-class values and as challenging the dominant narrative of America as a meritocracy where opportunity is fairly distributed based on ability and hard work. The first time I met Mrs. Levy, she told me, "Kids from other countries value education. They don't take things for granted that American kids do. I had a student who was from Africa who didn't understand why African American students didn't value education." She added, "If I had to teach just Indian and Chinese kids, I'd pay to work here. They're such a delight. At my last school, African American kids, American kids of any color, would always say, 'Why do we have to do this?'" Twice in this conversation, the category of "African American" was used when comparing immigrant students to "American" students. The assimilation of any immigrant student—black, white, Asian, or Latino—at the high school into "black America" was viewed as undesirable because it was "a process that implies inherent downward social and cultural mobility" (Pierre 2004, 150). In the school context, African American students were often identified as a particularly troubling group of American students.

The marking of African American students as embodying a troubling form of American identity sometimes occurred in the context of discussions about the influence of American culture on other countries as well as on Garfield students from other countries. In the following conversation, Mrs. Levy and her colleague Mr. Roberts, a US-born white social studies teacher, discussed their concerns about the particular kinds of American culture being adopted by culturally and racially diverse youth both within and outside the US. While the teachers generally condemned the corrupting influence of "American" culture, this American culture was coded explicitly and implicitly as cultural practices originating from African American urban youth.

In the English Department office, John, the senior who moved to US from India when he was five, and Anthony, a senior who identified as black and Puerto Rican, discussed the morning's assembly speaker. Another student listened in, as did two teachers—Mrs. Karen Levy and Mr. Christopher Roberts.

John said: He sounded so gay!

I glanced at Mrs. Levy, who shook her head. She said: "You know, John breaks every stereotype you have about Indo-Pak kids, he's so Americanized, he knows all the words. ALL the words. . . . And tell me this, why is it that every student regardless of color or ethnicity ends up sounding African American? Is that all we are exporting everywhere?"

Mr. Roberts: Yup.

The teacher's comments about the "Indo-Pak" student's full adoption of American language posited the use of specific terminology—in this case, the word "gay" in a derogatory sense—as a key aspect of Americanization. The use of the term "gay" as indicating something undesirable or uncool seemed prevalent among both US-born and immigrant students at the high school, across racial lines (Chikkatur, 2009); however, the use of this term

by John, who was positioned as not American, was seen as resulting from
his adoption of African American youth culture. Further, the teacher's
comment, "Is that *all* we are exporting everywhere?," casts a negative light
on this cultural influence. Mrs. Levy's comment also implies that there is
only one way to "sound African American," which ignores the impact of
class, geography, and the level or type of education on how a person speaks
and sounds. Additionally, as Smalls (this volume) notes, youth—including
black-identified youth—tend to draw on a communicative repertoire that is
influenced by culturally diverse sources.

The conversation continued:

Mrs. Levy: Oh, you'll love this, Anita, so they're trying to get together the
              multicultural show and every kid wants to do a hip-hop dance.
              And the teacher's telling them, "No, I want to see something
              traditional from your culture, I don't want to see ten hip-hop
              numbers."
Anita: Well, they do have Chinese and Japanese rap, so that is sort of
              their culture.
Mrs. Levy: I guess so. We had a student do a presentation on Japanese rap
              for her senior project.
Anita: Yup, they had Japanese rap and hip-hop when I was there a
              few years ago.
Mrs. Levy: They want something from their culture.
Anita: It is their culture, it's youth culture and I guess it's kind of the
              same everywhere.

(Fieldnotes, May 2007)

Here, there was a seamless transition from speaking about immigrant
youth in the US to speaking about youth "all over the world." Asian
youth, in particular, were identified by teachers as being "non-American"
regardless of whether they resided within or outside the US, reflecting
long-standing views of Asian Americans as "perpetual foreigners" (Lee
2005; Takaki 1989; Tuan 1998). As noted earlier, Mrs. Levy's explanation that the students were expected to perform "something from their
culture" positions the students' cultures as unchanging and static, an idea
I tried to challenge by pointing out how youth cultures across the globe
have cross-cultural influences. Unfortunately, my attempted challenge still
defined culture as a set of static practices that are adopted without being
mediated by contexts or individuals, because I said that youth culture is
"kind of the same everywhere."

Additionally, in the conversation, the ability of Asian and Asian American students to be "American" was questioned, whereas African American
youth were viewed as unquestionably American, but as corrupt Americans. This difference reflects how African Americans and Asian Americans
are dissimilarly positioned in the nation's political imagination and racial

structures. As Tuan (1998) notes, "for Asians, nativism and the stigma of foreignness further compounds racial marginalization. Blacks may be many things in the minds of whites, but foreign is not one of them" (8). Tuan's observation about contemporary racial realities resonates with the historical position of African Americans and Asians in the nation's political and legal structures (Carbado 2005).

The teachers' comparisons of immigrant and African American students also echoed historical comparisons between these groups within the US that have tended to exploit race-specific stereotypes and to extol meritocracy, often to the detriment of both groups (Lee 2005). As Ngo (2006) argues, "Asian Americans, we are told, are able to 'make it' on their own, without special assistance or anyone's help. Implicitly, historically marginalized groups (e.g. African Americans) are told that their failure is not due to the fact that the USA is fundamentally a racist society" (60). This pervasive myth about Asian and other immigrants in the US "keep[s] the American Dream alive, upholding popular beliefs in a meritocratic economy. . . . If the immigrant can do it, starting with nothing and not knowing the language, surely anyone can" (Honig 1998, 4). Within the educational system, this myth translates into a belief that if recent immigrant students can come to the US and "make it" in the educational system, anyone can. The failure of US-born racial minority students to achieve is attributed to their personal shortcomings rather than to inequalities or negligence on the part of the educational system. This explanation ignores the long history of segregation and unequal funding that have negatively impacted the education of African Americans. It also obscures the class-specific contours of immigration laws that have afforded many—although certainly not all—Asian immigrants access to the cultural, social, and economic capital not widely available to racialized US minorities, such as African Americans, Mexican Americans, and Native Americans (Prashad 2000; Q. Chen, this volume; Visweswaran 1997).

CONCLUSIONS AND IMPLICATIONS FOR POLICIES AND PRACTICE

Racially and ethnically diverse public schools such as Garfield constitute an important learning context for this generation of students, including the large numbers of children of immigrants, who "will be the first to live in an America that is truly multiracial and has no racial majority group" (Orfield 2009, 27). Schools can also be relatively safe, public spaces where marginalized youth can feel comfortable expressing and exploring their political views (Maira 2009). It is crucial, therefore, that there is curricular and extracurricular space for students to explore the enduring power of the meritocracy myth alongside persistent race and class differences in life opportunities and outcomes. As MacLeod (2009) notes, rather than reinforcing the myth of a color-blind meritocracy that obscures "the existence of barriers to success, schools should acknowledge them explicitly" (265). Public schools can provide information about the complicated relationship between education and economic mobility, particularly for groups such as African Americans and Native Americans who have been historically marginalized in schools and in society. For example, while more formal education does lead to higher earnings and lower unemployment rates for all, there is still racial inequity in the ability to translate educational credentials into salaries and status. For example, whereas 8% of whites with a high school degree were unemployed in November 2009, 13.7% of blacks with high school degrees were unemployed ("The Jobless Rate for People like You" 2009). As Tuan (1998) notes, "race remains an inescapable marker of difference that has consequences even for middle-class blacks" (7). In the post–civil rights era, racial discrimination is often insidiously subtle, taking the form of microaggressions (D. Solorzano, Ceja, and Yosso 2000), for example, and tends to be targeted at members of racial minority groups who refuse to assimilate into the dominant cultural norms (Yoshino 2006). While students can still be taught about individuals from their groups who succeed despite barriers, "the obstacles against which these figures prevailed" need to be emphasized when discussing their stories (MacLeod 2009, 265).

While the extent to which African American and other racial minorities are actually hostile to mainstream educational institutions might be less than what is perceived by teachers, peers, and researchers (Spencer et al. 2001), there are also good reasons for why such youth should be suspicious of schools. As Valenzuela (1999) found in her study of Mexican American youth, students can "oppose a schooling process that disrespects them: they oppose not education, but *schooling*" (5). Rather than attributing the oppositional attitude of African American students to laziness or a devaluing of education, teachers might reframe such attitudes as a critique of an education that fails to respect students, their families, their communities, and their histories and experiences with educational institutions. With their students, they might examine critically the role that school policies and practices play in creating or exacerbating tensions among students from different racial groups; between immigrant and US-born students (Carhill-Poza, this volume); and within racial groups (Rosenbloom and Way 2004; Smalls, this volume; Valenzuela 1999).

Attributing lower academic achievement among US-born racial minority students solely to their effort, attitude, or cultural practices only serves to reinforce harmful stereotypes about these groups. It also places immigrant students in the untenable position of contributing to anti–African American discourses as a way to bolster their standing in a society that continues both to idealize and stigmatize immigrants. What Toni Morrison (1993) observed nearly two decades ago still resonates: "A hostile posture toward resident blacks must be struck at the Americanizing door before it will open" (57). Those in positions of power in educational institutions need to ensure that the inclusion of immigrant students does not continue or exacerbate the exclusion of other marginalized groups of students. It therefore remains imperative that public schools enable, rather than discourage, immigrant and US-born students "to realize the complex cultural, economic, political, and ideological interests of their community, kin, and selves" (Fine 1991, 198). Rather than overlooking the continued impact of race and racism on all students' lives, schools can help students learn about the racialized histories and stories of different groups as the first step in creating more positive and productive relationships across immigrant statuses, generational lines, and racial backgrounds.

NOTES

1. The names of all the teachers and students have been changed.
2. I talked about my research project in the three focal classes and interviewed all the students who volunteered and obtained parental consent (if they were under eighteen). I did interview three ESOL students who were not in Ms. Parker's class, because only four students in her ESOL class volunteered to be interviewed.
3. Demographic information about the school and the district was available on the school district's website and reflects the information on the website at the time of the study.
4. This law changed the rules for who could enter the country legally. While there are other categories of migrants to the US, my study mainly focuses on immigrant students whose families entered the US legally either through preference categories or through refugee quotas. As far as I know, only one student I interviewed entered the US without proper legal authorization and did not have legal residency status at the time of my study.

REFERENCES

Bettie, Julie. 2003. *Women without Class: Girls, Race, and Identity*. Berkeley: University of California Press.

Brayboy, Bryan M. J., Angelina Castagno, and Emma Maughan. 2007. "Equality and Justice for All? Examining Race in Education Scholarship." *Review of Research in Education* 31 (1): 159–194. doi:10.3102/0091732X07300046159.

Carbado, Devon W. 2005. "Racial Naturalization." *American Quarterly* 57(3): 633–658. doi:10.1353/aq.2005.0042

Carter, Prudence L. 2005. *Keepin' It Real: School Success beyond Black and White*. Oxford: Oxford University Press.

Chikkatur, Anita. 2009. "Difference Matters: Race, Immigration and National Identity at a Diverse, Urban Public High School." PhD diss., University of Pennsylvania.

Das Gupta, Monisha. 2006. *Unruly Immigrants: Rights, Activism, and Transnational South Asian Politics in the United States*. Durham, NC: Duke University Press.

Delpit, Lisa D. 2006. *Other People's Children: Cultural Conflict in the Classroom*. New York: New Press.

52   *Anita Chikkatur*

Fine, Michelle. 1991. *Framing Dropouts: Notes on the Politics of an Urban Public High School*. Albany, NY: SUNY Press.
Gibson, Margaret A. 1988. *Accommodation without Assimilation: Sikh Immigrants in an American High school*. Ithaca: Cornell University Press.
Glenn, Evelyn N. 2002. *Unequal Freedom: How Race and Gender Shaped American Citizenship and Labor*. Cambridge, MA: Harvard University Press.
Haney-López, Ian. 1996. *White by Law: The Legal Construction of Race*. New York: NYU Press.
Hernandez, Donald J., Nancy A. Denton, and Suzanne E. Macartney. 2009. "School-Age Children in Immigrant Families: Challenges and Opportunities for America's Schools." *Teachers College Record* 111 (3): 616–658.
Holdaway, Jennifer, and Richard Alba. 2009. "Introduction: Educating Immigrant Youth: The Role of Institutions and Agency." *Teachers College Record* 111 (3): 597–615.
Honig, Bonnie. 1998. "Immigrant America? How Foreignness 'Solves' Democracy's Problems." *Social Text* 56: 1–27.
Jacobsen, Rebecca, Erica Frankenberg, and Sarah W. Lenhoff. 2012. "Diverse Schools in a Democratic Society: New Ways of Understanding How School Demographics Affect Civil and Political Learning." *American Educational Research Journal* 49 (5): 812–843. doi:10.3102/0002831211430352.
"The Jobless Rate for People like You." 2009. *New York Times*, November 6. Accessed January 9, 2012. http://www.nytimes.com/interactive/2009/11/06/business/economy/unemployment-lines.html.
Ladson-Billings, Gloria. 2006. "From the Achievement Gap to the Education Debt: Understanding Achievement in U.S. Schools." *Educational Researcher* 35 (7): 3–12. doi:10.3102/0013189X035007003.
Lareau, Annette. 2000. *Home Advantage: Social Class and Parental Intervention in Elementary Education*. Lanham, MD: Rowman & Littlefield Publishers.
Lee, Stacey J. 2005. *Up against Whiteness: Race, School, and Immigrant Youth*. New York: Teachers College Press.
Levinson, Bradley A., Douglas E. Foley, and Dorothy C. Holland. 1996. *The Cultural Production of the Educated Person : Critical Ethnographies of Schooling and Local Practice*. Albany, NY: SUNY Press.
Lewis, Amanda E. 2003. *Race in the Schoolyard: Negotiating the Color Line in Classrooms and Communities*. New Brunswick, NJ: Rutgers University Press.
Louie, Vivian S. 2004. *Compelled to Excel: Immigration, Education, and Opportunity among Chinese Americans*. Stanford, CA: Stanford University Press.
MacLeod, Jay. 2009. *Ain't No Makin' It: Aspirations of Attainment in a Low-Income Neighborhood*. Boulder, CO: Westview Press.
Maira, Sunaina. 2009. *Missing: Youth, Citizenship, and Empire after 9/11*. Durham, NC: Duke University Press.
Morrison, Toni. 1993. "On the Backs of Blacks." *Time*, December 02.
Ngai, Mae M. 2004. *Impossible Subjects: Illegal Aliens and the Making of Modern America*. Princeton, NJ: Princeton University Press.
Ngo, Bic. 2006. "Learning from the Margins: The Education of Southeast and South Asian Americans in Context." *Race Ethnicity and Education* 9 (1): 51–65. doi:10.1080/13613320500490721.
Olsen, Laurie. 1997. *Made in America: Immigrant Students in our Public Schools*. New York: New Press.
Orfield, Gary. 2009. *Reviving the Goal of an Integrated Society: A 21st Century Challenge*. Los Angeles: The Civil Rights Project/Proyecto Derechos Civiles at UCLA. Accessed August 1, 2013. http://civilrightsproject.ucla.edu/research/k-12-education/integration-and-diversity/reviving-the-goal-of-an-integrated-society-a-21st-century-challenge/orfield-reviving-the-goal-mlk-2009.pdf.

Payán, Rose M., and Michael T. Nettles. n.d. "Current State of English-Language Learners in the U.S. K–12 Student Population." Accessed June 15, 2012. http://www.ets.org/Media/Conferences_and_Events/pdf/ELLsympsium/ELL_factsheet.pdf.

Perry, Pamela. 2001. "White Means Never Having to Say You're Ethnic: White Youth and the Construction of 'Cultureless' Identities." *Journal of Contemporary Ethnography* 30 (1): 56–91. doi:10.1177/089124101030001002.

Pierre, Jemima. 2004. "Black Immigrants in the United States and the 'Cultural Narratives' of Ethnicity." *Identities: Global Studies in Culture and Power* 11: 141–170. doi:10.1080/10702890490451929.

Planty, Michael, William Hussar, Thomas Snyder, Stephen Provasnik, Grace Kena, Rachel Dinkes, Angelina KewalRamani, and Jana Kemp. 2008. *The Condition of Education (NCES 2008–031)*. Washington, DC: National Center for Education Statistics, Institute of Education Sciences, US Department of Education.

Portes, Alejandro, and Min Zhou. 1993. "The New Second Generation: Segmented Assimilation and Its Variants." *Annals of the American Academy of Political and Social Science* 530: 74–96. doi:10.1177/0002716293530001006.

Prashad, Vijay. 2000. *The Karma of Brown Folk*. Minneapolis: University of Minnesota Press.

Roediger, David R. 2005. *Working toward Whiteness: How America's Immigrants Became White: The Strange Journey from Ellis Island to the Suburbs*. New York: Basic Books.

Rosenbloom, Susan R., and Niobe Way. 2004. "Experiences of Discrimination among African American, Asian American, and Latino Adolescents in an Urban High School." *Youth & Society* 35 (4): 420–451. doi:10.1177/0044118X03261479.

Solorzano, Daniel, Miguel Ceja, and Tara Yosso. 2000. "Critical Race Theory, Racial Microaggressions, and Campus Racial Climate: The Experiences of African American College Students." *Journal of Negro Education* 69 (1–2): 60–73.

Spencer, Margaret B., Elizabeth Noll, Jill Stoltzfus, and Vinay Harpalani. 2001. "Identity and School Adjustment: Revisiting the "Acting White" Assumption." *Educational Psychologist* 36 (1): 21–30. doi:10.1207/S15326985EP3601_3.

Takaki, Ronald T. 1989. *Strangers from a Different Shore: A History of Asian Americans*. Boston: Little & Brown.

Tuan, Mia. 1998. *Forever Foreigners or Honorary Whites? The Asian Ethnic Experience Today*. New Brunswick, NJ: Rutgers University Press.

Tyack, David B., and Larry Cuban. 1995. *Tinkering toward Utopia: A Century of Public School Reform*. Cambridge, MA: Harvard University Press.

Valenzuela, Angela. 1999. *Subtractive Schooling: U.S.-Mexican Youth and the Politics of Caring*. Albany, NY: SUNY Press.

Visweswaran, Kamala. 1997. "Diaspora by Design: Flexible Citizenship and South Asians in U.S. Racial Formations." *Diaspora: A Journal of Transnational Studies* 6 (1): 5–29. doi:10.1353/dsp.1997.0016.

Wacquant, Loïc. 2007. *Urban Outcasts: A Comparative Sociology of Advanced Marginality*. Malden, MA: Polity Press.

Wilson, William J. 2009. *More than Just Race: Being Black and Poor in the Inner City*. New York: W. W. Norton & Co.

Zolberg, Aristide R. 2006. *A Nation by Design: Immigration Policy in the Fashioning of America*. New York: Russell Sage Foundation.

4 "Spanish Speakers" and "Normal People"
The Linguistic Implications of Segregation in US High Schools

Avary Carhill-Poza

Immigrant children and youth today comprise 22% of the US school-aged population, and demographic trends anticipate continuing growth over the next decade (Mather 2009). Whether recently arrived or born in the US, immigrant students draw from a range of experiences in their sending and receiving contexts as they adapt to life and schooling in their new country. Among the myriad challenges encountered by this diverse group, learning English is viewed as one of the most critical (August and Shanahan 2006). More than five million immigrant students speak a language other than English at home and are classified at school as having limited proficiency in English (NCELA 2011).

Despite an emphasis on communicative methods in language teaching, acquiring academic English is still largely conceptualized as an individual learning achievement, and the role of bilingual peers in language learning has received limited attention. While the importance of peers in socializing immigrant youth to academic engagement and attainment has been established (e.g., Gándara and Contreras 2009; Gibson et al. 2004; Suárez-Orozco, Suárez-Orozco, and Todorova 2008), research on peers as resources for learning the language of schooling is scarce. This chapter draws on data from a three-year mixed methods study of the English language development of first generation immigrant Spanish-speaking youth in New York City public high schools (Carhill-Poza 2011). Vignettes from case studies demonstrate that schools shape peer social networks in unintentional ways. In particular, policies designed to support language development are shown to isolate language learners from mainstream students as well as from bilingual peers, creating boundaries with profound repercussions for access to education and the development of peer relationships, a crucial resource for learning the language used in school. Examining the role of language support policies in creating peer groups is important for understanding how schools serve language minority youth and yields implications for policy and practice.

Current education policy, built on assumptions that learning English is an individual learning achievement, fails to take account of the role of social context in language learning, particularly the importance of access to supportive and knowledgeable peers. As demonstrated by Smalls (this volume) and Chikkatur (this volume), it is essential to understand the opportunities and constraints immigrant youth negotiate to claim belonging, identities, and resources in US schools. This chapter contributes to the growing literature on the ways in which policies designed to support immigrant students fail to consider the spaces of intersectionality they inhabit and instead create boundaries with profound repercussions for access to education. Spanish speakers represent an important focus for research on the effects of education policy because they comprise the majority of students classified as English language learners (ELLs) in the US (80%) and are the fastest-growing group of school-aged adolescent English learners (National Center for Educational Statistics 2010).

LITERATURE REVIEW

For immigrant youth in the US, inequalities in access to educational opportunity have been documented in an extensive body of research linking low levels of English proficiency to low GPAs, grade repetition, and low graduation rates (e.g., National Center for Educational Statistics 2010). The public narrative around the academic achievement of immigrant students has focused almost exclusively on bolstering individual English proficiency levels enough to transition language minority youth into mainstream curriculum, and English proficiency is viewed as a prerequisite to learning grade-level academic content alongside monolingual and English proficient peers (Gándara et al. 2010; Olsen 2010). Learning English has been constructed as a decontextualized individual learning achievement, obscuring the sociocultural context of language development while sustaining a narrow focus on measuring language proficiency and applying language support services, an approach similar to the autonomous model of literacy discussed by Street (1995).

Over the last decade, No Child Left Behind legislation, the latest reauthorization of the Elementary and Secondary Education Act (ESEA), has embodied this narrative by holding public schools accountable for ELLs' linear progress toward proficiency in English in the shortest possible time (Menken 2008). As the ESEA comes up for reauthorization, emphasis is again on the "consistent statewide identification of students as English Learners, and to determining eligibility, placement, and duration of programs and services based on states' valid and reliable English Language proficiency assessment" (US Department of Education 2011, 3). While information about the needs of students not yet fluent in English is essential to providing them with consistent support, the interpretation of such information needs thoughtful examination.

Contrary to national and state education policies, linguists have long argued that the process of language learning is complex and that discrete language proficiency measures need to be interpreted in context. Learning to use English to do well in school cannot be separated from academic content-area learning or the contexts of schooling immigrant students (Lantolf and Appel 1994; Leung 2010). Scholars distinguish between the specialized academic language used in schooling and language used for non-schooling purposes in other conversational contexts (Bailey and Butler 2002; Cummins 1979; Scarcella 2003). To acquire academic English, which includes learning to organize, link, and densely pack complex information, express nuance and personal stance in relation to what one says or writes, and use thousands of new words (Berman 2004; Clark 2003; Nippold et al. 2005), students need to accumulate meaningful experiences using English with their teachers, texts, and peers as they learn challenging subject-area content. While English as a second language (ESL) coursework can provide valuable support for language learners, particularly emergent bilinguals, adolescents confront immense linguistic challenges throughout the high school curricula, which necessitate coherent support and consistent opportunities to learn academic English across a broad range of subject areas and contexts (Olsen 2010).

Many of the boundaries that shape the opportunities of immigrant youth to learn English through engagement in schooling have been investigated over the last two decades. It is well documented that immigrant youth consistently attend the poorest schools in the nation, where few resources are available to meet their educational needs (Gándara and Contreras 2009; Orfield and Lee 2006; Suárez-Orozco, Suárez-Orozco, and Todorova 2008). Students who are learning English are frequently separated from mainstream students in a "school within a school" (Olsen 1997; Valdés 2001) and tracked into an unchallenging curriculum that does not prepare them for college or the workforce and does not use the same kinds of language as more academic curricula (Harklau 1994; Mehan et al. 1996; Valenzuela 1999).

CONCEPTUAL FRAMEWORK

The current study draws on an ecological perspective (Bronfenbrenner 1977), together with theories of language development which emphasize interaction (Lantolf and Appel 1994; Swain 1993; Vygotsky 1978), to conceptualize individual language learning as fostered in tandem with cognitive development within multiple social contexts. In this view, adolescent second language learners are nested within interrelated social systems, including peer groups, schools, and homes, which shape their individual language learning processes and outcomes. School environments affect language learning both directly and indirectly through school influence on peer-group formation. As adolescents spend most of their time with peers and develop close-knit communities where language and other social norms are developed as part of everyday activity (Eckert 1989; Carnegie Council on Adolescent Development 1995), peers represent a primary context for conversations about academic topics and for interactions that can lead to learning academic English (Carhill, Suárez-Orozco, and Páez 2008).

Peers also form an important conduit for transmitting the expertise needed for academic achievement and participation in schooling (Berndt 1999; Gee 1996), an especially important resource for immigrant youth whose parents may not yet speak or write English well and often have limited understanding of US schools (Kao and Tienda 1995; Suárez-Orozco, Suárez-Orozco, and Todorova 2008). This study makes use of a social capital framework to describe how social relationships can be leveraged to provide resources for learning academic English as well as how social relationships are mediated by structural systems (Bourdieu and Passeron 1977). Relationships with supportive and knowledgeable peers are theorized to link immigrant students to academic and institutional resources (Stanton-Salazar 1997) including academically engaged and more proficient conversational partners who can provide language learners with opportunities to use and learn academic English. In this sense, social networks index the kinds of opportunities for learning academic English that immigrant youth encounter. Although friends of friends (weak ties) have been shown to provide some educational resources to immigrant youth (Enriquez 2011), social networks consisting of close relationships (strong ties) are better indicators of the linguistic resources afforded language minority youth (Bortoni-Ricardo 1985; Milroy 1987). Schools shape the development of a particular form of social capital—peer relationships—by explicitly and implicitly structuring access to academically engaged and more proficient peers (Gándara and Contreras 2009; Stanton-Salazar 2004).

THE CURRENT STUDY

The current study took as a starting point the notion that adolescent language minority youth negotiate multiple social contexts which influence their choices, opportunities, and language learning outcomes. The case studies illustrated in this chapter show that some students had more—and others fewer—opportunities at school to use English and Spanish in ways that supported developing academic English. Two primary research questions framed this inquiry: (1) How do school policies support or impede the development of peer social networks that facilitate development of academic English? (2) How do classroom practices enact school policies that support or impede engaging peers as resources for learning academic English?

RESEARCH CONTEXT AND METHODS

Data presented in this chapter are drawn from an interdisciplinary and mixed method study of 102 Spanish-speaking immigrant youth which linked the development of academic English to linguistic peer support (Carhill-Poza 2011). The students were recruited from four public high schools in New York City representing typical secondary school contexts for Spanish-speaking immigrant youth, and case studies of each school were developed. One focal adolescent was selected from among study participants in each school to illustrate the interaction of school setting and student agency in the development and use of peer linguistic resources. School data include fieldnotes collected over one year at each school, interviews with faculty and students, and statistics. Student data include official transcripts and records from the school, a formal interview and numerous informal interviews with each student conducted in Spanish and English, ethnographic fieldnotes collected during more than five days of participant observation with each student, artifacts, and transcripts of audio-recorded student interactions.

During three years, I visited the school research sites at least once each week and conducted participant observations in classes with Spanish-speaking immigrant youth, as well as in the hallways, lunchrooms, offices, and faculty meetings of the schools. To gain an understanding of students' language use throughout their school day, I shadowed focal students for a week and audio-recorded them throughout their school day using a digital audio-recorder that stayed on all day. I used formal interviews to elicit a description of social networks (Suárez-Orozco, Suárez-Orozco, and Todorova 2008) and corroborated these data through observation. Quantitative analysis was used to establish patterns of peer resources and aided the selection of case study participants with average linguistic peer resources at each school.

The examples in this chapter document the unique multilayered experience of individuals in their schools but draw on themes prominent across all four case studies and in the larger data set through an analytic inductive approach to data analysis (LeCompte and Preissle 1993). Themes that emerged were analyzed within and across the four case studies to account for the linguistic resources available to Spanish-speaking adolescents through their peer social networks and to document the impact of implicit and explicit school policies and other school factors on the ways focal students engaged with and developed peer linguistic resources. Validity was ensured through the use of multiple sources of evidence and through participants' checking of drafts of the case studies (Yin 2003).

An important aspect of the case studies was establishing focal students' use of academic English. Transcripts of participant interactions were analyzed for the use of Spanish and English and for academic language use in both languages. In order to establish and contrast the kinds of opportunities to use and learn academic language each participant encountered across five school days, students' language use was examined in context (interaction setting, interlocutors, topic of talk, text references) using event maps to detail patterns of language use across settings (Erikson and Schultz 1981).

Most importantly, vignettes of case studies emphasize the perspective of the student participants as they draw on their multilingual repertoires to use and learn academic language in high school. Javier and Jasmin were chosen to highlight the ways many layers of social context came together to form the conditions under which immigrant students were learning English in their schools. They entered their schools with similar English proficiency levels but over three years had confronted divergent policies which shaped access to peer linguistic resources. Pseudonyms are used to protect the identity of participants.

THE SCHOOL CONTEXT

New York City public schools at the time of this study served more than 1.1 million students, 41% of whom spoke a language other than English at home. Of the one in six students who were classified as ELLs, the majority (65%) spoke Spanish (New York City Department of Education 2005). These Spanish-speaking immigrant youth had roots in the Dominican Republic, Ecuador, Central America, and Mexico. All language minority students were administered an English proficiency test, the New York State English as a Second Language Assessment Test (NYSESLAT), each year to determine the number of mandated periods of ESL they would be required to take until they tested at the proficient level and were no longer eligible for language support services.

Schools in this study were chosen to exemplify average learning environments for Spanish-speaking immigrant students in New York City public schools (see Carhill-Poza 2011 for more detail on research site selection). Based on School Report Card data, the four school research sites had graduation rates and standardized test scores comparable to city-wide averages (New York City Department of Education 2005). School size (range from 2026 to 3352 total students) and the density of newcomer immigrant students (7% of students on average) were as equitable across research sites as possible. All schools in this study had a majority of Latino students (around 60%), around 30% Black students and a minority of White students. The schools that immigrant youth in this study attended served many more poor students than the city average (70% of students received free or reduced lunch compared to 49% across New York).

CASE STUDY 1, JAVIER: "WE DON'T DO THAT"

Javier's experience in high school typified that of many students at the lowest English proficiency levels in his school: his peer social network included bilingual peers who did not engage with him in academic talk or activities. During the spring semester of 2008, he was eighteen years old and in the eleventh grade at West Side High School, a public high school in New York City. Javier had left the Dominican Republic to join his father in the US three and a half years earlier and, with little knowledge of the realities he would encounter, was sent to West Side High School by the Department of Education's central office. Javier's parents spoke only Spanish with him and had not completed high school in the Dominican Republic. Working long hours and with little knowledge of public schools in New York City, Javier's parents frequently encouraged him to do well in school but did not question his assignment to West Side.

Outside the Mainstream

Javier was grouped with other ELLs in a small learning community (SLC) that met for classes mainly in the east wing of the fourth and fifth floor. In addition to the structural separation from mainstream students instantiated by the SLC, Javier found that the halls and lunchroom of West Side High School were not welcoming spaces for newcomer students to practice their English or get to know mainstream peers. Security searched students with metal detectors as they entered the building, and fights occurred in the halls several times during the 2008–2009 school year, some including knives and one, during a memorable visit, a gun (Fieldnotes, March 23, 2008).

Violence in the school and widespread acceptance of social division along linguistic and racial lines impeded the development of peer relationships, including those with English-proficient students. In the halls and lunchroom, Javier worried about violence from the English-speaking students and stayed close to his Spanish-speaking friends for protection. When asked to describe his experiences at West Side High School, he explained that the violence was a problem: "*Demasiado racismo, algo asi. Diferentes colores* are always fighting. *Todo eso. La pelea no me gusta de esta escuela ahora. Siempre es como una guerra*" [Too much racism, you know? People with different skin colors are always fighting. All that stuff. I don't like the fighting in this school now. It's always like a war] (Interview, March 4, 2008). In addition to highlighting concerns about safety in his school, Javier showed awareness of covert racial and linguistic boundaries. School staff emphasized the role of the SLC in providing a safe haven for newcomer students within an inhospitable school environment, and Javier liked being part of the Spanish-speaking community at West Side High School: "*Todo el mundo me conoce*" [Everyone knows me] (Interview, March 4, 2008). For Javier, "everyone" included the Spanish-speaking youth in his SLC, but not the wider school community.

After-school clubs, sports, and other extracurricular activities, which could have facilitated greater inclusion of language minority students in the life of the school, were restricted by school staff. Trash littered the halls and stairwells throughout West Side High School, and the walls showcased xeroxed pages prohibiting students from wearing hats and using cellular phones, but little student work or notifications of extra-curricular activities. When questioned about the pronounced lack of information on school activities in Javier's SLC, the principal replied, "They need tutoring, not anime (Japanese animation) club" (Interview, June 9, 2008). In his response, the principal referenced school policy which emphasized after-school tutoring for ELLs in preparation for high-stakes assessments, and the exclusion of students who were not yet proficient in English from extracurricular activities. Javier did sometimes attend tutoring for the American History Regents Exam, but did not participate in any of the extracurricular activities at his school which could have resulted in opportunities to interact with more pro-ficient peers or those with a wider range of experiences and cultural capital. Underlying the separation of English learners from mainstream students was the view that bilingual peers who had not yet mastered academic English were not valid resources for learning.

Learning English, Then Learning Content

School staff consistently articulated a vision of learning English which isolated language development from content-area learning. Both bilin-gual core content courses and language support courses structured classroom activities in ways that allowed limited student participation. Project-based learning, peer collaboration, and peer talk were viewed as classroom luxuries when language minority students needed to pass high-stakes exams. Javier's core content classes were bilingual courses taught and assessed fully in Spanish, which provided few opportunities for acquiring academic English or using academic language (in English or Spanish) productively. His ESL classes were a case study in missed opportunities, the teachers focusing on English grammar and vocabu-lary to the exclusion of age-appropriate academic content.

Based on his scores on the NYSESLAT and his grade level, West Side High School had placed Javier in four ESL periods per day. He found that his lengthy schedule, shown in Table 4.1, was a problem, particu-larly for afternoon classes, *"porque siempre llego cansado y no le pongo mucho caso al maestro"* [because I always arrive tired and don't pay much attention to the teacher] (Interview, March 4, 2008). Indeed, his teachers commented on his report card that he was "excessively absent" from early classes and showed a "lack of participation" later in the day.

Table 4.1   Javier's Schedule 2007–2008

Period	Time	Class
1	8:04–8:57	P.E.
2	9:01–9:48	School Service
3	9:52–10:39	English—Transitional ESL 10
4	10:43–11:30	English—Transitional ESL 10
5	11:34–12:21	Bilingual Economics
6	12:25–1:12	Bilingual Earth Science
7	1:16–2:03	No 7th-Period Class
8	2:07–2:54	Bilingual American History
9	2:58–3:45	Lunch
10	3:49–4:37	English—ESL 10
11	5:41–6:29	English—ESL 10

Javier's schedule was nearly identical to seventeen Level 2 ELLs in tenth grade. School staff had limited flexibility to craft schedules for English learners that included the required four periods of language support classes as well as the content-area coursework needed to graduate within four years. Javier's ten-hour schedule offered no electives and contained some redundant coursework: Javier had passed Bilingual American History the previous year, but was enrolled again in preparation for retaking the Regents Exam, which he had not passed. He had also already passed Economics but was taking the class again because nothing else fit his schedule.

Javier was acutely aware of and disappointed in his ESL placement in 2008–2009. He had been confident he would move up to Level 3, which he thought would offer more interesting instruction. Javier reported that he was bored in his classes and struggled to pay attention: *"Que no sean tan aburridos. Que no solamente den las clases o escriban en la pizarra, sino que lo explicquen"* [They should not be so boring. Not just lecture or write on the board, but explain things] (Interview, May 13, 2008). During the week of observation, Javier spoke most often in class when joking with friends in Spanish or singing popular *bachata* and *raggaetón* songs. He found that his current academic English skills were an obstacle for him to do many things at school, particularly understanding class lectures in English, paying attention in class, and completing homework assignments. Javier explained that he found homework especially hard, because *"no todos los maestros hablan español. Y si tu necesitas algo tienes que aprender alto ingles o intentarlo como tu puedas. Si no, busca otra persona que lo diga por ti"* [not all the teachers speak Spanish. And if you need something you have to learn a high level of English or try to do it however you can. If not, you look for another person to say it for you] (Interview, March 4, 2008). His comments show awareness of the hierarchy of English proficiency levels, in which higher levels provided more access to the resources and support he needed to engage in school and do well academically.

Peer Support

Javier spent most of his time in class with four Dominican peers with whom he spoke Spanish. He described his friends as *"agresivos. Peleoneros.* [laughs] Cool. *Siempre hacen mucho coro y todo. Divertidos"* [violent. They like to fight. (laughs) Cool. They always play around. Funny] (Interview, May 15, 2008). Only one peer, his younger sister, interacted with him regularly in academic tasks. Javier's peers provided emotional support and safety at school, but very little linguistic support. In the lunchroom and in the halls, Javier talked and joked in Spanish with his friends and other groups of Spanish-speaking students. Over five school days, I did not observe Javier talk about homework, an academic concept, or school with his friends. When I asked him about this, he said, "We don't do that. *Saludarse. Hablar.* Look for girls. Just play around" [We don't do that. We say hello, talk, look for girls. Just play around] (Interview, May 15, 2008).

Although "everyone" knew Javier, he had few academically engaged friends and few friends whom he spoke English with regularly. His friends supported him in important ways at school, providing emotional and social support, but his social network contained few linguistic or academic resources for him to leverage. When Javier didn't understand his homework or what classes he needed to take to graduate, he had no knowledgeable peers in his network to seek support from. Nor did his peer social network offer him opportunities to talk about academic concepts or collaborate on academic tasks, a mechanism for learning academic English. Javier's network represents his marginalized status in school and the related lack of social capital he could have exchanged for the linguistically rich experience of engaging challenging subject-area content with teachers, texts, and peers.

CASE STUDY 2, JASMIN: "SPANISH SPEAKERS" AND "NORMAL PEOPLE"

Jasmin was representative of students who had developed an academically oriented bilingual peer network. Her network referenced some structural exclusion alongside school policies which valued bilingual peers as resources for learning. Jasmin had come to New York City from a small town in Ecuador to join her mother and an older sister three years prior to the study. In April 2009, she was fifteen years old and in tenth grade at a large public high school in New York City. As in Javier's family, Jasmin was attending a higher level of schooling than either of her parents had completed. Although no one in Jasmin's family spoke English or was familiar with US Schools, Jasmin's friend in eighth grade had helped her navigate the school selection process; New Riverside High School was her first choice because of its new sports facilities and extensive team sports program.

Outside the Mainstream

At New Riverside High School, the 15% of the students who were classified as ELLs were separated from mainstream students in an ELL program. ELLs attended most of their classes on the fourth floor, an arrangement similar to the structural segregation Javier experienced. In contrast to Javier's school, however, Jasmin felt safe in the halls and lunchroom, and staff and security created a welcoming atmosphere by greeting students and visitors entering the school. Also in contrast to Javier's school, the faculty at New Riverside promoted after-school clubs and sports with notices in the bilingual area of the school, some containing Spanish and Chinese text. The hallways of New Riverside were clean and, in addition to notices about activities for students, student work and photo montages of students participating in school events were displayed.

Despite these school policies intended to support greater participation among immigrant youth in the life of the school, Jasmin and her ELL peers formed a school within a school. Jasmin highlighted this separation when she commented on the unfairness of her long school day, which in addition to creating a tiring schedule for her, precluded her from participating in any after-school clubs or sports because they began an hour before she finished class:

Jasmin: They should give less periods. Because you see, the normal people, they have less periods, and us, we could even have 1 through 11 and they don't care.
Avary: What did you call the other people?
Jasmin: The normal people. [laughs] The English-speaking people. The normal English people.
Avary: Well what are you guys then?
Jasmin: Spanish speakers.   (Interview, May 18, 2009)

Jasmin's comments highlight that the separation from mainstream students constructed and enacted through the lengthy schedules caused an even more intense social separation. For Jasmin, having so many class periods was a punitive action taken by the school against students not proficient in English (see Table 4.2). Categorization as an ELL by the school restricted the range of peers she could interact with in extracurricular activities and in classes, while positioning ELLs as abnormal in their school.

Based on her reading and writing scores on the NYSESLAT, New Riverside High School had placed Jasmin in two periods of ESL despite advanced Listening and Speaking scores. Jasmin, like Javier, was fully aware of her place in the English proficiency hierarchy. Because she had passed her high-stakes subject-area exam in English (the English Language Arts Regents) and routinely used English to accomplish academic tasks, she thought her ESL placement was a mistake. Academically, Jasmin was a good student; she had a 98% attendance rate for the 2008–2009 school year and a B average. Jasmin explicitly connected her ESL level to limitations placed on her coursework and socialization opportunities.

Table 4.2   Jasmin's Schedule 2008–2009

Period	Time	Class
3	8:45–9:33	Spanish 2
4	9:37–10:23	Bilingual Earth Science
5	10:27–11:13	P.E.—Swimming
6	11:17–12:03	Bilingual Global History
7	12:07–12:53	Jr. ROTC/Ceramics
8	12:57–1:43	English—Transitional ESL 4
9	1:47–2:33	Lunch
10	2:37–3:25	English—Transitional ESL 4
11	3:29–4:15	Bilingual Geometry

Learning English and Learning Content

Throughout her school day, Jasmin, like Javier, spoke mostly Spanish. However, school policies did not promote the same rigid separation of learning English from academic content that Javier experienced. Although most of Jasmin's core content classes were bilingual courses preparing students to take standardized state exams in Spanish, some made use of English textbooks (Geometry and Earth Science) or lectured and wrote notes in both English and Spanish (Global History). In these bilingual classes, academic content was taught in ways that supported academic language development: visual models were used, concepts were introduced by building on students' existing knowledge, and higher-order thinking skills were scaffolded to generate questions and discussion around the academic content in Spanish with some explanation of English terms or spelling differences if the words were cognates.

For example, the Global History teacher began a class about the colonization and independence of India by asking students, *"Nosotros Latinos se llamaron Indios. Por que?"* [They call us Latinos "Indians." Why?]. In a spirited whole-class discussion, she elicited what students knew about India and wrote their responses on the board in the language students had used: *"Musulmanes* [Muslims], many religions, food, Gandhi, *Hindues* [Hindus], *ropa hindu* [Indian clothes]" (Fieldnotes, April 3, 2009). By structuring classroom discourse inclusively, bilingual students were recognized as valid resources for learning, contributing to classroom knowledge and skills in both languages.

Peer Support

Jasmin had regular contact with five peers, including her recently arrived twin brother and her older sister, both of whom she described as friends as well as siblings. Jasmin's friends were from Ecuador and Colombia, and she noted that they talked mostly in Spanish at lunch or in the hallways between classes.

She described them as successful students who "cut, but not often" (Interview, May 18, 2009). Jasmin explained that to be successful in her school, a new student had to "have your friends, but, you know how some people are telling you to cut classes and do many bad things? Not to listen to them, just be the person that you were in Ecuador" (Interview, May 18, 2009).

Despite speaking mostly Spanish with Jasmin, her friends provided important academic language support for her. She worked on homework with all five peers in her network and all of them were interested in her progress in at least one of her classes. Her peers also helped her to find information she needed for her schoolwork, talked with her about books and articles they had read, and looked over her writing in English to help her correct mistakes. Because conversations with her peers centered on academic concepts, Jasmin used academic language in English and in Spanish. Jasmin engaged in several interactions each day with other bilingual youth at lunch while they sat together talking, eating, texting on their sidekicks, and doing homework together, and these conversations provided essential opportunities for her to develop her academic English.

CONCLUSIONS AND IMPLICATIONS FOR POLICY

The concept of social capital has been used to understand how immigrant students accumulate the resources and experiences which over time differentiate academic trajectories (Conchas 2006; Stanton-Salazar 2004). Whereas many of the boundaries that limit access to education for language minority students have been documented, the role of bilingual peers in language learning has received limited attention. Current education policies, which pay little attention to the role of social inequalities in language development outcomes, are central to understanding the academic outcomes of immigrant youth who have not yet learned academic English.

The ecological framing of this study aids in elucidating how multiple layers of social context together constructed the conditions under which Javier and Jasmin were learning English and shows that school policies as well as values enacted at the classroom level moderated students' access to and choice of peers. Javier and Jasmin attended neighborhood schools because they lacked connections to knowledgeable adults and peers to guide them in selecting smaller, more resourced schools. Within their schools, both students encountered a tremendous degree of structural exclusion. ELLs were physically separated from mainstream students throughout the day, and while facilities and instruction varied from school to school, exposure to mainstream peers was consistently limited. Students were both isolated and protected within a bilingual house or small learning community. Classrooms and hallways also sent a clear message to immigrant students about racial and linguistic boundaries. The case studies show that while school safety was not sufficient for creating an inclusive environment where students could develop friendships across linguistic and racial lines, the lack of it contributed to the segregation of English learners from mainstream peers (Gibson et al. 2004; Suárez-Orozco, Suárez-Orozco, and Todorova 2008). As research has long shown, the structural separation of English learners from mainstream peers constrained language learning opportunities (Harklau 1994; Olsen 1997; Valdes 2001).

Student schedules provided an interesting artifact of school policies which grouped students by language proficiency; the long class schedules of English learners—which combined as many as four mandated periods of ESL with coursework equivalent to a mainstream student of the same grade level—left Javier and Jasmin unable to participate in electives or extracurricular activities which could have provided opportunities to develop relationships with a wider range of peers. In effect, academically weaker students and those less proficient in academic English were further weighed down by the longest schedules and cut off from social capital. Mirroring findings by Gándara and Contreras (2009) and Menken (2008), these practices resulted in a different curriculum for English learners than for mainstream students. Failing to recognize alternative forms of social capital that immigrant students brought to their schooling experience, subtractive schooling policies allocated resources needed by ELLs to succeed to students more proficient in English (Conchas 2006; Valenzuela 1999).

Not only did Javier and Jasmin encounter a tremendous degree of structural exclusion in their schools, but classroom practices often delegitimized peers as resources for learning. Jasmin's experience shows that bilingual peers provided meaningful academic experiences using both Spanish and English to complete homework assignments and participate in classes. Despite less than optimal school environments, Jasmin and Javier made use of limited resources to work toward their goals of learning academic English, succeeding at school, and feeling safe at school. Schools can support the development of peer social networks with academically engaged, supportive peers through policies which integrate students in the school community and build positive identities and roles for bilingual peers (Conchas 2006; Gibson et al. 2004; Mehan et al. 1996). When administrators and teachers were able to foster peer collaboration around academic concepts and academic tasks, students benefited doubly: they were apprenticed into ways of doing and talking about school and they had the opportunity to use academic English productively and meaningfully.

REFERENCES

August, Daniel, and Timothy Shanahan. 2006. *Developing Literacy in Second Language Learners: Report of The National Literacy Panel on Language-Minority Children and Youth.* Mahwah, NJ: Lawrence Erlbaum Associates.

Bailey, Alison, and Francis Butler. 2002. *An Evidentiary Framework for Operationalizing Academic Language for Broad Application to K–12 Education: A Design Document* (CSE Tech. Rep. No. 611). Los Angeles: University of California, National Center for Research on Evaluation, Standards, and Student Testing (CRESST).

Bartlett, Lesley. 2007. "Bilingual Literacies, Social Identification, and Educational Trajectories." *Linguistics and Education* 18: 215–231.

Bartlett, Lesley, and Ofelia Garcia. 2011. *Additive Schooling in Subtractive Times: Educating Dominican Immigrant Youth in the Heights.* Nashville: Vanderbilt University Press.

Berman, Ruth. 2004. *Language Development across Childhood and Adolescence.* Vol. 3 of *Trends in Language Acquisition Research.* Amsterdam: John Benjamin Publishers.

Berndt, Thomas. 1999. "Friends' Influence on Students' Adjustment to School." *Educational Psychologist* 34 (1): 15–28.

Bortoni-Ricardo, Stella. 1985. *The Urbanisation of Rural Dialect Speakers: A Sociolinguistic Study in Brazil.* Cambridge: Cambridge University Press.

Bourdieu, Pierre, and Jean-Claude Passeron. 1977. *Reproduction in Education, Society and Culture.* Beverly Hills, CA: Sage.

Bronfenbrenner, Uriel. 1977. "Towards an Experimental Ecology of Human Development." *American Psychologist* 32: 513–531.

Carhill, Avary, Carola Suárez-Orozco, and Mariela Páez. 2008. "Explaining English Language Proficiency among Adolescent Immigrant Students." *American Educational Research Journal* 45 (4): 1155–1179.

Carhill-Poza, Avary. 2011. "Opportunities and Outcomes: The Role of Peers in Developing the Academic English Proficiency of Adolescent English Learners." PhD diss. New York University. Accessed August 01, 2011 from Proquest Dissertations Database.

Carnegie Council on Adolescent Development. 1995. *Great Transitions: Preparing Adolescents for a New Century.* New York: Carnegie Corporation.

Clark, Eve. 2003. *First Language Acquisition.* Cambridge: Cambridge University Press.

Conchas, Gilberto. 2006. *The Color of Success: Race and High-Achieving Urban Youth.* New York: Teachers College Press.

Cummins, Jim. 1979. "Linguistic Interdependence and the Educational Development of Bilingual Children." *Review of Educational Research* 49: 221–225.

Eckert, Penelope. 1989. *Jocks and Burnouts: Social Categories and Identity in the High School.* New York: Teachers College Press.

Enriquez, Laura. 2011. "'Because We Feel the Pressure and We Also Feel the Support': Examining the Educational Success of Undocumented Immigrant Latina/o Students." *Harvard Educational Review* 81 (3): 476–499.

Erickson, Frederick, and Jeffery Schultz. 1981. "When Is a Context? Some Issues and Methods in the Analysis of Social Competence." In *Ethnography and Language in Educational Settings,* edited by Judith Green and Cynthia Wallat, 147–160. Norwood, NJ: Ablex Publishing Corporation.

Gándara, Patricia, and Frances Contreras. 2009. *The Latino Education Crisis: The Consequences of Failed Policies.* Cambridge, MA: Harvard University Press.

Gándara, Patricia, Daniel Losen, Diane August, Miren Uriarte, Cecilia Gómez, and Megan Hopkins. 2010. "Forbidden Language: A Brief History of U.S. Language Policy." In *Forbidden Language: English Learners and Restrictive Language Policies,* edited by Patricia Gándara and Megan Hopkins, 20–33. New York: Teachers College Press.

Gee, James. 1996. *Social Linguistics and Literacies: Ideology in Discourses.* 2nd ed. London: RoutledgeFalmer.

Gibson, Margaret, Livier Bejínez, Nicole Hidalgo, and Cony Rolón. 2004. "Belonging and School Participation: Lessons from a Migrant Student Club." In *School Connections: U.S. Mexican Youth, Peers and School Achievement,* edited by Margaret Gibson, Patricia Gándara, and Jill Koyama, 129–149. New York: Teachers College Press.

Gibson, Margaret, Patricia Gándara, and Jill Koyama, eds. 2004. *School Connections: U.S. Mexican Youth, Peers and School Achievement.* New York: Teachers College Press.

Harklau, Linda. 1994. "ESL and Mainstream Classes: Contrasting Second Language Learning Contexts." *Linguistics and Education* 6: 217–244.

Kao, Grace, and Marta Tienda. 1995. "Optimism and Achievement: The Educational Performance of Immigrant Youth." *Social Science Quarterly* 76 (1): 1–19.

Lantolf, James, and Gabriele Appel. 1994. *Vygotskian Approaches to Second Language Research.* Norwood, NJ: Ablex Publishing Corporation.

Lecompte, Margaret, and Judith Preissle. 1993. *Ethnography and Qualitative Design in Educational Research.* 2nd ed. San Diego, CA: Academic Press.

Leung, Constant. 2010. "English as an Additional Language: Learning and Participating in Mainstream Classrooms." In *Conceptualising Learning in Applied Linguistics*, edited by Paul Seedhouse, Steve Walsh, and Chris Jenks, 182–205. Basingstoke, Hampshire: Palgrave Macmillan.

Mather, Mark. 2009. *Children in Immigrant Families Chart New Path.* Washington, DC: Population Reference Bureau.

Mehan, Hugh, Irene Villanueva, Lea Hubbard, and Angela Lintz. 1996. *Constructing School Success: The Consequences of Untracking Low Achieving Students.* Cambridge: Cambridge University Press.

Menken, Kate. 2008. *English Language Learners Left Behind: Standardized Testing as Language Policy.* Clevedon, UK: Multilingual Matters.

Milroy, Lesley. 1987. *Language and Social Networks.* 2nd ed. Oxford: Blackwell.

National Center for Educational Statistics. 2010. *The Condition of Education 2010.* Washington, DC: US Department Of Education.

NCELA. 2011. *The Growing Numbers of English Learner Students 2009/10.* Washington, DC: National Clearinghouse for English Language Acquisition and Language Instruction Educational Programs.

New York City Department of Education. 2005. *Annual School Reports.* New York: Division of Assessment and Accountability, New York City Department of Education.

Nippold, Marilyn, Linda Hesketh, Jill Duthie, and Tracy Mansfield. 2005. "Conversational versus Expository Discourse: A Study of Syntactic Development in Children, Adolescents, and Adults." *Journal of Speech, Language and Hearing Research* 48 (5): 1048–1064.

Olsen, Laurie. 1997. *Made in America: Immigrant Students in Our Public Schools.* New York: The New Press.

———. 2010. *Reparable Harm: Fulfilling the Unkept Promise of Educational Opportunity for California's Long-Term English Learners.* Long Beach, CA: Californians Together.

Orfield, Gary, and Chungmei Lee. 2006. *Racial Transformation and the Changing Nature of Segregation.* Cambridge, MA: The Civil Rights Project at Harvard University.

Passel, Jeffrey. 2011. *Demography of Immigrant Youth: Past, Present, and Future.* Washington, DC: NCELA. Accessed January 18, 2012. http://www.ncela.gwu.edu.

Portes, Alejandro, and Ruben Rumbaut. 2001. *Legacies: The Story of the Immigrant Second Generation.* Berkeley: University Of California Press.

Ruiz-De-Velasco, Jorge, Michael Fix, and Beatriz Clewell. 2000. *Overlooked and Underserved: Immigrant Students in U.S. Secondary Schools.* Washington, DC: Urban Institute.

Rumbaut, Ruben. 2004. "Ages, Life Stages, and Generational Cohorts: Decomposing the Immigrant First and Second Generations in the United States." *International Migration Review* 38 (3): 1160–1205.

Scarcella, Robin. 2003. *Academic English: A Conceptual Framework* (Technical Report 2003–1). Irvine, CA: University of California Linguistic Minority Research Institute.

Stanton-Salazar, Ricardo 1997. "A Social Capital Framework for Understanding the Socialization of Racial Minority Children and Youths." *Harvard Educational Review* 67 (1): 1–40.

———. 2004. "Social Capital among Working-Class Minority Students." In *School Connections: U.S. Mexican Youth, Peers and School Achievement*, edited by Margaret Gibson, Patricia Gándara, and Jill Koyama, 129–149. New York: Teachers College Press.

Street, Brian. 1995. *Social Literacies*. London: Longman.

Suárez-Orozco, Carola, Marcelo Suárez-Orozco, and Irina Todorova. 2008. *Learning a New Land: Educational Pathways of Immigrant Youth*. Cambridge, MA: Harvard University Press.

Swain, Merril. 1993. "The Output Hypothesis: Just Speaking and Writing Aren't Enough." *Canadian Modern Language Review* 50: 158–180.

US Department of Education. 2011. *ESEA Reauthorization: A Blueprint for Reform*. Accessed December 14, 2011. http://www2.ed.gov/policy/esec/leg/ blueprint/faq/ diverse-learners.pdf.

Valdés, Guadalupe. 2001. *Learning and Not Learning English: Latino Students in American Schools*. New York: Teacher College Press.

Valenzuela, Angela. 1999. *Subtractive Schooling: U.S.-Mexican Youth and The Politics of Caring*. Albany, NY: SUNY Press.

Vygotsky, Lev. 1978. *Mind in Society*. Translated by M. Cole. Cambridge, MA: Harvard University Press.

Yin, Robert. 2003. *Case Study Research: Design and Methods*. 3rd ed. Thousand Oaks, CA: Sage Publications.

5 Problematizing My Position as a Researcher

Studying the Construction of Class by Chilean and Colombian International Students

Ana Luisa Muñoz-García[1]

"I am a turtle; wherever I go I carry 'home' on my back."

(Anzaldua 1999, 43)

Although people in Latin America are "well trained" to identify class, establish class differences, and make sense of life based on class, it is an uncommon topic in academia and other public domains. Class is a "practice of living," a fundamental organizer of social experience, both "objective" and "subjective," an organizer that has been largely eclipsed in scholarly literature over the past twenty-five years, particularly in the US, by other forms of interrogation and analysis, no matter how important" (Weis 2008, 3). As a Chilean woman, I question how Latin American society has constructed class and how mobility (through class and space) allows reflections about the naturalization of class and class privilege in specific contexts. The ways in which class can be reshaped through the process of mobility is emerging as an area of academic interest, and postsecondary education is a crucial site for engaging with issues of access, equity, and opportunity in the global context (Arum, Gamoran, and Shavit 2012; Li 2011; Weis 2012).

In this chapter, I focus on how international students from the Andes Mountains, a region that has its own historical, social, and cultural characteristics, construct class at home and reshape those constructions abroad. This focus serves as one example of the complexity of the dynamics of internationalization, understanding internationalization as a reified discourse of practices and policies of higher education (Matus and Talburt 2009). I argue that mobility allows international Chilean and Colombian scholars to transform their notion of class abroad and that through their movement across international borders and their encounters with the "other," students experience a process of deconstruction of class. Drawing on interviews I conducted with twelve international graduate students from two Andean countries, I interrogate how class is negotiated (or reworked) through both education and space, challenging the ways we understand the relationship between class and education in a global context. While the focus of the study is scholar mobility, I simultaneously offer a detailed parallel critical analysis of the main dilemmas that I have faced as a feminist female Chilean scholar from a working-class background studying class issues with scholars from Chile and Colombia. I critically question my co-constructed positionality.

This chapter contributes to the discussion about the complex ways immigrant students negotiate identities in the process of mobility. Like Smalls and Chikkatur (both in this volume), I focus on the ways education becomes a space of reworking identities. While Smalls and Chikkatur focus on the negotiations and discourses of race and ethnicity within schools, I look at class with international students from Chile and Colombia. However, in all three chapters it is possible to observe the complexities of the everyday and educational lives of students who are not considered domestic. Carhill-Poza (this volume) critiques the ways educational institutions in the US homogenize Latino students, an issue that international scholars—a group represented by participants in my study—challenge every day. Like Q. Chen's work (this volume), this study is framed by the literature on international scholar mobility. Both of us analyze the ways international scholars are positioned in the discourses of mobility and immigration, and the ways that they negotiate their positionalities as privileged immigrants.

First, I review the literature related to class and international student mobility. I then briefly explain the main methodological issues and dilemmas of studying class abroad and reflect critically about the complexities of studying issues of class from my working-class perspective. Then, I focus on one of the relevant findings of this study, how international students rework class abroad, and conclude with future considerations for studying class in the global context and policy implications for universities and governments, which have decided to incorporate the aims of internationalization into higher education policies.

CLASS REPRODUCTION AND SOCIAL MOBILITY

International students' schooling experiences has become the focus of an emerging body of higher education studies as increasing numbers of students attending US universities and colleges are from abroad. However, South American international students have been nearly absent from this scholarship. Furthermore, discourses about Latin American students in the US have focused mostly on the children of immigrants. International students from Latin America are also often viewed as a homogenous group, when, in fact, a high level of diversity exists among Mexican, Caribbean, and South American students.

Studies have shown how the presence of international students across the globe primarily from the so-called "developed countries" has increased during the last few decades; according to the Organization for Economic Co-operation and Development (OECD), in 2009 the number of international students worldwide was 3.3 million, and the US led this ranking with 20% of the international students (Guruz 2011; OECD 2011). As relevant "actors" in the global economy, institutions of higher education have promoted internationalization policies as a desirable standard, privileging the movement of students and academics (Fahey and Kenway 2010a; Rizvi 2011). The influence of scholars who are "going abroad," returning to their home countries, and then emigrating to others challenges institutional practices and policies (Matus 2009). Recent studies have shown that international students in the US have diverse experiences that often change the ways they see and understand the world, influencing their beliefs and their constructions of others and themselves (Fahey and Kenway 2010a; Matus 2004; Rizvi 2010).

The choices we make and the values that guide those choices, indeed the boundaries around the options from which we make choices, are all shaped by class structures (hooks 2000; Weis 2008, 2012). Many have theorized and illustrated ways in which schools have historically functioned as sites of class reproduction (Anyon 1981; Bourdieu 1977; Bowles and Gintis 1976; Lareau 1987; Weis 1990; Willis 1977); however, how class travels across borders is an underexplored phenomenon. In particular, individual class mobility—or the ability to move from one social class to another—can influence family and community relations, as well as individuals' relationships with their class of origin and the class of destination (Sympson 1970). Over time, and in the aggregate, mobility can affect class structures. Currently, the policies of redistribution (Fraser 1997) that allow students from the working class to enter the higher education system and obtain a degree provide paths of upward mobility. However, a discussion of how movement across places can challenge class structures is absent from the literature.

INTERNATIONAL STUDENT MOBILITY

Studying abroad is not a new phenomenon (Bhandari and Blumenthal 2011; Kim 2007, 2010; Rizvi 2010). However, the number of international students around the world has increased considerably during the past few decades (Altbach 2001; Bhandari and Blumenthal 2011; Broks and Waters 2011; Delicado 2011; Fahey and Kenway 2010a; Goodman and Gutierrez 2011; Guruz 2011; Kim 2010; Rizvi 2010). In different analyses of internationalization in higher education and student mobility around the world, there is agreement that international education has become a marker of success and social status (Findlay et al. 2011; Ong 1999; Rizvi 2011; Waters 2008). Traditionally, the literature about mobility has focused on the narratives of human capital development (CONICYT 2010; Cox 2010; OECD and World Bank 2009). Securing higher education abroad has emerged as a "natural" way to develop human capital, especially for those whose native countries do not have a well-established higher education system. Recently, however, scholars have begun to use critical perspectives to challenge the naturalized assertions of international student mobility (Epstein et al. 2008; Fahey and Kenway 2010a, 2010b; Matus 2009; Rizvi 2010, 2011; Rizvi and Lingard 2010; Sidhu 2006). Currently, governments and universities around the world express and make public their commitment to the internationalization of higher education and recognize the benefits that internationalization brings to them. For this reason, it is necessary to highlight that many national as well as university policies focus their efforts on internationalizing their institutions in order to meet the demands of the new social, political, economic, and cultural landscape. Moreover, it is important to recognize the complexity of implementing these strategies within universities (Matus and Talburt 2009).

METHODOLOGICAL CONSIDERATIONS AND THE RESEARCHER'S POSITIONALITY

In this qualitative study, conducted during the spring of 2011, I focused on collecting the meanings, interpretations, and processes of the social world (Eisner 1991; Glesne 2006). I conducted semistructured interviews with twelve international graduate students from two Andean countries which are connected, both economically and culturally. These students, all of whom were between the ages of 28 and 35, studied in two highly ranked public universities in the US. Seven students were from Chile and five were from Colombia. Most of them were from their capital cities, Santiago and Bogota, but a few were from smaller cities. Eight were female, and four were male. Seven students were studying social sciences, and five were in science and engineering. Eleven of them self-identified by their nationality, Chilean or Colombian, or as Latin American; one identified as Afro-Colombian. Five students considered themselves to be from a "poor family" or "working-class background," and one was from a "very poor environment." Three of them were from middle-class families, and two were from the upper class. Snowball sampling was used to select the participants. I am aware that grouping my participants can be seen as a homogenizing of international students from Latin America, so I specifically aim not to portray fixed, static, and essentialized pictures of them. On the contrary, I would like to share the complexity of their experiences. I expect that their narratives will convey the challenges of living in another culture. It will highlight that coming from an ethnic group can be positioned in various ways within the racialized context of the US. As a feminist researcher, I aimed to co-construct the interviews, attempting to equalize power relationships and carefully considering what I spoke about as well as how and why I spoke (Fine 1998).

As I sought to understand how these international graduate students talked about their own educational experiences at home and abroad, the interviews served as spaces where knowledge negotiation processes took place between the participant and the researcher. It is relevant to stress that the interviews took on the character of casual conversations with the participants. Furthermore, because they knew I was also an international student, more data sometimes emerged after the interviews, in informal conversation.

I transcribed the interviews, which I conducted in Spanish, and then I translated into English the data that could be incorporated into the study. After transcribing the interviews, I coded and organized data according to categories that emerged from the information collected. I identified forty-four codes and organized them into four categories: family background, class, education, and experiences studying abroad. Some of the major topics that emerged from the interviews were issues related to class in the participants' educational experience, classism, privilege, inequality, and narratives about being Latin American in the US, as well as stories embedded in their national history. I organized and reorganized the data according to these themes.

"YOU KNOW WHAT I MEAN"

Methodologically, this study invited me to reflect on my own situated identity in the research process and analyze the ways in which certain dimensions of this identity could play a relevant role in the fieldwork. As a researcher, particular aspects of my identity—gender, race, class, sexuality, and nationality—had significant effects on the type of information I collected, as well as on my interpretation of the information that was shared with me. "You know what I mean!" was one of the most common phrases; it indicated that we shared a common understanding. In fact, we did share a familiarity with the countries involved; I am from Chile and have visited Colombia. We also shared experiences about being international students studying in the US. To ask for more information, I sometimes had to say, "I may know what you mean, but I am not sure" or "Perhaps I know, but people who read this data might have no idea." As other scholars (Gaztambide-Fernandez 2009; Lee 2005) have argued, the identity of the researcher influences the research process. Participants use ethnicity, race, class, gender, and education to situate others. In my case, my nationality, Latin American identity, and class played strong roles.

Many of my participants made assumptions about who I was, and I wonder how the ways they were constructing me as a researcher impacted the ways they answered my questions. At the same time, what I chose to share with them about myself impacted the depth of my interviews and how

I analyzed the data. As Gaztambide-Fernandez (2009) writes, "how others present themselves to me, I present myself to them, and the interaction is shaped by the specific context of our encounter" (221). Most of these questions about my identity did not come from the Colombian-born students; the Chilean-born students asked them. Thus, one of the relevant issues this study raised is how our encounter would have been different if I had asked the same questions in the participants' home countries. In other words, I wonder how the international context—that is, living in a temporary location at a particular point in time—impacted the types of narratives participants constructed about themselves and others.

Another issue I faced was that of language. According to Srivastava (2006), the topic of translation is often not identified or discussed in research that involves more than one language, although it is highly relevant: "It seems that while there is an emerging focus on diasporic or mixed-background researchers, there is very little dialogue on how such researchers (often multilingual) employ language and understand and mediate its role in analysis" (Srivastava 2006, 216). Thus, one concern of this study was how the languages we acquired played a significant role in shaping our worldview and the type of vocabulary we used. To this end, we avoided making assumptions that we shared the same meanings of words and phrases. For example, in some cases the use of idioms by the participants, and my requests for clarification, provided an "open door" for in-depth discussion of complex issues. As Mullings (1999) writes, "a researcher's knowledge is therefore always partial, because his/her positionality (perspective shaped by his/her unique mix of race, class, gender, nationality, sexuality and other identifiers), as well as location in time and space, will influence how the world is viewed and interpreted" (337).

OUTING CLASS

When class is such a naturalized and taken-for-granted phenomenon, it can be complex and difficult to probe, irrespective of whether one grew up in an environment where money was never an issue or in one where it was a concern all of the time. I had to be careful about the ways in which I brought up issues, and when the topic of class came up in conversation, to take advantage of the opportunity to dig deeper. In several different interviews, I heard phrases like "I never talked about these issues in Chile or Colombia" and "I never thought about it before" (Interview, Claudio, Chile, March 5, 2011), "Sorry, this can be embarrassing but I grew up in a very classist environment" (Matias, Chile, March, 4, 2011), "I do not want to sound classist, but . . ." (Nicole, Colombia, March 4, 2011), and "I know that this may seem very classist, I am not classist, but . . ." (Emilia, Chile, March, 3, 2011). The participants recognized that class is a salient issue even though they did not talk about it in their countries. They were very clear about how they recognize a person from a different class background, what type of questions help to identify someone's class, and which phenotypes indicate which class. Outside their home countries they found it more difficult to identify the class background of other students. Interestingly, they also questioned how they notice themselves asking the same questions that they used to ask in their home countries in order to identify someone's class background.

PROBLEMATIZING MY POSITIONALITY

As a light brown–skinned Chilean woman who is an international student doing a PhD in the US but also from a working class background, I took up different and contradictory positionalities in the fieldwork with different participants, sometimes as an equal, and sometimes "looking up" to their privilege. Like my participants, I was studying for a doctorate; however, whereas most of them came from an upper class background, I did not. In a similar vein, Gaztambide-Fernandez (2009) notes that "the power relations that shaped my work were far more complex than metaphors of verticality allow. If anything, I might say that I was researching, up, down, sideways, and all around" (222). Certainly, being a fellow PhD student gave me some insider status. I also speak Spanish, am from Latin America, and in some cases shared the participants' scholarly focus. However, there were always areas of difference: I was from the south; I studied at a different, less well-known university for my bachelor's degree, but then completed my master's degree at a university that most of the Chilean participants had attended. Recognizing that I am from Chile, students from Colombia usually compared their experiences with those of people from Chile, using expressions like "I know that this means another thing in your country," "We do have another type of state violence, different from Chile in the dictatorship," "Chileans are more serious than Colombians," and so on.

In this sense, there is not a binary notion of insider and outsider. Positionality allows for a multifaceted identity, and one necessary question in this research might be how those fluid parts of one's identity are hierarchized and blurred outside of the home country, and how my situated self intersects at different points and in different ways with each participant. This is beautifully described by Smalls (this volume) as "the 'intersubjective' work that transpires between the researcher and the researched," a phrase that expresses the multiple ways the researcher gets involved in the process of constructing knowledge. As I've already argued, research positionality is always in flux, and it is linked to my constructions of myself in real life, outside of the field. "The critical point for our discussion is that the multiplicities of identities (some shared, and others not) opens up a space for researchers to facilitate exchange by creating shared positionalities with participants" (Srivastava 2006, 212). In addition to this discussion about positionality, some scholars have focused their attention on the process of reflexivity. Mullings (1999) aptly notes that reflexivity becomes an important process for clarifying the landscapes of power within which much research is conducted. Similarly, Cousin (2010), with her notion of "greying positionalities," problematizes the primacy of the "master status," discussing how overidentification with "inherited" positionality can produce "intellectual and emotional laziness" rather than invite reflexivity. One of the points Cousin makes is that "reflexivity in the research process also includes suggesting to subjects 'possible horizons of meanings' and perhaps the skill of the researcher to do so may be more important than their personal biography and status as insider or outsider" (15). For me, the most important task has been to think about the ways in which my positionality allows me to ask reflexive questions—for example, about how I construct the voice of my participants and how I bring myself into the research process.

ANALYSIS AND FINDINGS: REWORKING CLASS IN THE PROCESS OF MOBILITY

In this study, participants considered the ways they think class travels with them abroad, but they also acknowledged that traveling abroad makes them think about how social class and class differences work in Chile and Colombia. Their narratives suggested that their experiences abroad allowed them to meet different group of people, which caused them to confirm and challenge their construction of class. In other words, these scholars see themselves asking the same types of questions that they ask in their home country to get information about class, but in the US, these questions do not help them to easily recognize the class backgrounds of people who are not Chilean or Colombian. Therefore, one issue that is central to this study is how class is denaturalized abroad. Removed from the familiar "classed context" of "home," one has to learn to understand a different set of class constructions. How does the process of identification with or differentiation from "the other" allow them to begin to interrogate the ways they understand class? To address these concerns, we first need to know how class and class differences are constructed at home, and the ways those constructions are negotiated and challenged both at home and abroad. In this sense, space is transformed into a new site where meeting "others" abroad remains crucial to comprehending how class travels and how it is challenged by place. In order to understand this process of "reworking class" I now discuss how these participants understand and negotiate class at home and how their sense of class traveled abroad.

Between Two Classes: The Challenge of Reworking Class at Home

The participants I interviewed were students from a range of social class backgrounds, and because of this I heard different types of narratives that prompted questions and conversations related to class, place, and positions. The primary goal was to understand how their educational and social backgrounds shaped the educational experiences of the participants abroad. There are two main issues that participants in this study considered relevant to constructing class at home: first, there was a process of negotiating class through their education, and second, there was a shared consciousness about privilege and the fact they grew up in an unequal society. Matias, who is Chilean, provided an example of how a student from a working-class background negotiates class at school in his home country:

A particular situation happened in high school. We did a science project between two high schools; the other high school was public. The girls of the other high school came to exhibit their work at our school. Then among my classmates, they began to do a lot of comments that the girls were ugly, they were browner or that their uniforms were ugly, do you know what I mean?, that they speak different, and so forth. I did not participate in that conversation, but I felt part of it. I felt part of these other girls. But I was also part of my group at school, so it was a complex situation, this was a matter of class, I was in the middle. I understood the two groups, do you understand? I did not know which place I belonged. (Interview, March 4, 2011)

Despite coming from a working-class background, Matias's parents made the effort to enroll him in a charter school where most of the students were from middle- and upper-class families. Being in a different social/cultural environment at school, Matias had to negotiate his class with his peers. As he put it: "More than learning knowledge, I learned how to adapt to social situations." The stories were complex; many times, he added, "I do not know if you understand this?" or "do you know what I mean?" He gave many examples of how moving between social classes was complicated and full of tension for him. This kind of movement from one class to another can be even more complex in a society where the class issues are felt strongly, but are completely omitted from conversation. In these contexts, the idea of class is more than having purchasing power. It has to do with issues like last names, phenotypes, neighborhoods, and the ways people made their fortunes.

Florencia, a PhD student in the social sciences, offered a similar narrative. Like Matias, she had to pause at certain moments in the interview, when the memories brought up feelings and emotions that made clear the struggle experienced by a student who felt "out of place." Florencia grew up in a working-class family in a neighborhood in Colombia. When she entered a private and elite university in Bogota, she faced different issues related to class. She described feelings of loneliness and discrimination in a place where she felt she did not belong. Florencia's reflections about her educational experience in the university went further. She dealt with various issues of class in her educational institution, but she dealt with another issue upon coming back to her parents' home and neighborhood. She recalled:

> I see who my family is, who are my friends in the neighborhood, and who are my friends from school, and I feel that the university took me away from them in many ways. Because the university made me think about other things, it made me learn to love other forms of life. Not that I do not like theirs, but I am no longer in their lives. [. . .] At the university I met the father of my son, and he had a very similar story . . . we were drawn together at the university and then we shared in this solitude, the loneliness of not being who we were in our families, but also not being part of people of the university, not being part of those networks. (Interview, March 3, 2011)

Florencia's description of her classmates contrasted starkly with the narratives of students from Chile and Colombia who self-identify as upper class. While they also reworked class in their educational experience, for them the university in their home country was the place where they could "go outside of their bubble" and "meet with people from other socioeconomic backgrounds." They were in the same institution, but the construction of their educational experience in those institutions was quite different from that of students who did not belong to the middle or upper class.

As in other studies, the stories about how the participants from working-class backgrounds negotiated class at home bring up two relevant concerns. First, schools become a place where class is negotiated and where students learn how to read class. A significant area of inquiry related to this study, then, is the consequences of how the education system completely omits class discussion, thus naturalizing class and leaving class inequality untouched. Second, new policies of redistribution in higher education in some countries in Latin America are developing doctoral scholarships which incorporate the possibility of learning English, which is changing the type of students who can pursue the opportunity of studying abroad (OECD and World Bank 2010). Some of the participants are enrolled in these programs, and it is important to know how the class construction of these participants travels with them.

Coming from an Unequal and Classist Society

Thus far I have discussed how students from working-class backgrounds negotiate their class in their educational experience at home. The narratives of the students from the upper class provided a contrast to these experiences, illustrating instead how differently class is lived in the everyday life of these students. Take the stories of Nicole and Javiera, who not only shared a class background but also both attended elite private universities.

Both of them were in social sciences, and in both cases, their mothers had a strong influence on their education. Nicole remembered her mother asking her to read the *Open Veins of Latin America of Galeano* when she was eight years old, and Javiera connected her memories of her mother reading the newspaper and talking about the news. Because of that, both of them had a strong consciousness about the history of their own countries. Both of them grew up in upper-middle-class neighborhoods. Nicole lived "in the north of the city in Bogota," and Javiera lived "east of Italian Square, close to the mountains in Santiago." Both cases exemplify the importance of geography in how class is experienced and how the division within cities gave them clues to situate the "other." Bogota and Santiago are divided into neighborhoods known to most residents, and saying which side of the city you live in gives your audience information about socioeconomic status, about where you "belong." Even though they were living in a "bubble," as Javiera mentioned, they were aware of how class works. For example, Nicole's family moved from a middle-class to an upper-middle-class neighborhood when she was in primary school. Her family's move and the massacre of an entire political party during the 80s were two significant and informative memories from Javiera's childhood. Every participant from Colombia talked widely about the massacre; however, the fact that Nicole put the massacre and her family's move to a new home on the same level, as the two most important events in her life, did not make sense to me until she related the following narrative:

> [I was] at a private university, probably the most elite university of the country. It is one of the leading universities, but it is also one of the universities that reproduce inequality in the sense that it is a social network. [. . .] Living in a country with social inequality and class discrimination, the pressure (where do you live) was high. So, the chances and the pressure of socialization that one felt at the university had much to do with socioeconomic background. (Interview, March 4, 2011)

Nicole's narrative illustrates how important it was for her that her parents made this upward improvement by changing their neighborhood, and how that affected her opportunities at the university. Additionally, the stories Nicole and Javiera shared give us some clues about the segregation of the education system—and the cities in Colombia and Chile—and the few possibilities these students had to interact with people from a different class background. As discussed below, the question that follows is how class constructions, shaped by students' educational experience, travel abroad.

"Unprotected by Class": Neither Mexican nor Immigrant

One of the major themes in the narratives of the participants is who they are in the US. Some feel like "second-class citizens," (Interview, Claudio, March

5, 2011), or that they are treated like an "illegal immigrant from Mexico" (Emilia, March 3, 2011; Nicole, March 4, 2011). However, these international graduate students did not feel "Mexican" or "undocumented." Mexican, immigrant, illegal immigrant, and Mexican illegal immigrant were the terms these participants used to explain how people in the US read them and the effects those constructions had in their daily lives as international students. For example, Claudio, who felt categorized as a "second-class citizen," used his position as a PhD student to distinguish himself from "immigrants." An important question that the narrative of Claudio raises for this study is what made him feel that it was necessary to distinguish his position from that of people who decide to move to the US to look for a job or, in general, a better life. Emilia described a similar situation of feeling like an outsider who is also considered Mexican in the US. She recognized the order of her identities in the US as an order that does not work in her home country. At the same time, she compared racism in the US to classism in her country:

> Some people yelled at me in the street, "Mexican, Mexican" as derogatory term, as if they were saying "asshole." Also, when my partner became ill, we were here, she was a super blonde woman in the Chilean context, and they told her what she had was probably due to the lack of hygiene in our countries when she really had cancer! . . . But it has been not so much; no one ever hit me [in the US], ever. In that sense I think that discrimination against lesbians is much higher in Chile that I have felt discrimination from racism in the US, but I can see the racism in this country, and I find it extremely surprising, as surprising as classism in our society (Interview, March 3, 2011)

There are a number of issues that Emilia brought up in her narrative. First, she was surprised that someone yelled at her in the street, using "Mexican" as a derogatory word. Also, she positioned her girlfriend as "blonde"— which is associated with the upper class in Chile. Yet her girlfriend was discriminated against in the US hospital because the staff constructed her as being from a poor Latin American country, and she did not receive the proper treatment. Finally, however, for Emilia, "it was not so much" because she did not experience violence. In this sense, she was constructing racism based on her own experience of discrimination: "racism here is like classism in our society" and "discrimination against lesbians is much higher in Chile that I have felt discrimination from racism in the US." The question of how these international students dealt with being positioned as undocumented people and the nature of their reflections on those experiences emerged from Emilia's narrative. Her narrative also forces us to think about how students' multifaceted identities take different forms in different spaces. As these students began to think critically about their positions in the US, they often tried to take refuge in the privilege offered by socioeconomic class in their home country, a class privilege that did not always translate in the US. In their experiences as doctoral students from Latin America, they felt "unprotected" by their class. This was present whether they were from working-, middle-, or upper-class backgrounds, because they had the "privilege of education." For example, Nicole found herself thinking critically about the dynamics between Latin Americans in Latin America, and between people from the US and Latin America. She thought of herself as Colombian, stating, "I look in the mirror and I see a Colombian person, but never close to 'Mexican,' or 'illegal immigrant,' I had never seen myself like that, but here [in the US] I am [seen as] an illegal Mexican immigrant." In the US she is seen as Mexican, and she had many experiences in which she was treated like an undocumented person, something that did not happen to her husband, whose skin is lighter. She struggled with her reasons for not wanting to be seen as an immigrant, and the reasons she wanted to be seen differently. For her, it had been emotionally challenging and was difficult to articulate, as she noted in the following exchange:

Nicole:	I basically went through a process where I try to be consistent with myself. I think: ok, you see me, and if you see an undocumented person, that's good, because I position myself in solidarity with those people . . . Because at first my reaction was: "But there are class markers which are different!!" But it is disgusting that I'm thinking that way!!!
Ana Luisa:	What do you mean when you say: there are markers of class? Do you feel in a different class than immigrants from Colombia or other countries?
Nicole:	Of course! Basically because if you compare a person who has to immigrate to the US, and I do not understand why they come to find a work in a place like this, but they come for economic reasons. It is not my situation; it is not the reason why I came. I do not want to stay. I'm not trying to conquer any American dream. It is not what I believe in, nothing like that, but in that sense there are differences, and it is what I am appealing to. What comes to my mind when I think about it, it is horrible, because it is a class distinction that I condemn in everyday life in Colombia and the US, but these are the contradictions . . .
Ana Luisa:	Do you appeal to your class to settle racial discrimination?
Nicole:	Yes, but it happens only in my head, because obviously for others it does not have sense. That for me, for example, this has been emotionally very difficult, I mean all this [classist attitude] for me has always been unacceptable and I stop it at various times in my family, and in my job in Colombia. Suddenly, when I feel on the vulnerable side, what I am saying is that I'm different!! I never felt that before, because I had that never been in that situation . . . (Nicole, March 4, 2011)

International students take their class structure with them when they travel abroad; in this migration their class constructions are challenged. The privilege and security some participants found in their class status in their home countries does not work in the US. In the US, these students tried to rely on the same class paradigm they sought to reject in their home countries.

CONCLUSION: RETHINKING CLASS ABROAD

The participants in this study did not represent one homogeneous group, either in terms of class or race or in terms of gender and/or sexuality. As I mentioned earlier, very little research exists on international students from Latin America and specifically on students from Andean countries. The data from this research touches on class issues, the sense of mobility, race and class discrimination, and many other concerns. I heard stories about class mobility through education, the possibilities for reworking one's own class position in one's home country, and what it meant for the participants to be international students from Latin America living in the US. I heard happy stories as well as not so happy ones, but more importantly, I heard narratives about how participants attempted to use their class status to counteract the racial discrimination they experienced in the US. How they experienced class in their home countries and how they experienced it in the US are two major themes of this study. The stories presented in this chapter invited me to situate an analysis of how the inequality, power, and privilege in socially and economically stratified societies, like those of Chile and Colombia, travel abroad and are challenged. Because the participants in this study were international students, it also invites reflection about how policies of internationalization are being thought about and the significant issues scholars from different class backgrounds face. More importantly, policies and programs should consider discourses about students' class mobility as another type of migration process with all the complexity that it implies.

Methodologically, this study brings to the fore a conversation about how the positionality of the researcher might be discussed in terms of language issues, as well as in terms of context and space. As an international student, I have also questioned my own situatedness and multiple locations in order to preserve my integrity in discursive terms and to ensure the reliability of my studies. This work reaffirms the importance of reflexivity regarding the role of a researcher's multiple identities in the context of fieldwork. The voices of these students prompted me to reflect on classism, power, and resistance, but also on solidarity, love, and consciousness. I chose class as a focal point because it is one of the most challenging parts of my identity. The poor have no voice in writing circles, and when they do, it is because they are not poor anymore. I am one of them. I was poor; I grew up below the poverty level. Today, I am displaced by class. I am a well-educated woman, I can have a voice, and I am no longer poor. That fact positions me in a dilemma for which I do not yet have a solution or answer. Moreover, as a doctoral student from an underclass family, I continue to struggle with class issues and assumptions about who I am or should be.

Finally, the relevant finding in this research concerns how international students tried to use their class positions to counteract racial discrimination. However, the class privilege they were used to at home did not work for them in the US, which left these students unprotected by class. This study leaves open several important questions: What types of social and cultural skills do international students need in order to deal with "global diversity" and to confront the different ways in which they are being positioned as people from Latin America? What type of conversation within academia is necessary to bring to light how class is being redefined through internationalization processes? How it is possible to articulate the policies of internationalization in higher education? Moving abroad allows students to interact with a wider variety of classes because of the internationalization of universities, but students still operate within institutions governed by racism, patriarchy, homophobia, and xenophobia. More research is needed about this specific process. Finally, even though these participants are in the constant process of identity construction, the "home" they carry to the US as international students plays an important role in the construction of their experience in this country. A significant first step is an understanding of how these "turtles" have constructed their home in terms of class, gender, race, and sexuality and of the ways they carry it on their backs abroad.

NOTES

1. I gratefully acknowledge the editorial assistance of Bethany Van Hooser, who not only provided editorial support, but also discussed the ideas in this chapter with me extensively.

REFERENCES

Altbach, Philip. 2001. "Higher Education and the WTO: Globalization Run Amok." *International Higher Education.* (23): 2–4.

Anyon, Jean. 1981. "Social Class and School Knowledge." *Curriculum Inquiry* 11 (1): 3–42.

Anzaldua, Gloria. 1999. *Borderlands/La Frontera: The New Mestiza.* San Francisco, California: Aunt Lute Books.

Arum, Richard, Adam Gamoran, and Yossi Shavit. 2012. "Expanded Opportunities for All in Global Higher Education Systems." In *Social Class in Education Global Perspectives*, edited by Lois Weis and Nadine Dolby, 15–36. New York: Routledge.

Bhandari, Rajika, and Peggi Blumenthal. 2011. "Global Student Mobility and the Twenty-First Century Silk Road: National Trends and New Directions." In

International Students and Global Mobility in Higher Education, edited by Rajika Bhandari and Peggi Blumenthal, 1–23. Chennai, India: McMillan.

Bourdieu, Pierre. 1977. "Symbolic Power." In *Identity and Structure: Issues in the Sociology of Education*, edited by D. Gleson, 112–117. Driffield: Nafferton Books.

Bowles, Sam, and Herb Gintis. 1976. *Schooling in Capitalist America: Educational Reform and the Contradictions of Economic Life*. New York: Basic Books.

Broks, Rachel, and Johanna Waters. 2011. *Student Mobility and Internationalization of Higher Education*. London: Palgrave-Macmillan.

CONICYT. 2010. "Balance Gestion Integral: Comision Nacional de Investigacion Cientifica." Accessed March 20, 2012. http://www.conicyt.cl.

Cousin, Glynis. 2010. "Positioning Positionality: The Reflexive Turn." In *New Approaches to Qualitative Research: Wisdom and Uncertainty*, edited by Maggi Savin-Baden and Claire Howell Major, 9–19. London and New York: Routledge.

Cox, Loreto. 2010. "Becas para Postgrados en el Extranjero: Un Analisis Critico de la Justificacion y el Diseno del Sistema en Chile." 1–17. Published electronically June 2010.

Delicado, Ana. 2011. "The Consequences of Mobility: Careers and Work Practices of Portuguese Researchers with a Foreign PhD Degree." In *Analysing the Consequences of Academic Mobility and Migration*, edited by Fred Dervin, 163–181. Newcastle: Cambridge Scholars Publishing.

Eisner, Elliot. 1991. *The Enlightened Eye: Qualitative Inquiry and the Enhancement of Educational Practice*. New York: Macmillan.

Epstein, Debbie, Rebecca Boden, Rosemary Deem, Fazal Rizvi, and Susan Wright, eds. 2008. *Geographies of Knowledge, Geometries of Power: Framing the Future of Higher Education*. New York: Routledge.

Fahey, Johanna, and Jane Kenway. 2010a. "International Academic Mobility: Problematic and Possible Paradigms." *Discourse: Studies in the Cultural Politics of Education* 31 (5): 563–575.

———. 2010b. "Thinking in a 'Worldly' Way: Mobility, Knowledge, Power and Geography." *Discourse: Studies in the Cultural Politics of Education* 31 (5): 627–640.

Fazal, Rizvi, and Lingard Bob. 2010. *Globalizing Education Policy*. New York: Routledge.

Findlay, Allan, Russel King, Fiona Smith, Alistair Geddes, and Ronald Skeldon. 2011. "World Class? An Investigation of Globalisation, Difference and International Student Mobility." *Transactions of the Institute of British Geographers* 37 (1): 118–131.

Fine, Michelle. 1988. "Working the Hyphens: Reinventing Self and Other in Qualitative Research." In *The Landscape of Qualitative Research: Theories and Issues*, edited by Norman Denzin and Yvonna Lincoln, 130–155. Thousand Oaks, CA: Sage.

Fraser, Nancy. 1997. *Justice Interruptus: Critical Reflections on the Postsocialist Condition*. New York and London: Routledge.

Gaztambide-Fernandez, Ruben. 2009. *The Best of the Best: Becoming Elite at an American Boarding School*. Cambridge, MA: Harvard University Press, 2009.

Glesne, Corrine. 2006. *Becoming Qualitative Researchers*. 3rd ed. New York: Longman, 2006.

Goodman, Allan, and Robert Gutierrez. 2011. "The International Dimension of U.S. Higher Education: Trends and New Perspectives." In *International Students and Global Mobility in Higher Education: National Trends and New*

Directions, edited by Rajika Bhandari and Peggy Blumenthal, 83–106. New York: Palgrave-Mcmillan.

Guruz, Kemal. 2011. *Higher Education and International Student Mobility in the Global Knowledge Economy*. Albany, NY: SUNY Press.

hooks, bell. 2000. *Where We Stand: Class Matters*. New York: Routledge.

Kim, Terri. 2008. "Transnational Academic Mobility in a Global Economy: Comparative and Historical Motifs." In *Geographies of Knowledge, Geometries of Power: Framing the Future of Higher Education*, edited by Debbie Epstein, Rebecca Boden, Rosemary Deem, and Fazal Rizvi, 319–337. New York: Routledge.

———. 2010. "Transnational Academic Mobility, Knowledge, and Identity Capital." *Discourse: Studies in the Cultural Politics of Education* 31 (5): 577–591.

Lareau, Annette. 1987. "Social Class Differences in Family-School Relationships: The Importance of Cultural Capital." *Sociology of Education* 60 (2): 73–85.

Lee, Stacey. 2005. *Up against Whiteness: Race, School, and Immigrant Youth*. New York: Teachers College Press.

Lin, Shumin. 2011. "Class Wreckage and Class Re-positioning: Narratives of Japanese-Educated Taiwanese." In *Social Class in Education: Global Perspectives*, edited by Lois Weis, 73–90. New York: Routledge.

Matus, Claudia. 2004. "El Sujeto Importado: Complejidades, Fragmentaciones y Redefiniciones del Estudiante Internacional en Universidades Estadounidenses." *Revista Calidad de la Educación* 21: 287–301.

———. 2009. "Time as Becoming: Women and Travel." *Journal of Curriculum Theorizing* 25 (2): 7–21.

Matus, Claudia, and Susan Talburt. 2009. "Spatial Imaginaries: Universities, Internationalization, and Feminist Geographies." *Discourse: Studies in the Cultural Politics of Education* 30 (4): 515–527.

Mullings, Beverley. 1999. "Insider or Outsider, Both or Neither: Some Dilemmas of Interviewing in a Cross-Cultural Setting." *Geoforum* 30: 337–350.

OECD. 2011. *Society at a Glance 2011—OECD Social Indicators*. Paris: OECD Publishing.

OECD and World Bank. 2009. *Reviews of National Policies for Education: Tertiary Education in Chile*. Paris: OECD Publishing.

———. 2010. "Reviews of National Policies for Education: Becas Chile Scholarship Program." Paris: OECD Publishing.

Ong, Aihwa. 1999. *Flexible Citizens: The Cultural Logics of Transnationality*. London: Duke University Press.

Rizvi, Fazal. 2010. "International Students and Doctoral Studies in Transnational Spaces." In *The Routledge Doctoral Supervisor's Companion: Supporting Effective Research in Education and Social Sciences*, edited by Pat Thomson and Mélanie Walker, 35–50. New York, NY: Routledge.

———. 2011. "Theorizing Student Mobility in an Era of Globalization." *Theory and Practice* 17 (6): 693–701.

Sidhu, Ravinder. 2006. *Universities and Globalization: To Market, to Market*. Mahwah, NJ: Lawrence Erlbaum.

Srivastava, Prachi. 2006. "Reconciling Multiple Researcher Positionalities and Languages in International Research." *Research in Comparative and International Education* 1 (3): 210–222.

Waters, Johanna. 2008. *Education, Migration, and Cultural Capital in the Chinese Diaspora: Transnational Students between Hong Kong and Canada*. Amherst, NY: Cambria Press.

Weis, Lois. 1990. *Working Class without Work: High School Students in a Deindustrializing Economy.* New York: Routledge.

———. 2008. *The Way Class Works: Reading on School, Family, and the Economy.* New York: Routledge.

———. 2012. *Social Class in Education: Global Perspectives.* New York: Routledge.

Willis, Paul. 1977. *Learning to Labour: How Working Class Kids Get Working Class Jobs.* Farnborough, UK: Saxon House.

6 Negotiating the Meaning of Citizenship

Chinese Academics in the Transnational Space

Qiongqiong Chen

An increased transnational flow of people, ideas, images, technologies, and monies is one of the marked features of contemporary globalization (Appadurai 1996). These flows have broken the physical boundaries of nation-states, shrunk the distances between people around the world, and obscured the links between the state and its citizens. As Sassen (2002) observes, in a world of mass migration, global commoditization, and destabilizing of national state–centered hierarchies of power, territorial sovereignty has become increasingly decoupled from citizenship practices and identities, as well as from discourses of loyalty and national attachment. The literature on transnational migration and flexible citizenship has suggested that people are able to live simultaneously in more than one nation-state and have multiple senses of belonging and affiliation (Ong 1999; Bosniak 2000; Levitt and Glick Schiller 2004). Thus, the assumption that there is a one-to-one relationship between territory, sovereignty, identity, and citizenship can no longer be held. This requires a new explanation of citizenship and of the way that people reimagine identities and boundaries in the increasingly globalized world.

In response, this chapter provides a cultural analysis of the relations between mobility and the current transformations of citizenship through an empirical study of Chinese academics who are working in the United States (US). It aims to explore how these scholars narrate their experiences of displacement and dwelling and of constructing "homes away from home" (Clifford 1997, 244). My intention here is not only to highlight the transnational connections among Chinese knowledge diasporas (Chen and Koyama 2013), but, more fundamentally, to question the very meaning of citizenship and social incorporation in the context of globalization and transnational migration. I argue that the Chinese academics in this study are flexible agents who are creating a new social space where they can live and work in the host country, while at the same time remaining engaged with development at "home" and producing new conditions for their academic life and public scholarship.

To develop this argument further, I first review literature on transnationalism, diaspora, and citizenship to establish an analytic framework for understanding the case of Chinese academics in the US. I then present empirical data to show how these Chinese academics navigate the different regions of family, workplace (here, academia), and nation-state to negotiate the meaning of citizenship through their transnational practices. I argue that their narratives have challenged both the old notion of formal citizenship as a basis of migrants' sense of belonging and identity (Teo 2011) and the overly liberating powers of cosmopolitanism attached to diasporic identity. In the conclusion, I discuss the implications of the new emergence of transnational subjects and space for reconceptualizing the meaning of citizenship, as well as for rethinking policies that deal with the global movement of academics.

TRANSNATIONALISM, DIASPORA, AND FLEXIBLE IDENTITY

The recognition of transnationalism has revitalized the study of international migration, shifting from the linear assimilationist paradigm of migration to an emphasis on transnational connections, simultaneous belonging, and multiple identities (Kriesberg 1997; Smith 2001; Ma 2003; Levitt and Glick Schiller 2004; Vertovec 2009; Teo 2011). Levitt and Glick Schiller (2004) have conceptualized transnationalism as the process by which immigrants build social fields that connect and position them in more than one country. They argue that the boundaries of a social field are not necessarily contiguous with national boundaries and that the field itself is created by actors through their daily practices and transnational relations. Ma (2003) interprets this social field "as space with contested cultural boundaries, flexible citizenship, and intensive flows of people, capital, subcontracted goods, technology and information" (5), all tied in their own ways with the emigrants and their social networks. To them, it is the paradox of separation and entanglement, of living *here* and connecting *there*, that requires scholars to look beyond national borders to understand the process of migration and the formation of diasporas.

The language of diaspora, originally used to describe the Jewish deportation and exile, is now used more loosely to refer to a dispersed people who maintain a connection with a prior home (Dufoix 2003). To Clifford (1997), this diasporic connection "must be strong enough to resist erasure through the normalizing processes of forgetting, assimilating, and distancing" (255). In this sense, diaspora exists in a lived tension of being both here and there, of maintaining local communities and "having collective homes away from home" (251). This understanding of diaspora has arisen as part of the postmodern project of resisting nationalism and celebrating cosmopolitism as a result of traveling, dwelling, and attaching to multiple locales (Tölölyan 1996). Particularly in cultural studies research, there is considerable discussion on "diaspora consciousness" marked by dual or multiple identifications (Vertovec 2009). Such work looks at the subjective experiences of displacement and hybridity, as well as of the rearticulation and restructuring of new identities. It implies that identity is not a fixed essence, but constantly in the process of changing and being remade.

In the context of Chinese diaspora, this understanding of transnational networks and flexible identities is widely acknowledged in recent literature on global Chinese migrations. For instance, in her studies of transnational Chinese managers and professionals, Ong (1999) uses the notion of flexible citizenship to grasp the new identities of the elite transnational subjects and the strategies they devise to circumvent the constraints of social structures. She claims that China's strategy of negotiating with global capitalism, entailing a combination of the developmentalist nation-state, the careful cultivation of diasporic networks, and economic competition with the West, has produced a "distinctive Chinese modernity linked to overseas Chinese" (36). In a more focused study of the Chinese knowledge diaspora, Yang and Welch (2010) look at the policy implications of China's diaspora option and the diasporic identities of Chinese scholars in a prestigious Australian university. In a related vein, Chen and Koyama (2013) seek to understand the relations among academic mobility, knowledge circulation, and identity formation based on their US samples of Chinese scholars. They argue that their movement is not simply a transfer from one place to another, but constitutes a new space of transnational engagement and subjectivity building.

The studies mentioned above highlight the flexibility of and connectivity among members of the Chinese diaspora, but what is missing is a discussion of the changing role of the nation-state and the meaning of citizenship within the border transformations of global conditions. The following section focuses on the concepts of citizenship and nationality to further complicate the issues of diasporic identity and belonging.

REPOSITIONING CITIZENSHIP

Most of the scholarship on citizenship has been associated with the idea of the nation-state (Sassen 2002). Traditionally, citizenship has been understood as the legal relationship between the individual and the state. From this perspective, the four basic components of citizenship—rights, responsibilities, participation, and identity—come together, forming a unity of function. However, this understanding of citizenship is not sufficient to capture the layered nuances of migrants' belonging and identity in the transnational moment.

Current developments in globalization, especially the changing nature of the nation-state, have challenged the nature of the social contract between the state and its citizens (Robertson 2009). In order to grasp this new expression of civic ties and cultural identities, scholars have invoked alternative interpretations of citizenship, such as "postnational citizenship" (Soysal 1994), "cultural citizenship" (Rosaldo 1994), "denationalized citizenship" (Sassen 2002), and "flexible citizenship" (Ong 1999). Soysal (1994) privileges global over national dynamics by using the term "postnational" to formulate an emergent model of universal membership. She explains that "national citizenship is no longer the main determinant of individual rights and privileges" (12) and "incorporation into a system of member rights does not inevitably require incorporation into the national collectivity" (3). Similarly, Delanty (2000) argues that citizenship has become deterritorialized and fragmented into the separate discourses of legal rights, duties, and identity. To him, the fundamental criterion of citizenship is no longer birth but residence and the cultivation of identity. From this postnational perspective, citizenship is no longer exclusively about the struggle for social rights, but also about cultural identity and demands for the recognition of differences.

In contrast, Sassen's (2002) concept of "denationalized citizenship" represents a rejection of the notion of postnational citizenship and returns the argument to the framework of the nation-state. She argues that global-level changes do not necessarily entail deterritorialization with respect to the national state; instead, the practices of citizens are still largely confined to national institutions. Thus, she strives to understand the transformations of the institutions of citizenship through national channels, rather than waiting for a "global" state. Similarly, Ong (1996) questions the notion of cosmopolitanism by arguing that the construction of citizenship cannot escape from state power and other forms of regulation. Ong explains citizenship as a cultural process of "subjectification" in the Foucauldian sense, a dual process of "self-making and being-made by power relations" (737) linked to the nation-state and civil society. Ong (1999) coins the term "flexible citizenship" to "refer especially to the strategies and effects of mobile mangers, technocrats, and professionals seeking to both circumvent and benefit from different nation-state regimes by selecting different sites of investments, work, and family relocation" (112). She looks at the cultural logics of capitalist accumulation, travel, and displacement that induce subjects to respond opportunistically to the changing political-economic conditions.

Framed by Ong's theory of flexible citizenship, I use an in-depth interview approach to explore the ways in which Chinese scholars with American passports, on one hand, and those with green cards, on the other, negotiate the meaning of citizenship and their transnational identities. In doing so, I hope to provide not only a more nuanced understanding of the complexities of transnational academic mobility, but also some critical scrutiny of the national and global policies that frame such mobility.

METHODOLOGY

Because I place my study in the broader frame of the cultural analysis of mobility and citizenship, I choose to use qualitative methods to examine the "global everyday" (Appadurai 2001) of Chinese academics in the US. To empirically investigate their perceptions of their daily experiences, I conducted in-depth interviews with Chinese professors in an American research university. I selected North University (a pseudonym) due to its large number of academics from Mainland China and its research-intensive qualifications. I made an initial selection of participants on the basis of the surnames of Chinese faculty listed in the directories of North University's website, and I then emailed these faculty members an invitation to participate in the study. Once interviews began, a snowball sampling technique emerged as interviewees suggested colleagues who might be willing to participate in the research. Additional participants were recruited during a meeting of the Chinese Professionals and Scientists Association at North University and during activities held by the local Chinese community.

This research is ongoing, and the data I used in this paper was collected between October 2010 and September 2011. The sample comprises fifteen primary participants from North University, varying in academic discipline, professional rank, gender, and age. All of them (ten males and five females) came to the US during the 1980s and 1990s, with at least a bachelor's degree from Chinese universities. Eleven earned their PhD degrees in the US (four in the social sciences and seven in the natural sciences and engineering), one earned a PhD in Canada in a social science field, and the other three came as postdoctoral fellows in the natural sciences. Among them, six were American citizens, seven were permanent residents, and the other two held a H-1B work visa. Their ages varied from thirty-five to sixty, and their ranks varied from assistant to full professor.

In total, I conducted fifteen in-depth interviews. Each interview lasted between two and four hours. Most of the interviews were conducted in the participants' offices or homes. Interviews were conducted in Mandarin Chinese, with the exception of one conducted in English upon the participant's request. All interviews were recorded and transcribed into Chinese (except the one in English). I analyzed the data through a manual inductive coding approach and organized it on the basis of common themes that emerged from the raw Chinese text. I did not translate the entirety of the transcripts from Chinese into English, but only the excerpts used as quotations in the article. The use of Chinese and English created methodological challenges for this study. The dilemma was that the use of Chinese might have captured the richness of the participants' life stories and shed light on the relevant issues; however, in the process of converting and transforming data into English research text, part of the meaning and cultural flavor were, inevitably, lost in translation. Thus, the quotations I present in the next section are not original words, but involve language translation,[1] cultural decoding, and my own linguistic interpretation.

BEING AN AMERICAN CITIZEN: "I'M A CHINESE WITH AN AMERICAN PASSPORT"

> I see myself as a Chinese, consciously, genetically, or biologically. . . .
> I am a one hundred percent Chinese, with an American passport.
> (Interview, Dr. Liu, February 18, 2011)

When asked about their national identifications, participants with or without American citizenship unanimously declare that they regard themselves primarily as Chinese. For them, national identity is not so much an issue of citizenship as of feelings of attachment to their homeland, a country where they grew up (Teo 2011). For example, Dr. Liu is a professor in biomedical science and has lived in the US since the early 1990s. He didn't apply for American citizenship until 2005, when he married a woman from his hometown in China. He reveals:

> It's easier for me to arrange for my wife come to the US and stay with me permanently if I have an American status, so I applied. Since China does not recognize dual citizenship, I'm forced be to a non-Chinese [laughs]. . . . It was hard for me to get a passport to leave China in early 90s, but now I need a visa to go back. Isn't life ironic? (Interview, February 18, 2011)

Although Dr. Liu has been an American citizen for several years, his lifestyle has not changed. According to him, he still speaks Chinese at home, reads Chinese newspapers, watches Chinese cable TV, and socializes with the Chinese community. He maintains professional relationships with his American colleagues, but seldom socializes with them away from campus. "I am always active in work, but kind of isolated in life," he says. As for the issue of social incorporation, he states frankly that he lives a relatively independent life in the US and doesn't care much about what he calls the mainstream lifestyle. He further explains:

> Although I have lived here for almost twenty years, I am far away from being integrated into this society. But I don't really care about that, and sometimes I feel I'm already there, at least in my field; in this sense, yes, I guess I'm well integrated. Many research institutions, even those in Singapore or in Israel, contacted me to review papers and grants. Do they know me personally? No, but they can locate my papers, and trace me to review proposals. I have my own area and in this area I am in the mainstream. But in the broader American society, I still think of myself as Chinese, although I hold an American passport. (Interview, February 18, 2011)

Dr. Liu's response questions the prevalent notion of mainstream society. For him, the mainstream is not a lifestyle to follow, but a space created through everyday practices. Dr. Liu strategically claims his citizenship when it helps him integrate into academic communities. When it comes to social communities, he chooses to maintain belonging to his home culture. As a proactive social agent, he knows where it is strategic to claim his citizenship and how to integrate into the host society tactically.

Like Dr. Liu, Dr. Zhu, a full professor in biology, became an American citizen for family reasons. During the interview, she explained how her father had died in a car accident in the US when he came for her graduation commencement. She continues to carry this trauma and wants to take care of her mother for the rest of her life:

> I felt so sorry for my mom. I don't want her stay alone in China. . . . For a long time, I had managed to arrange for her to come to the US, but her visa was rejected three times. Finally, I decided to turn myself into an American citizen and have her live with me permanently. (Interview, February 11, 2011)

As an immigrant who has been living in the US for more than twenty years, Dr. Zhu still regards herself as Chinese, even though her nationality is now American. "To me, citizenship is more like a membership; I mean I earned a membership here," she notes. "I think my identity to the US is largely based on interest, because my lab is here and my whole family is here." Clearly, Dr. Zhu uses citizenship as a tool to gain benefits from her host country rather than perceiving it, like many immigrants, as a goal to strive toward.

In reflecting upon her experiences as an international female professor in a predominantly male department, she frankly acknowledges that she doesn't feel strongly marginalized as a minority:

> That's right, I'm Chinese, but I feel more as a biological researcher in my work. . . . I think most people think of me based on my work, not on my national origin. If you are strong in research, you will be respected anyway. The real key thing is more about work. But when I go out, say, go shopping, people still judge me by my face. Although they didn't say straightly, "Oh, you are a foreigner, you are inferior," sometimes I can feel that way. (Interview, February 11, 2011)

Interestingly, contrary to the popular discourse in which minority faculty are devalued, depreciated, and attacked (Hsu 2000), Dr. Zhu sees the university as a safe space where she can pursue her research interest freely and escape from certain racial discriminations in the larger society. Knowing that outstanding research capability is the major factor in being accepted by the American academy, she works hard and uses certain strategies to create her own space in her academic field, which she perceives as relatively merit based.

In contrast to Dr. Liu and Dr. Zhu, Dr. Wu claims that his professional life plays a critical role in his decision to be an American citizen. Dr. Wu is a full professor in computer science and also a board member of the local Chinese school. He is well known both in the Chinese community and as a senior Chinese professor at North University. Sharing his story of becoming a US citizen, he recalls:

> I was quite naive at that time. I thought there would be more opportunities to get grants with citizen status, because many national grant

programs have citizenship requirements, such as DOD [Department of Defense] grants. But later, I realized it was not what I thought at all. I never got any DOD grants even though I changed my nationality. If I had chance to choose again, I would just apply for a green card [permanent residence] and keep my Chinese passport. I think this is an ideal combination, especially for those who travel a lot between the two countries. (Interview, June 9, 2011)

Dr. Wu is a participant in China's Thousand Talents program, which is a governmental project to attract top overseas Chinese academics to participate in China's development. Reflecting upon his experience as an honored overseas scholar, Dr. Wu expresses that he enjoys working with his Chinese colleagues and students, but prefers to have his base in the US: "I want to bring my expertise to China and I think this temporary visit works well on me. . . . If I return permanently, people might no longer treat me as a guest, but as a competitor," he states. As a "knowledge carrier" (Yang and Welch 2010), Dr. Wu enjoys the flexibility of movement between geographical and virtual spaces as well as the opportunities given scholars in a globalized world.

When I asked what citizenship means to him, he joked, "It means every time I visit China, I need to apply for a Chinese visa." As for citizenship practices, he says,

> I voted several time, but to be honest I don't really care much how I vote. I won't feel very sad if I don't have the right to vote, or maybe a little bit, and equally, I won't feel extremely proud of the right to vote. Yeah, maybe I'm a fake American [laugh]. (Interview, June 9, 2011)

How do we theorize the meaning of citizenship in his narrative? The answer to this question, as Bosniak (2000) proposes, depends on how we understand citizenship itself. If we understand it from the perspectives of national and political identities, we might see Dr. Wu as an inauthentic American who doesn't have a strong attachment to the country. However, if we locate citizenship in the domain of "common good" and "local participation," his claim of citizenship is entirely legitimate. As a scientist, he engages actively in his research field—he operates a lab, advises students, and publishes papers—and he also does volunteer work in his community, pays taxes, and is involved in local activities. In his case, an American status or passport has become less and less important to confirm his citizenship, let alone to profess loyalty to the protective states (Ong 1999).

Individuals negotiate identities and citizenship differently in specific contexts. Some want to or have to become legal American citizens, but not all choose to do so. There are Chinese professors who are content with having their green cards and prefer to keep their original nationality. In this sense, citizenship is likely tied more closely to cultural belonging and identity than to nation of residence.

BEING A PERMANENT RESIDENT: "IT'S EASIER TO GO BACK AND FORTH BETWEEN CHINA AND THE US WITH A GREEN CARD"

In contrast to those who gained citizenship status, other Chinese professors are practicing their own ways of integrating into US society. Due to the denial of dual citizenship in China, many scholars believe that holding a green card can make traveling and working in China more convenient. Dr. Yang is one of them. He is a full professor at North University and also functions as an advisory professor in several Chinese universities. He has worked at North University for more than fifteen years but still maintains contact with his colleagues and friends in China. He describes himself as a "bridge," a cultural mediator, who links China and the US through his teaching, research, and public activities. As one of the early professors hired by North University from Mainland China, he has actively participated in initiating cooperative programs between his school and several Chinese universities. He also helped to arrange for visiting scholars and exchange students from China to study at North University. In contrast to those who became American citizens, Dr. Yang still holds a green card because he believes it is better for his travel and work:

> I am still holding the green card. It's easier to travel and work in China. You know, since I'm still a Chinese citizen, people trust my loyalty to the country, and they would forgive me when I grumble a little or let out my criticism. However, if I become a US citizen, things would become more complicated. People in China would look at me as a foreigner, especially those who are working in the governmental sections. They would be more cautious about their comments on certain things, and would not take my suggestions seriously. I mean, people would just not trust me. It's a political issue. (Interview, March 1, 2011)

Dr. Yang strategically chose to keep his Chinese citizenship in order to gain cultural and social capital in both the US and China. When I asked about his life experience "between" the two countries, he corrected my Chinese word choice of "between" to the word "in":

> To me, "between" is a passive world, neither here nor there; but "in" is more active, which indicates both here and there. I don't think I can be apart from either China or the US. Yeah, I think I belong to both cultures. As you know, every culture has its own merits. Chinese culture carries good traditions and American culture has many advanced things to learn. I try to embrace the good aspects from each culture and leave the bad ones. . . . I feel pretty comfortable living in the US and at the same time I keep pace with what's going on in China. I watch CCTV News and ABC News every day. I

think I know more about China than many local people [in China].
(Interview, March 1, 2011)

Unlike many immigrants whose dream is to obtain American citizenship,
Dr. Yang is content with his green card; he believes that it gives him more
flexibility in his work. His narratives challenge the old models of "straight-
line" assimilation in which immigrants are understood to move from one
place to another, experiencing "foreign strangeness to assimilation and citizenship" (Lowe 1996, 6). Immigration scholars once argued that to move
up the social ladder, immigrants would have to abandon their own language, ties to their homeland, and identities. Dr. Yang's displacement and
transnational connections, however, have a positive impact on his career
development. He is catching up in the dialectic of embedding and disem-
bedding (Giddens 1990, as cited in Ong 1996), a situation which enables
him to escape from certain constraints of his home country, and at the same
time help him to engage in developments at "home."

Whereas Dr. Yang is a professor who adeptly navigates the transnational
space and intentionally keeps his Chinese citizenship, Dr. Bai, an assistant
professor in management, is still weighing the locations of her citizenship.
At the time of the interview, she held a green card and was unsure whether
she would change it. She claims that her citizenship status does not make a
big difference to her current life, as the following passage illustrates:

I am thinking to do that [apply for American citizenship], but I am not
sure. You know both of my parents are still in China now. Sometimes,
I would think what if my parents get sick, I need to go there on the next
day, so the green card would help me better . . . and also it costs a lot to
be a citizen. I am really not sure [long pause]. So far, there's no specific
reason for me to become an American citizen. The immigration process
is pretty loose now and I don't think I have to be hurry yet. . . . To me,
I really don't care how people look at me. Are you a Chinese citizen
or US citizen? Yes? To me, I don't care. I feel okay I just do whatever
convenient for me. (Interview, April 15, 2011)

Similarly, Dr. Xu, an assistant professor in economics, is also considering
where to claim his citizenship. During the conversation, he expressed several times his confusion of being caught in the cracks between two cultures.
In his words: "Culture is a complicated thing. You never know whether you
finished adjusting or not. . . . It's a never-ending process." When asked if he
considered returning to China, he answered:

I just felt the longer I live here, the harder it is to return. The tension
is always there, and becomes more complicated after establishing my
family here [the US]. Initially, I wanted to go back after several years'
working, but then I got my son; now he goes to school; it's almost

impossible for me to go back now. The education in China is so competitive and tough; I don't want him to grow up in such a rigid system. (Interview, March 22, 2011)

For Dr. Xu, his primary consideration is his son's education and future. This echoes studies of the Chinese diaspora in which children are shown to be the central axis of families' journeys, and often a critical reason for the decision to migrate (Orellana et al. 2001). Although Dr. Xu's knowledge capital offers him more possibilities and mobility, his daily activities and decision making are still largely governed by the regime of family. As to the issues of citizenship, he admits that he has no plan to change his legal nationality and will wait and see.

Dr. Xu's story, to some extent, reflects the ambivalence of social identity with which many immigrants grapple. His ambivalence is articulated partly in his affection for his homeland and partly in his desire to continue to live and work in a new land which he assumes could provide better economic prospects and opportunities for his child's future.

Again, although Dr. Yang, Dr. Bai, and Dr. Xu tell different stories and map different itineraries, to some extent they all play the dual roles of describing and reflecting a distinct collective experience of being noncitizens living in the US. While citizenship remains a largely national enterprise, the fact that citizenship status has been affected by various forms of globalization should not be denied. Thus, these narratives help to broaden our understanding of the meaning of substantive citizenship, and by extension, to push us to rethink policies on academic mobility in a nuanced way.

DISCUSSION AND CONCLUDING THOUGHTS

The above narratives illustrate the divergent ways in which Chinese scholars interpret and understand their own experience of claiming citizenship through their transnational practices. Nevertheless, these narratives collectively show that the Chinese academics in this study are flexible subjects who navigate adroitly among the different regions of family, workplace, and nation-states in order to gain better opportunities for their careers and their families. As active social actors, they are able to move between national spaces, play off one nation-state against another (e.g., being an American citizen or not), and seek the tactical advantages of both host and home countries. They know that it is easier to become a citizen here than there, and that there exist more legal and political rights in one country than in the other (Ong 1999). They also know how to accumulate, convert, and "cash in" their capital, which can take the form of economic, cultural, symbolic, linguistic, educational, and social capital (Bourdieu 1986).

However, not all immigrants have this luxury and flexibility in the US. The practices of citizenship are highly diverse among different groups of people, depending on various factors including migration channels, political circumstances in the home country, and legal, social, and economic status in the host society (Vertovec 2009). Unlike what is commonly portrayed in the public sphere that American citizenship is the ultimate goal for immigrants, the participants in this study use citizenship as a tool rather than as a goal. As a group of privileged people in terms of education, financial capital, and professional connections, they are able to make a choice about whether to become a citizen or not. For them, the meaning of citizenship in the profound sense of duty and national identifications has become minimal.

This citizenship practice not only complicates the notion that American citizenship is the ultimate goal and privilege for those who are living in the US, but also challenges the assumption that one's country of residence is one's only site of affiliation. The participants' narratives show that people are able to live dual or hybrid lives—moving easily between different cultures and pursuing interests that require a simultaneous presence in both. They are creating new forms of citizenship identity that are, in a very real sense, both here and there (Bosniak 2000; Levitt and Glick Schiller 2004). Thus, their incorporation into a given society has been decoupled from the national identity and sovereignty that have been linked to citizenship.

Further, this chapter argues that the policy discourse on mobility, especially on the movement of highly skilled researchers and university academics, remains locked within the boundaries of nation-states, framed by the assumption that there is a one-to-one relation between social identity and nation-states. This is evident in the popular languages of brain drain, gain, or circulation in the policy discourse which assumes that "the 'brains' involved are not only a resource for the nation-state but in a sense they belong to it and can thus be lost to or gained by it" (Fahey and Kenway 2010, 566). Such an understanding has led nations to compete for highly skilled talents by developing policies to best tap into the global talent pool. For example, the US has revised its immigrant law to attract more highly educated professionals and keep them working in the country. By contrast, in the case of China, the government deploys diasporic options to entice overseas Chinese talents to bring their skills and expertise back to China (Zweig 2006; Welch and Zhang 2008). This strategy has strengthened China's links with its intellectuals abroad both physically and emotionally in order to ensure their continued national membership and loyalty.

As demonstrated here, people's activities, practices, and belongings are not rooted in a single nation-state, but in a transnational space which relies more on connectivity and cooperation than on competition. Thus, we need to rethink the role of nation-states in dealing with global flows of people and in defining citizenship; this role is now more international and liberal, and it allows for forms of citizenship other than the strictly juridical (Sassan 2005). This has implications for imagining global policies on academic mobility that go beyond the framework of nationalism and support global cooperation for the sake of a better mobilizing of talent and knowledge. As more and more people are on the move, as transnationalism and flexibility have been increasingly recognized, nation-states need to have the capacity to pursue a broader international agenda and policies that allow individuals and groups to better achieve their interests, dreams, and aspirations in this growing, interconnected world.

NOTES

1. I am the translator of all quotations.

REFERENCES

Appadurai, Arjun. 1996. *Modernity at Large*. Minneapolis: University of Minnesota Press.

———. 2001. "Grassroots Globalization and the Research Imagination." In *Globalization*, edited by Arjun Appadurai, 1–21. Durham, NC: Duke University Press.

Bosniak, Linda. 2000. "Citizenship Denationalized." *Indiana Journal of Global Legal Studies* 7 (2): 447–510.

Bourdieu, Pierre. 1986. "The Forms of Capital." In *Handbook of Theory and Research for the Sociology of Education*, edited by John Richardson, 241–258. New York: Greenwood.

Chen, Qiongqiong, and Jill P. Koyama. 2013. "Reconceptualising Diasporic Intellectual Networks: Mobile Scholars in Transnational Space." *Globalisation, Societies and Education* 11 (1): 23–38.

Clifford, James. 1997. *Routes: Travel and Translation in the Late Twentieth Century*. Cambridge, MA: Harvard University Press.

Delanty, Gerard. 2000. *Citizenship in a Global Age: Society, Culture, Politics*. Buckingham: Open University Press.

Fahey, Johannah, and Jane Kenway. 2010. "International Academic Mobility: Problematic and Possible Paradigms." *Discourse: Studies in the Cultural Politics of Education* 31 (5): 563–575.

Hall, Stuart. 1996. "Introduction: Who Needs 'Identity'?" In *Questions of Cultural Identity*, edited by S. Hall and P. du Gay, 1–17. London: Sage Publications.

Hsu, Ruth. 2000. "'Where's Oz, Toto?' Idealism and the Politics of Gender and Race in Academe." In *Power, Race, and Gender in Academe: Strangers in the Tower?* edited by Shirley Geok-lin Lim and Maria Herrera-Sobek, 183–206. New York: Modern Language Association.

Kenway, Jane, and Johannah Fahey. 2006. "The Research Imagination in a World on the Move." *Globalisation, Societies and Education* 4 (2): 261–274.

———. 2011. "Getting Emotional about 'Brain Mobility.'" *Emotion, Space and Society* 4 (3): 187–194.

Kriesberg, Louis. 1997. "Social Movements and Global Transformation." In *Transnational Social Movements and Global Politics*, edited by Jackie Smith, Charles Chatfield, and Ron Pagnucco, 3–18. Syracuse, NY: Syracuse University Press.

Levitt, Peggy. 2003. "Keeping Feet in Both Worlds: Transnational Practices and Immigrant Incorporation in the United States." In *Toward Assimilation and*

Citizenship, edited by Christian Joppke and Ewa Morawska, 177–194. New York: Palgrave Macmillan.

Levitt, Peggy, and Nina Glick Schiller. 2004. "Conceptualizing Simultaneity: A Transnational Social Field Perspective on Society." *International Migration Review* 38 (3): 1002–1039.

Lowe, Lisa. 1996. *Immigrant Acts: On Asian American Cultural Politics*. Durham, NC: Duke University Press.

Ma, Laurence. 2003. "Space, Place, and Transnationalism in the Chinese Diaspora." In *The Chinese Diaspora : Space, Place, Mobility, and Identity*, edited by Laurence Ma and Carolyn Cartier, 1–50. Lanham, MD: Rowman & Littlefield.

Ong, Aihwa. 1996. "Cultural Citizenship as Subject-Making: Immigrants Negotiate Racial and Cultural Boundaries in the United States." *Current Anthropology* 37 (5): 737–762.

———. 1999. *Flexible Citizenship: The Cultural Logics of Transnationality*. Durham, NC: Duke University Press.

Orellana, Marjorie Faulstich, Barrie Thorne, Anna Chee, and Wan Shun Eva Lam. 2001. "Transnational Childhoods: The Participation of Children in Processes of Family Migration." *Social Problems* 48 (4): 572–592.

Rizvi, Fazal. 2005. "Rethinking 'Brain Drain' in the Era of Globalisation." *Asia Pacific Journal of Education* 25 (2): 175–192.

Robertson, Susan L. 2009. "The Shifting Politics of Governance, Sovereignty and Citizenship." *Globalisation, Societies and Education* 7 (1): 1–3.

———. 2010. "Critical Response to Special Section: International Academic Mobility." *Discourse: Studies in the Cultural Politics of Education* 31 (5): 641–647.

Rosaldo, Renato. 1994. "Cultural Citizenship and Educational Democracy." *Cultural Anthropology* 9: 402–411.

Sassen, Saskia. 2002. "The Repositioning of Citizenship: Emergent Subjects and Spaces for Politics." *Berkeley Journal of Sociology* 46: 4–25.

———. 2005. "Regulating Immigration in a Global Age: A New Policy Landscape." *Parallax* 11 (1): 35–45.

Smith, Michael Peter. 2001. *Transnational Urbanism: Locating Globalization*. Oxford: Blackwell.

Soysal, Yasemin Nuhoglu. 1994. *Limits of Citizenship: Migrants and Postnational Membership in Europe*. Chicago: University of Chicago Press.

Teo, Sin Yih. 2011. "'The Moon Back Home Is Brighter'? Return Migration and the Cultural Politics of Belonging." *Journal of Ethnic and Migration Studies* 37 (5): 805–820.

Tölölyan, Khachig. 1996. "Rethinking Diaspora(s): Stateless Power in the Transnational Moment." *Diaspora* 5 (1): 3–36.

Vertovec, Steven. 2009. *Transnationalism*. London and New York: Routledge.

Welch, Anthony, and Zhang Zhen. 2008. "Higher Education and Global Talent Flows: Brain Drain, Overseas Chinese Intellectuals, and Diasporic Knowledge Networks." *Higher Education Policy* 21 (4): 519–537.

Yang, Rui, and Anthony Welch. 2010. "Globalisation, Transnational Academic Mobility and the Chinese Knowledge Diaspora: An Australian Case Study." *Discourse: Studies in the Cultural Politics of Education* 31 (5): 593–607.

Zweig, David. 2006. "Learning to Compete: China's Efforts to Encourage a Reverse Brain Drain." *International Labour Review* 145 (1–2): 65–89.

Part II
Place-Taking

7 "Luchando por una Vida Nueva"

A Socio-Spatial Analysis of Academic Aspirations among Rural Latino Students in the US South

Melissa Wicks-Asbun and Rebecca Torres

In the past two decades, the Latino population in the southern US has increased dramatically, particularly in North Carolina, where the number of Latinos living in the state doubled between 2000 and 2010 (US Census Bureau 2010). This boom has naturally affected the education system: the growth of Latino students enrolled in North Carolina public schools increased nearly fivefold between 1999 and 2009 to more than 150,000 (NCPS 2009). In some counties, Latino students currently account for more than 25% of the total student population (see Figure 7.1). Projections suggest that both the total number and proportion of Latino students in North Carolina public schools will continue to grow. Such a rapid increase created well-documented struggles between residents and newcomers in the new destination communities, and are particularly focused on how both could begin to build community and schools together (Villenas 2002).

Despite having demonstrated positive progress in academic achievement and better performance on statewide federally mandated End-of-Course Tests than other minority groups (NCDPI 2007), foreign-born Latino students have the highest dropout rate in North Carolina public schools (NCDPI 2010). Furthermore, relatively few Latino students continue their education after high school. Despite making up 8% of the student body in K–12, just over 2% of students enrolled in North Carolina public universities are Latino (UNC-GA 2007).[1] This cannot be attributed completely to lower academic performance; End-of-Course Test results indicate that Latino students are able to keep up with their peers academically, suggesting that other factors are constraining high school completion and continuation to higher education.

While aspirations play an important role in educational attainment, a gap between aspirations and attainment can provide evidence of policy, financial, and informational barriers that limit students' access to higher education. In this chapter, we utilize data from a survey conducted with Latino high school students in rural eastern North Carolina and qualitative interviews with students and parents to show that students as well as parents, despite limited formal education, express a strong desire for students to continue their studies at the college or university level, thereby implying that there are structural barriers to making these aspirations a reality for more young people. As discussed in other chapters in this section, the

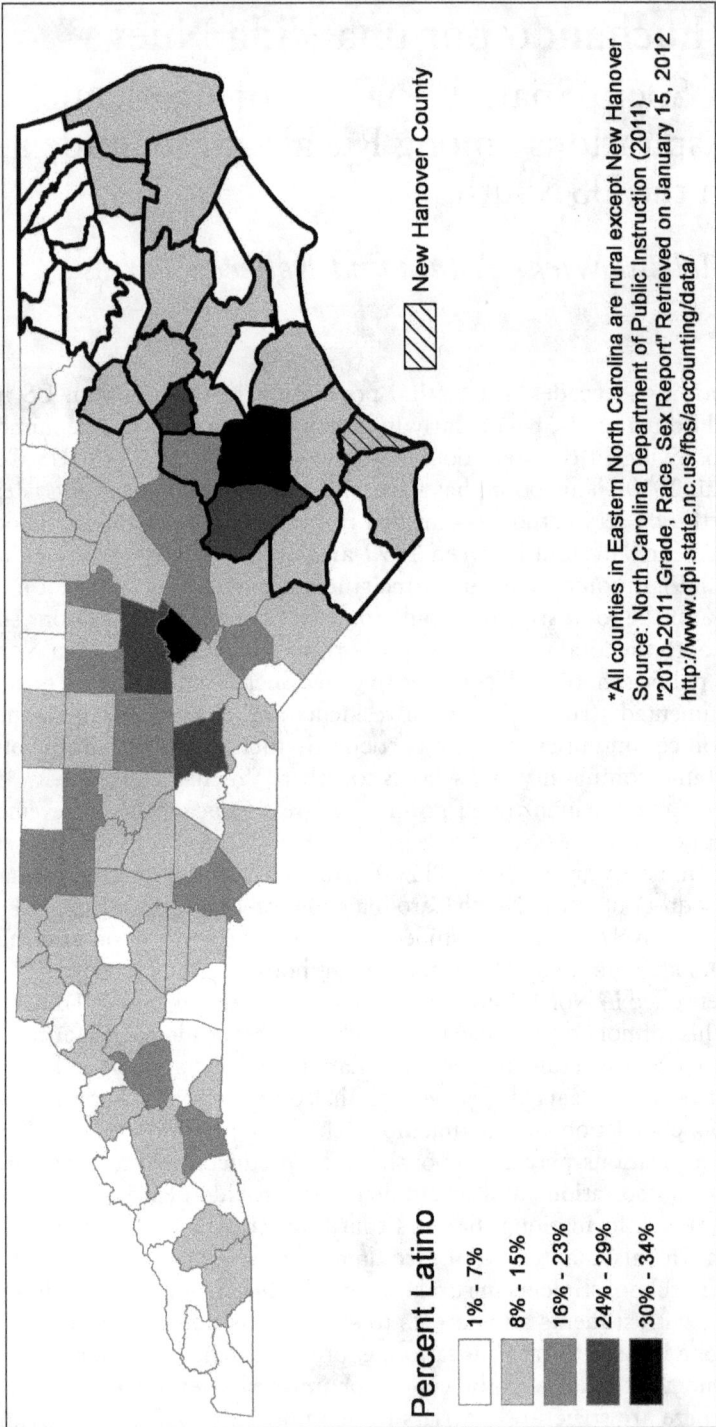

Figure 7.1   Percent Latino of total student population, 2011.

Percent Latino

- 1% - 7%
- 8% - 15%
- 16% - 23%
- 24% - 29%
- 30% - 34%

New Hanover County

*All counties in Eastern North Carolina are rural except New Hanover
Source: North Carolina Department of Public Instruction (2011)
"2010-2011 Grade, Race, Sex Report" Retrieved on January 15, 2012
http://www.dpi.state.nc.us/fbs/accounting/data/

structures creating these barriers come from an interlocking set of federal and local policies related to immigration, education, and national security.

Educators must have a nuanced understanding of students' goals and the multiple factors that shape them in order to help students fully achieve their aspirations. In the past, studies that focused on adult perspectives have documented how educators and administrators interpreted the high dropout rate among Latinos as evidence of apathy regarding their education (Bohon, Macpherson, and Atiles 2005). Our findings trouble these results by indicating that foreign-born Latino students have high aspirations, but find the barriers to achieving these goals insurmountable. Furthermore, participants questioned "the point of going" to college given that their documentation status would make it impossible for them to work in their chosen profession after graduation, illustrating their understanding of a lack of long-term financial stability. Understanding students' aspirations and how they are formed will help teachers and administrators comprehend the disconnect between aspirations and achievement among undocumented students that is often rooted in factors that extend beyond the classroom experience. Further, our analysis locates the issue within systems and structures created by policies rather than individual failings such as a lack of academic preparedness or ambition.

Our study focuses on rural eastern North Carolina (counties highlighted in Figure 7.1), an area that has one of the highest percentages of Latino students in the state.[2] It is also one of the most economically disadvantaged regions, with more than 60% of students eligible for free or reduced lunch (NCDPI 2009). Our findings suggest that foreign-born Latino students in the rural southern communities of the study area have high academic aspirations, but operate within legislative and institutional structures that create significant barriers to achievement. Placing student perspectives at the center of our research, we found that factors at the individual and local scales, such as parents and teachers, had the greatest positive influence on students' aspirations. Conversely, factors at the state and national scales, including immigration and education policies, were among the greatest inhibitors to academic aspirations. Lack of resources and funding—often directly related to documentation status—presented additional barriers. We argue that an enhanced understanding of aspirations and constraints in attainment is an important step in identifying the tools, resources, and policies needed to help students overcome those obstacles.

SOCIO-SPATIAL PERSPECTIVES ON ACADEMIC ASPIRATIONS

Understanding student aspirations and the factors that shape these aspirations has long been a topic of interest with implications for public policy decisions related to education, migration, and development. Studies have taken various approaches, focusing on minority students, student school environment, home life, and other issues (Burnell 2003; Chang et al. 2006; Howley 2006; Hurtado-Ortiz and Gauvain 2007; Kandel and Kao 2001; Kao and Tienda 1998; Phelan, Davidson, and Yu 1993; Qian and Blair 1999; Valencia and Johnson 2006). However, there is a paucity of studies that consider ethnicity and geography when addressing student aspirations, with notable exceptions including Wortham (2002), Kandel and Parrado (2006), and Kandel and Kao (2001). Utilizing socio-spatial perspectives provides a holistic approach that reveals the interconnections of factors at multiple scales—uncovering the role of seemingly unrelated and distant factors in the perceptions, decisions, and everyday practices of Latino students.

Drawing upon an adaptation of elements from both Matthews and Limb's socio-spatial model (1999) and Bronfenbrenner's original social ecological systems paradigm (1977) of child development, we developed a place-specific socio-spatial model for Latino children's development of academic aspirations in the rural south (Figure 7.2). The Bronfenbrenner model of ecological theory (1977) approaches a student's academic experience through the use of three separate but interrelated systems, proposing that achievement is the product of multiple environmental influences. The model's three systems are the microsystem (family, religious setting, classroom, and peers), the exosystem (school, community, mass media, and health agencies), and the macrosystem (economic system, society, political system, culture, and nationality). Given the somewhat ambiguous and diverse policy-level and community responses to Latino immigration across different spatial scales of neighborhood, community, region, state, and nation-state, we refined the Bronfenbrenner model to capture the multiple socio-spatial factors at these different levels. Like Matthews and Limb (1999), we base our model on finer-grained socio-spatial spheres in order to better capture the complexities specific to the economic, social, and physical landscapes of our study communities in the rural south. Our conceptualization includes five interrelated concentric spheres of influence (the *autosphere*, the *microsphere*, the *mesosphere*, the *exosphere*, and the *macrosphere*), along with a sixth, the *transnational sphere*. The boundaries between these spheres are not as neatly defined as depicted in Figure 7.2, but rather are blurred. Given space limitations, our discussion of the model is brief; however, Figure 7.2 provides a spatial representation, and details of each socio-spatial sphere are presented in Table 7.1.

Based on Matthews and Limb (1999), our model commences with the *autosphere*, that is, the physical, emotional, intellectual, and socially constructed body of the student. While some versions of the social ecological model collapse the *mesosphere* into the microsystem, for the purposes of our model, we chose to use both *microsphere* and *mesosphere* to permit a finer-grained spatial analysis. Using Matthews and Limb's

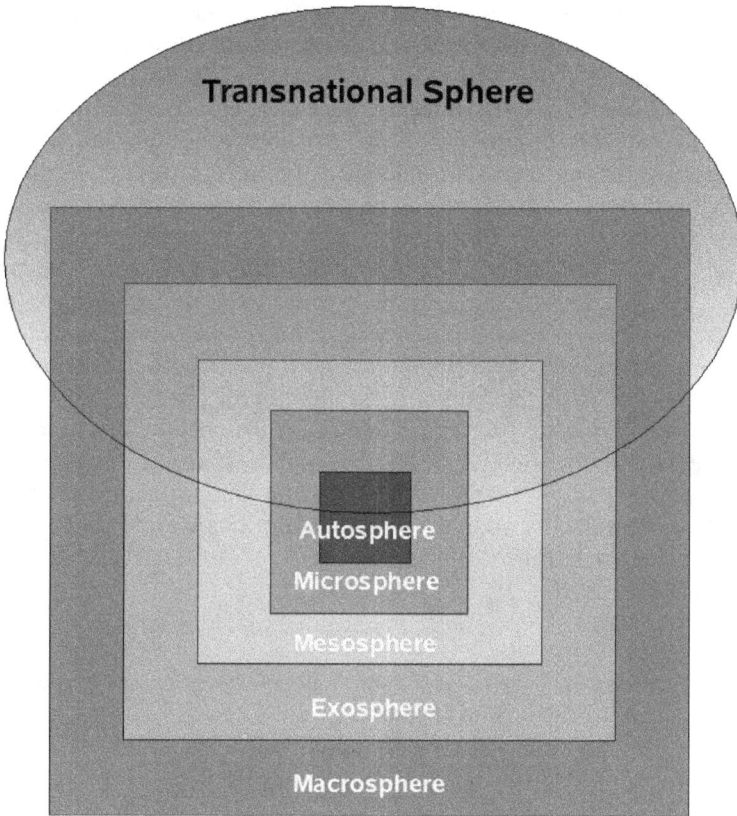

Figure 7.2 Socio-spatial context for Latino children's development of academic aspirations in the rural south.

(1999) notion of *microsphere*, which is based on Bronfenbrenner's (1977) *microsystem*, we conceive the *microsphere* to include the embodied student (the *autosphere*), her closest relationships within the home—with parents, siblings, and other household members—and the values, customs, and belief systems that affect the student. Because previous research demonstrates the strong influence of the nuclear family on Latino students' academic aspirations, for this study, the most relevant *microsphere* factors are the roles of parents and family (Brewster and Bowen 2004; Chenoweth and Galliher 2004; Goldenberg 2001; Ibáñez et al. 2004; Kao and Tienda 1998; Qian and Blair 1999; Teachman and Paasch 1998).

Drawing again on Bronfenbrenner's (1977) original model, we conceive the *mesosystem* in a more spatialized and place-specific manner as the *mesosphere*. This is the socio-spatial context in the child's *microsphere*, that is, the home and immediate neighborhood, which connects to and interacts with the wider community, extended family, church, school teachers, peers of similar or distinct backgrounds, employers, etc. In our model, the *exosphere*, also adapted from Bronfenbrenner (1977), includes the parents' employment opportunities, which are contingent upon the regional economy; the socioeconomic status of the community; and the active presence of advocacy groups, state agencies, and civil society, which are often concentrated in the urban capital with little reach into marginalized rural areas. The *macrosphere* includes factors such as the national economy, society, legislation, and public debate. We also stretch the spatial boundaries of analysis to include a *transnational sphere* that extends across the border of nation-states and all other socio-spatial spheres and ranges from the cultural practices and performances in the home to the neoliberal practices and policies that both regulate and propagate migration from Latin America. Table 7.1 presents a detailed elaboration of the socio-spatial influences of our model that are unique to the issue of Latino student aspirations in the context of the specific social, economic, political, and environmental landscapes of the rural south.

Table 7.1 Socio-Spatial Context for Latino Children's Development of Academic Aspirations in the Rural South

Influences on Latino Students	*Transnational Sphere*
Autosphere	
· Biological Body · Social Body (i.e., ethnicity, race, gender) · Emotion · Cognitive Development · Identity · Individual Documentation Status	· Mexican Cultural Norms & Practices · Values & Beliefs
Microsphere	

· Family Structure & Relations
· Family Documentation Status
· Household Income & Poverty
· Home Language Use
· Parental Educational Attainment
· Parental Educational Values & Attitudes
· Sibling Education & Attitudes
· Neighborhood & Neighbors (i.e., attitudes, race, ethnicity, socioeconomic status)
	· Mexican Household Economic
	  Dependency on Remittances
	· Communications
	· Travel & Visits
	· Documentation Status (mobility/
	  immobility, return migration)
	· Exchange of Ideas, Information,
	  Consumption Patterns, etc.
	· Family Transnational Ties
	  (household)

(continued)

Table 7.1 (continued)

Influences on Latino Students	Transnational Sphere

Mesosphere	
· Community Attitudes & Relations · Race Relations · Family Social Networks · Family Participation in Civil Society (i.e., church, community organizations, Latino organizations) · Family Participation in Community (i.e., events, spaces) · Parent-School Relations · School ESL/DLI/Outreach Programs · Teachers' Experience, Education, & Attitudes · Schoolmates (i.e., ethnicity, language use, attitudes, documentation status) · Employer Labor Requirements	· Trafficking Networks & Flexible Credit for Smuggling Costs · Emigration from New Sending Regions · Transnational Civil Society Projects · Mexican Education System · Dependency on Remittances, Social Security Network

Exosphere	
· Regional Economic Restructuring (i.e., traditional industries—CAFOs, processing, tobacco, construction; new industries; skilled or unskilled) · Emigration to Cities of Traditional Low-Skilled Workers · State & Regional Anti-Immigration Ordinances · State Agencies' Cooperation with Immigration Authorities · Anti-Immigration Media · Anti-Immigration Political Agenda · Energizing Latino Civil Society · Immigration Health, Education, & Support Nonprofit Programs · Small Business Demand for Immigrant Labor · State Rejection of the DREAM Act · Community College Denial of In-State Applicants · Civil Society & Service Vacuum · Education Programs (Head Start, More at Four, pre-K, adult literacy) · Lack of Latino Leadership & Political Representation · History of Racial Inequality & Racial Prejudices · School System Immigration Program & Funding · DPI Duality	· US/Mexico Neoliberal Project · Mexican Neoliberal Policy (agrarian reform) · Loss of Jobs in Mexico & Overseas

(continued)

Table 7.1   (continued)

Influences on Latino Students	Transnational Sphere
Macrosphere	
· Neoliberal Economy (i.e., services, manual labor, capital overseas, overseas jobs, demand for cheap goods, free market & trade) · Immigration Policy—Past and Present · Militarization of Border · Post-9/11 Homeland Security · Federal DREAM Act and Immigration Reform Failed · National Anti-Immigration Discourse & Politics · Political Representation Concentrated in New Gateway States · National Economic Dependence on Immigration Labor	· US/Mexico Neoliberal Project · Debt Relief, NAFTA · Mexican Neoliberal Policy (agrarian reform)

The most important *macrosphere* dimension for our study is the local political expression of national and state laws and regulations, in particular federal immigration policy. Our findings suggest that the influences of *macro-* and *transnational sphere* factors contain some of the most negative impacts on aspirations—yet, little research has examined these spheres. Consequently, we will focus this chapter on these two spheres.

As noted earlier, the transnational sphere cuts across all scales of our model. At the level of the *autosphere*, transnational influences are transmitted to children through their parents' and family's culturally based ontologies, epistemologies, norms, practices, values, and beliefs. These are culturally constructed, and reconfigured within the context of the host culture, generating new manifestations of subjectivities, practices, and performance. The transnational dimensions of the *microsphere* are strong in households that maintain ties to home communities. Those bonds, in turn result in stronger ethnic identities among children. The transnational dimensions that cut across the *mesosphere* include experiences in communities of origin; prior schooling in the country of origin; hardships on families struggling to pay off smuggler debts or maintain families in origin communities; and hometown associations that fortify home ties and support youth in sending and receiving communities, among other factors. For example, studies have found that prior schooling in Mexico played an important role in the academic achievement of Mexican immigrant children compared to US born coethnics (Padilla and Gonzalez 2002). Other transnational components of the *mesosphere* include neoliberal policies and practices both in the US and Mexico. For example, Mexican austerity programs that reduced support for smallholder farmers led to increased migration to the US, greater competition for jobs, increased anti-immigrant sentiments, overextended social services, and larger school enrollment, among other consequences. Finally, the *transnational sphere* intersects with the *macrosphere* at the level of bilateral agreements and relations, free trade agreements, and border controls, as well as other relationships. By reconfiguring the socioeconomic and political context in which migrants are situated, these *macrosphere* dimensions filter down to families on both sides of the border.

METHODOLOGY: STUDENT-CENTERED SURVEYS AND INTERVIEWS

We used a multimethod approach, triangulating findings from quantitative surveys and qualitative interviews with students and parents. The study included a survey of forty-four Latino high school students about their aspirations in one county and fifteen interviews with students and five parents in two additional counties. In geographical research, there has been a recent shift toward privileging the voices of youth who often have perspectives different from those of adults (Matthews, Limb, and Taylor 1998). In an effort to allow the students to speak for themselves, we focused our study on their words and points of view rather than on those of the adults around them.

Student surveys and interviews were conducted simultaneously in three eastern North Carolina counties. The counties were chosen because they were rural and had experienced significant increases over the last two decades in both the absolute number and proportion of Latinos. Until recently, geographical research and education research on aspirations rarely focused on rural areas (Burnell 2003; Howley 2006; Philo 1992). We administered a modified version of a survey developed by Portes and Rumbaut (2001) to students. It was designed to encapsulate students' own ideas regarding their academic aspirations and to extract their perceptions of what shaped their aspirations. Questions focused on such factors as home life, school environment, school activities, neighborhood, American society, and access to higher education. Surveys were administered individually in English or Spanish (according to participant preference) to high school students in a single school system. All Latino high school students in one county were invited to participate, with forty-four of eighty-one eligible students choosing to do so after obtaining parental consent. Participants ranged in age from fourteen to nineteen. Twenty-five were male and nineteen were female. Thirty-one students were foreign born, and all were from Mexico, except two (who were from El Salvador and the Dominican Republic). This was representative of the population in the study area, where the vast majority of Latinos are of Mexican origin. Students' academic levels ranged from self-reported A grade averages (making them honor-roll students) to self-reported D averages. Students were enrolled in diverse curricula, including participation in English as a second language (ESL), vocational tracks, and honors programs.

In-depth, semistructured interviews focused on the same issues as the survey but allowed for an elaboration of responses. All interviews were conducted between April and July 2007. One additional interview was conducted with Cesar (one of the original study participants) in December 2011, when the opportunity for a follow-up presented itself. Fifteen student interviews were conducted at school or in the home after seeking the approval of school officials and parents. Interview participants ranged in age from fourteen to eighteen; seven were male and eight were female. Eleven were foreign born, and all but one was from Mexico (the additional participant was from Guatemala). All students had lived in the US for five or more years. As with survey participants, students ranged in academic achievement from being honor-roll students (A averages) to those with C to D averages.

Additional interviews were conducted with five parents of the foreign-born students in their homes. All parents were foreign born and undocumented, which is representative of many Latino immigrants in relatively new destination communities (Kandel and Cromartie 2004; Passel, Capps, and Fix 2004). Parent interviews were semistructured to obtain adult perspectives on the same factors. These interviews helped to clarify and add texture to the information obtained from student surveys and interviews. One final interview was conducted with a foreign-born undocumented college graduate, aged twenty-seven, who had previously attended one of the high schools participating in the study. His successful graduation from college and subsequent pursuit of an MBA is not commonplace. This interview provided additional insight into the obstacles confronting Latino students following high school, throughout college, and after graduation; it also helped identify tools that might assist Latino students in overcoming systemic constraints to realizing their educational aspirations.

Students and parents were given surveys and interviews in either Spanish or English, depending on their comfort level. All Spanish language surveys and interviews have been translated into English in this paper.

SOCIO-SPATIAL FACTORS AFFECTING ASPIRATIONS

The socio-spatial factors influencing Latino student aspirations are numerous, place specific, and multidimensional. Given the variety of factors considered at multiple scales through a socio-spatial lens of analysis, it is not possible to provide a comprehensive discussion of all of the dimensions influencing students' educational aspirations. Therefore, we present an analysis of only the most significant issues shaping the study participants' aspirations for higher education.

Most foreign-born Latino students surveyed had high academic aspirations regardless of their self-reported grade point averages. In the survey, students were asked: "What is the highest level of education you would like to achieve?" Nearly 80% of students indicated that they would either like to finish college or obtain a graduate or professional degree. However, only 45% of foreign-born students thought they would be able to finish college or obtain a graduate or professional degree when asked: "Realistically speaking, what is the highest level of education you think you will get?" Nearly all foreign-born students participating in interviews also expressed a desire to continue studies after graduation, a response indicative of high academic aspirations.

While this may reflect a self-selection bias in that students with higher aspirations agreed to participate, after reviewing the sample, school administrators felt that the cross-section of students appeared to be typical of the wider study population. There were no noted differences between the height of the aspirations of the foreign-born students and that of the US-born students.

The following is a typical statement from a foreign-born student about his aspirations. The statements below express a sentiment echoed throughout the study: a desire to continue studying and pursue a career curtailed by barriers associated with documentation status.

Manuel, 9th grader (ESL Student): I want to do construction. . . . I wanted to be a police officer, but I don't think that is going to be possible [referring to his documentation status]. (Interview, September 10, 2007)

Raul, MBA: At some point in time, you may really wonder if it is worth it, because what happens when you finish? You have a degree but you may not be able to work in the profession you have chosen. (Interview, July 5, 2007)

Manuel, despite just beginning his high school academic career, tempers his aspirations to attend college with a "realistic" view of what he will be able to attain given his documentation status. At the same time, Raul posits a very real dilemma facing undocumented students: What is the value of an education when your employment prospects are so severely limited? In the end, is the time and effort worth it, if the employment outcome and opportunities will likely remain unchanged?

Students reported that parents had a greater influence on their aspirations than any other individual or group. All but one participant identified their parents' aspirations for them as their main reason for pursuing education beyond high school; 87% of survey participants also stated that their parents wanted them to finish college or go on to pursue a graduate or professional degree. This confirms the critical role the *microsphere*—the immediate household and family—plays in students' aspirations, and is consistent with previous research (e.g., Bandura et al. 2001; Ibáñez et al. 2004; Portes and Rumbaut 2001). According to the survey, students who perceived their parents to have high academic aspirations for them in turn had high academic aspirations for themselves. Twenty-eight foreign-born students out of thirty-one indicated that their parents expected them to finish at least some college, all of whom also indicated that they too would like to at least finish some college.

Juana, a mother of three, who has mainly worked in agriculture since coming to the US, expressed a sentiment common among parent partici-pates: "I want a better life for my children. I want them to have the oppor-tunities I did not have. They need to study and have a career, not work in the fields" (Interview, September 10, 2007). Similarly, many students attributed their aspirations to the sacrifices their parents were making to give them a better life, and expressed a desire to avoid disappointing them. David, an eleventh-grade student of foreign-born parents, said,

> They want me to be the one to succeed because they didn't have the opportunity. It will really make them happy if I just keep going and I won't have any regrets at the end of school. Being successful in life is my life, so education is very important. (Interview, April 30, 2007)

Students perceived higher education as a necessary step toward achieving a "better life," which was often framed against the experience of their par-ents and families remaining in their country of origin.

Teachers emerged as another key positive influence on students' forma-tion of academic aspirations. Typically, interactions with teachers occur in the students' *mesosphere*. The majority of students rated as high the quality of instruction, teacher interest in students, and access to informa-tion about college from teachers. This assessment was also supported by interview responses. When asked if her mother (a single mom) talks to her about going to college, Claudia, an eleventh grader, responded, "Not really, because she said that we have to pay a lot of money here" (Interview, May 9, 2007), referring to the cost of out-of-state tuition that undocumented students must pay in North Carolina. When asked if anyone has encour-aged her to go further, she answered, "My tenth-grade English teacher, she is always reminding me to do better" (Interview, May 9, 2007). These findings of the *mesosphere* are consistent with research indicating that ele-ments of the school environment, including teachers and students' feelings of belonging, influence their aspirations (Gándara et al. 2004). Addition-ally, Chen (this volume) documents the crucial role institutional allies can play in helping undocumented students navigate universities that are hostile to or unaware of their status.

While parental and teacher influence on student aspirations is well docu-mented, it has also been found that peers may influence students' aspirations, both in rural and urban settings, although not as strongly as parents (Buch-man and Dalton 2002; Gándara et al. 2004). In contrast, in this study, twenty-two of the thirty-one foreign-born students surveyed reported that they frequently discussed college with their friends. While most students (85%) noted that some of their friends had dropped out of school without graduating or did not plan to go to college, they were just as likely to indi-cate that they had as many friends planning to attend college (100%). The most common response (given by 78% of students) was that many or most of their friends planned to attend a community college, which served as an important pathway to higher education for Latino students because of the lower cost. Among the most frequent themes surrounding discussions of higher education with friends were the barriers to attending college, as reflected in ninth grader Manuel's comment:

> I have one friend who is really trying, taking honors, we hardly talk about it. I have had four friends that say, "I don't have a social security card, I can't go" and that's what is messing everyone up. They don't really think about it just because of that. I tell them that I want to go, but they say, "You can't if you don't have it."(Interview, September 10, 2007)

In the *exosphere*, the most significant factors to emerge were policies associated with students' undocumented status. Of the students surveyed, 70% indicated a belief that their documentation status would affect their ability to attend a university. Echoing the sentiments of other students, Sofia, an eleventh grader, noted, "Well, I am planning [on going to col-lege], but I don't know if me as an illegal gets to go to college" (Interview, October 4, 2007). According to Claudia, an eleventh grader, "People kept telling me I couldn't go to college because I'm not a US citizen. Right now, [students] say, 'I can't go to college so why does it matter?' I think it would give them hope [if laws were changed]" (Interview, May 9, 2007). Victoria, a tenth grader, lamented,

> I really haven't looked at any [four-year universities] because they are too much money. . . . It really aggravates me knowing that just because we are undocumented we don't have the same privilege. We cannot pay as much as everyone else, we have to pay more. I've heard there are some colleges, that won't let [undocumented] students in. Even if we get to go to college and graduate from college, it's still going to be hard to get a job for the same reason. It really worries me, because I don't want to waste money and waste time going to college if I can't get a job. (Interview, October 4, 2007)

With few exceptions, study respondents came from low-income fami-lies (mostly agricultural workers) with few or no assets to finance the costs of studying at a college or university level, a situation that becomes even more challenging for undocumented families that lack access to federal financial aid, or who may be charged out-of-state tuition because of their documentation status. Scholars have connected students' socio-economic status with aspirations, finding that students with fewer financial resources feel college is not an option, whether due to high cost or the need for an immediate income stream upon completing high school (Bowden and Doughney 2010; Haller and Virkler 1993; Kao and Tienda 1998). Similarly, in the survey, 90% of foreign-born students who expressed a desire to attend college indicated that money would be the principal reason for why they might not have the opportunity to continue their education after high school. Most stated they would look for schol-arships to help pay for college. However, due to restrictions on federal financial aid, undocumented students would have far fewer resources to draw upon when the time came to apply for assistance.

Interestingly, while concerns about financial ability to attend college did not appear to completely stifle academic aspirations (with twenty-six out of thirty-one foreign-born survey respondents stating they would like to at least finish college), lack of money was a key contributing factor in the gap between aspirations and students' perceived abilities to attain these aspira-tions. In the survey, twenty-eight out of thirty-one foreign-born students agreed with the statement "money will be a reason that I won't be able to continue studying after high school." Cesar, a tenth grader, expressed his frustration with the cost of college and the price difference for citizens and undocumented students. He stated, "I don't think it's fair. They charge other students from different countries more than citizens. I don't think it's fair" (Interview, April 30, 2007).

Thus far, only thirteen states nationwide have amended tuition rules to allow in-state status to undocumented foreign-born students (Chronicle of Higher Education 2011). North Carolina is not one of them, and continues to charge undocumented students out-of-state tuition. Enacting the rule change in North Carolina would provide some immediate help to undocu-mented students, but it would not remove a number of other constraints related to documentation status.

It is important to note that educational policies are not the only factors affecting students' abilities to access higher education. Like the teach-ers in Kamara and Monkman's study (this volume) and the college stu-dents in Thomas's study (this volume), participants in our study reported that their educational experiences and aspirations were mediated by the effects of policies related to citizenship and national security. Specifically, local policing of immigrants in response to national immigration debates and policies contributes to an anti-immigrant mindset that leads to dis-crimination that, in turn, can lower academic performance and aspi-rations (Portes and Rumbaut 2001). For example, federal immigration laws weigh heavily on the minds of undocumented students. As students grow from children into teenagers, they begin to realize the implications of their documentation status. With visible nervousness, Manuel spoke about his fears relating to his documentation status:

> Most of the times in the news I see it [deportations] and it gets me scared that they'll probably kick me out, they come and they go to people's house and take them back. I can't imagine immigration going to their [his parents'] work and taking them, how would we be able to live? (Interview, September 10, 2007)

Racist immigration policies negatively impact immigrants, their families, their communities, and our nation as a whole. For example, Immigration and Customs Enforcement (ICE) raids on homes and businesses create a climate of fear, hatred, and suspicion that carries into daily life, dividing communities with visibly present immigrant populations instead of unifying them. As Hing (2009:309) contends, "the structure of immigration laws has institutionalized a set of values that dehumanize, demonize, and criminalize immigrants of color". As a result, students often feel alienated and even ridiculed in their own community, a common pattern in immigrant destinations (Villenas 2002). Sergio, a twelfth grader, talks about life in his rural community, a place that has received Latino migrant farm workers for over thirty years. However, only recently has the town seen a more permanent and much larger immigrant population. Sergio describes the racist remarks he receives as an immigrant:

> I go into places and they talk to me differently. I love this [laughing] they always try to talk louder and use the o's constantly. It just makes me laugh. There have been times, I've been in stores and people look at me like what are you doing here? I just don't go back there, I don't feel like I want to put myself through that. There are some people that just don't understand yet. (Interview, April 30, 2007)

Sergio's examples show how policies exacerbate xenophobia, racism, and discrimination, and serve to infuse even the most mundane interactions between immigrants and locals with tension and misunderstandings.

Undocumented students who go on to college and complete a degree face the challenge of finding work because of their immigration status. For example, Raul, an undocumented MBA graduate who currently works as an accountant in a major national firm, has worked by using falsified documents. Other study participants, like Cesar, are now in college. He secured a partial scholarship to a small private college where he is majoring in mathematics. Cesar wanted to be an engineer, but the school does not have that major and he does not have the resources to pursue his education elsewhere. When asked if he would consider going back to Mexico to work after graduation, a country he has not set foot in since he was six years old, he said he could not imagine living there: "I don't really know much about

Mexico, I know more about this country. I think of myself as half and half, as Mexican American" (Interview, May 7, 2007).

Cesar is also facing a more immediate problem as a result of recent anti-immigrant state and local policies. He does not have a driver's license because of state laws prohibiting him from acquiring one without a valid social security number, and the route he takes between school and home frequently has license checkpoints. One of the counties he drives through participates in the Secure Communities program, a collaborative effort between local authorities and homeland security to round up undocumented residents. His mother has expressed concern about his safety but reiterates that it is absolutely necessary for him to complete his education. Cesar's college academic performance in the spring semester of 2011 was negatively impacted by having to pass through frequent license checkpoints, court dates related to driving without a license, and ultimately an encounter and detention with ICE: he failed three classes. Shaken, he said, "I'm scared. I'm trying to be optimistic. I just want to stay here and study" (Interview, January 25, 2012).

It is clear that the policies of the *exosphere* and *macrosphere* have an immediate impact on the student's *mesosphere*. The lack of opportunities for immigrants to pursue higher education and to attain jobs has far-reaching results on local economies and social service provision. New immigrant destinations such as North Carolina are experiencing a desperate need for bilingual professionals, which is exacerbated by inadequate access to higher education for foreign-born, bilingual Latino youth who are unable to complete the requirements to become nurses, doctors, lawyers, court translators, police officers, accountants, loan officers, social workers, teachers, and more. These professionals are needed to serve the growing Latino population. Recognizing this need, Cecilia, an eleventh grader, said during an interview,

> I want to be a nurse. I have always wanted to be a nurse since I was a little girl. I like the health-care profession and I like to help people. There are still so many people who cannot speak English, I can help them. (Interview, October 4, 2007)

This lack of bilingual professionals, with an understanding of the cultural context of Latino immigrants, erects barriers for families to avail themselves of medical, educational, and other public benefits. This not only harms immigrants, but also reduces the effectiveness, and thus the efficiency, of those existing resources and programs targeting Latino newcomers.

The shortage of Latino professionals also results in a dearth of role models who could help Latino youth cope with the disconnect between their home and their new culture. Such mentors can also fill some of the void left by immigrant parents, who are often working long hours and not as available to their children as they may once have been (Suarez-Orozco and

Suarez-Orozco 2009). The presence of skilled professionals and role models is just one of the many benefits that educating foreign-born Latino youth could offer to local areas.

CONCLUSION

The factors that positively and negatively affect the academic achievement of rural Latino students are complex and layered, straddling multiple spheres in students' lives. It is imperative that we begin to understand the factors that influence students' academic aspirations, regardless of their achievement, so that we might better provide them with the tools and resources needed to achieve those aspirations and succeed educationally. This will enrich not only their lives but also the communities in which they live, as they become productive members of society and fulfill important economic roles. Further, analyzing the structures within and outside educational institutions that intersect to limit students' opportunities and aspirations emphasizes the fact that the problem is not located in individuals. Rather, the problem is the result of interlocking policies that reduce the space students feel is available to them to pursue their dreams.

We found that within the communities in rural eastern North Carolina, foreign-born Latino students and their parents have high academic aspirations. Factors in the *microsphere* and the *mesosphere* were more likely to have a positive influence on students' aspirations. Irrespective of whether participants had been in the US two years or ten years, their parents' encouragement played the strongest role in the students' desire to continue their education beyond high school. Students reported that parents often stressed the importance of education in providing their children an opportunity for a better future than they themselves had. This is important because, as Goldenberg et al. (2001) indicates, educators often attribute low academic aspirations and low performance of Latino immigrant children to low parental education and expectations. This misconception conceals structural barriers to having and achieving high academic aspirations.

Factors in the *exosphere* and *macrosphere* were more likely to have a negative influence on students' perceptions concerning their ability to attain higher levels of education. Specifically, the dominant factors in these spheres were state and federal policies. While these policies did not diminish students' high academic aspirations, such factors limited what they considered to be achievable. This effectively creates a gap between aspiration and perceived possibility of attainment. Thus, lowering academic achievement expectations is found to be a negative effect of documentation status, which is consistent with McWhirter et al.'s (2013) findings in their study of nearly five hundred undocumented Latino students. This is particularly the case in North Carolina, a state that failed to pass legislation in 2003 and again in 2005 allowing undocumented students graduating from a North Carolina high school to pay the in-state tuition rate. At the level of the *macrosphere*, the federal DREAM Act has also failed to pass through Congress. However, some progress has been made as a result of the change in the federal immigration program called Deferred Action for Childhood Arrivals (DACA), which will be discussed further below. States granting in-state tuition status to undocumented Mexican youth saw an increase in college enrollment and, ultimately, educational attainment (Kaushal 2008). Indeed, society's "opportunity structures" have often been used to describe the difference between academic aspirations and the ability to attain those aspirations (Kao and Tienda 1998; Qian and Blair 1999). The lack of access to scholarships and state and federal student aid means that higher education is beyond reach for most of these students. While such a change would be an immediate help to undocumented foreign-born students with high aspirations, it would not be a long-term solution because they would have no way of working legally once they graduated.

It is imperative that several national policies be addressed immediately—both for the future of undocumented youth and the nation as a whole. The first necessary action is to pass the federal DREAM Act, which would give undocumented youth with high academic aspirations, who were brought by their parents to the US and raised there, a path to a legal documentation status if they pursue education or military service after high school. As explained above, this would benefit not only those students, but also the places they live by adding educated members to the community who ultimately will make contributions to society. The second policy that must be addressed relates to how undocumented immigrants are dealt with once in the US, particularly policies associated with policing and surveillance. As discussed, immigration policies such as ICE raids and the Safe Community Initiative (which ultimately places immigration "roundups" in the hands of local authorities) not only bring fear to the immigrant community and its members, but stigmatize and divide newcomers from other local residents. Institutions of higher education need to take a stand for these vulnerable students by lobbying for legislative change, carving out alternative funding sources, and conducting activist research to demonstrate the benefits of providing access to higher education to undocumented youth, and for the nation as a whole.

While recent policy changes regarding deportation of undocumented youth have the potential to be beneficial, they do not provide a permanent solution for young people who have spent most of their lives in the US. In June 2012, the Obama administration announced the DACA initiative, which offers a two-year renewable reprieve from deportation for qualified youth and gives them the opportunity to apply for a work permit so they may finally be able to work legally and enjoy protections such as a living wage. The new policy focuses on those who are under the age of thirty-one; entered the US before age sixteen; arrived prior to June 15, 2007; lived in the country consecutively the past five years; and have no convicted felonies or "significant" misdemeanors. They must currently be enrolled in school, have graduated high school, obtained a GED or served in the armed forces (USCIS 2013a). As of March 2013, 469,530 young adults had applied, and 245,593 had been approved. North Carolina was ranked sixth in the list of top ten states of applicant residence (USICS 2013b). While the new policy gives youth an opportunity to work legally for the first time, it does not change their residency status, nor does it give them a path to permanent legal status within the county. Furthermore, the policy leaves out entire populations over the age of thirty-one and those students who may have arrived in 2008 and after; this policy is therefore not a substitute for the DREAM Act.

Permanent changes in federal policy would be beneficial not only to undocumented students but also to their families and the communities in which they live, the state at large, and the nation. On average, an individual with a bachelor's degree earns $40,100 annually, in contrast to an individual with only a high school diploma, who earns only $25,000 per year (NCES 2010). Additionally, this change in federal policy would alleviate many of the pressures students feel about their documentation status and the divide that is being created in communities between new immigrants and the established community. As a nation, we must not punish the children of immigrants who have been raised as Americans. Instead, we must afford them the opportunity to achieve their aspirations and give back to the country they now call home. As this chapter shows, such a change requires comprehensive immigration and educational reform, rather than just one or the other.

Finally, it should be noted that, like the participants in the other studies in this volume, many students in our research pursued higher education and careers despite the structural barriers that they faced. Rather than accepting the limitations imposed by restrictive federal and local policies, students and parents made space for their dreams and ambitions by facing powerful and oppressive institutions like ICE. This chapter is a testimony to the power of immigrants to resist and remake their worlds even in the face of overwhelming obstacles. Imagine what these students would be capable of if even a few of these obstacles were removed.

NOTES

1. This statistic does not distinguish between Latinos who were foreign-born and those who were US citizens.
2. We are grateful to the students and parents who shared their experiences with us, as well as the school system that provided access to study participants. This research was made possible due to generous support from the National Science Foundation Geography and Spatial Sciences Program (Award # 0547725 and #1005927) and the University of Texas at Austin

Harrington Faculty Fellows Program and the College of Liberal Arts. The Department of Geography at East Carolina University provided much-appreciated graduate student support. We wish to thank Marina Islas for her assistance with producing our map and Velvet Nelson for providing feedback on an earlier version of the manuscript. Any errors or omissions remain solely our responsibility.

REFERENCES

Bandura, Albert, Claudio Barbaranelli, Gian Caprara, and Concetta Pastorelli. 2001. "Self-Efficacy Beliefs as Shapers of Children's Aspirations and Career Trajectories." *Child Development* 72 (1): 187–206.

Bohon, Stephanie, Heather Macpherson, and Jorge Atiles. 2005. "Educational Barriers for New Latinos in Georgia." *Journal of Latinos and Education* 4 (1): 43–58.

Bowden, Mark, and James Doughney. 2010. "Socio-Economic Status, Cultural Diversity and the Aspirations of Secondary Students in the Western Suburbs of Melbourne, Australia." *Higher Education* 59: 115–129.

Brewster, Ann, and Gary Bowen. 2004. "Teacher Support and the School Engagement of Latino Middle and High School Students at Risk of School Failure." *Child and Adolescent Social Work Journal* 21 (1): 47–66.

Bronfenbrenner, Urie. 1977. "Toward an Experimental Ecology of Human Development." *American Psychologist* 32 (7): 513–531.

Buchmann, Claudi, and Ben Dalton. 2002."Interpersonal Influences and Educational Aspirations in 12 Countries: The Importance of Institutional Context." *Sociology of Education* 75 (2): 99–122

Burnell, Beverly. 2003. "The 'Real World' Aspirations of Work-Bound Rural Students." *Journal of Research in Rural Education* 18 (2): 104–113.

Chang, Esther, Chuansheng Chen, Ellen Greenberger, David Dooley, and Jutta Heckhausen. 2006. "What Do They Want in Life? The Life Goals of a Multiethnic, Multi-generational Sample of High School Seniors." *Journal of Youth and Adolescence* 35 (3): 321–332.

Chenoweth, Erica, and Renee Galliher. 2004. "Factors Influencing College Aspirations of Rural West Virginia High School Students." *Journal of Research in Rural Education* 19 (2): 1–14.

Chronicle of Higher Education. 2011. "Rhode Island Board Approves In-State Tuition for Undocumented Students." Accessed January 27, 2012. http://chronicle.com/blogs/ticker/rhode-island-board-approves-in-state-tuition-for-undocumented-students/36706.

Conchas, Gilberto. 2001. "Structuring Failure and Success: Understanding the Variability in Latino School Engagement." *Harvard Educational Review* 71 (3): 475–504.

Gándara, Patricia, Susan O'Hara, and Dianna Gutiérrez. 2004. "The Changing Shape of Aspirations: Peer Influence on Achievement Behavior." In *School Connections: US Mexican Youth, Peers and School Achievement*, edited by Margaret A. Gibson, Patricia Gándara, and Jill Peterson Koyama, 39–62. New York: Teachers College Press.

Goldenberg, Claude, Ronald Gallimore, Leslie Reese, and Helen Garnier. 2001. "Cause or Effect? A Longitudinal Study of Immigrant Latino Parents' Aspirations and Expectations, and Their Children's School Performance." *American Educational Research Journal* 38 (3): 547–582.

Haller, Emil, and Sarah Virkler. 1993. "Another Look at Rural-Nonrural Differences in Students' Educational Aspirations." *Journal of Research in Rural Education* 9 (3): 170–178.

Hing, Bill Ong. 2009. "Institutional Racism, ICE Raids, and Immigration Reform." *University of San Francisco Law Review* 44: 1–49.

Howley, Caitlin. 2006. "Remote Possibilities: Rural Children's Educational Aspirations." *Peabody Journal of Education* 81 (2): 62–80.

Hurtado-Ortiz, Maria, and Mary Gauvain. 2007. "Postsecondary Education among Mexican American Youth." *Hispanic Journal of Behavioral Sciences* 29 (2): 181–191.

Ibáñez, Gladys, Gabriel Kuperminc, Greg Jurkovic, and Julia Perilla. 2004. "Cultural Attributes and Adaptations Linked to Achievement Motivation among Latino Adolescents." *Journal of Youth and Adolescence* 33 (6): 559–568.

Irvin, Matthew, Judith Meece, Soo-yong Byun, Thomas Farmer, and Bryan Hutchins. 2011. "Relationship of School Context to Rural Youth's Educational Achievement and Aspirations." *Journal of Youth and Adolescence* 40 (9): 1225–1242.

Kandel, William, and John Cromartie. 2004. "New Patterns of Hispanic Settlement in Rural America." United States Department of Agriculture (USDA), Economic Research Service, Rural Development Research Report No. 99. Accessed January 25, 2012. http://www.ers.usda.gov/ersDownloadHandler.ashx?file=/media/560863/rdrr99fm_1_pdf

Kandel, William, and Grace Kao. 2001. "The Impact of Temporary Labor Migration on Mexican Children's Educational Aspirations and Performance." *International Migration Review* 35 (2): 1205–1231.

Kandel, William, and Emilio Parrado. 2006. "Hispanic Population Growth and Public School Response in Two New South Immigrant Destinations." In *Latinos in the New South: Transformation of Place*, edited by Heather Smith and Owen Furuseth, 111–134. Burlington, VT: Ashgate Publishing.

Kao, Grace, and Marta Tienda. 1998. "Educational Aspirations of Minority Youth." *American Journal of Education* 106 (3): 349–384.

Kaushal, Neeraj. 2008. "In-State Tuition for the Undocumented: Education Effects on Mexican Young Adults." *Journal of Policy Analysis and Management* 27 (4): 771–792.

Matthews, Hugh, and Melanie Limb. 1999. "Defining an Agenda for the Geography of Children: Review and Prospect." *Progress in Human Geography* 23 (1): 61–90.

Matthews, Hugh, Melanie Limb, and Mark Taylor. 1998. "The Geography of Children: Some Ethical and Methodological Considerations for Project and Dissertation Work." *Journal of Geography of Higher Education* 22 (3): 311–324.

McWhirter, Ellen Hawley, Karina Ramos, and Cynthia Medina. 2013. "¿Y Ahora Qué? Anticipated Immigration Status Barriers and Latina/o High School Students' Future Expectations." *Cultural Diversity and Ethnic Minority Psychology* 19 (3): 288–297.

National Center for Education Statistics (NCES). 2010. "Table: Median Annual Earnings of Full-Time, Full-Year Wage and Salary Workers Ages 25–34, by Educational Attainment and Sex: Selected Years, 1980–2009." Fast Facts. Accessed January 25, 2012. http://nces.ed.gov/fastfacts/display.asp?id=77.

NCDPI. 2007. "Reports of Supplemental Disaggregated State, School System (LEA) and School Performance Data for 2005–2007: End of Course (Composite, All End of Course Subjects)." Accessed August 8, 2007. www.ncpublicschools.org/accountability/reporting/leaperformancearchive/.

———. 2009. "2009 Free & Reduced Meals Application Data." Accessed September 2, 2011. http://www.ncpublicschools.org/fbs/resources/data/.

———. 2010. "2009–2010 Consolidated Data Reports." Accessed January 13, 2012. http://www.dpi.state.nc.us/docs/research/discipline/reports/consolidated/2009–10/consolidated-report.pdf.

North Carolina Public Schools (NCPS). 2009. *2009 Statistical Profile*. Accessed January 13, 2012. http://www.dpi.state.nc.us/docs/fbs/resources/data/statisticalprofile/2009profile.pdf.

Passel, Jeffrey, Randolph Capps, and Michael Fix. 2004. "Undocumented Immigrants: Facts and Figures." The Urban Institute. Last modified January 12, 2004. http://www.urban.org/publications/1000587.html.

Phelan, Patricia, Ann Davidson, and Hanh Cao Yu.1993. "Students' Multiple Worlds: Navigating the Borders of Family, Peer and School Cultures." In *Renegotiating Cultural Diversity in American Schools*, edited by Patria Phelan and Ann Davidson, 52–88. New York: Teachers College Press.

Portes, Alejandro, and Ruben Rumbaut. 2001. *Legacies: The Story of the Immigrant Second Generations*. Berkeley and Los Angeles: University of California Press.

Qian, Zhenchao, and Sampson Blair. 1999. "Racial/Ethnic Differences in Educational Aspirations of High School Seniors." *Sociological Perspectives* 42 (4): 605–625.

Suarez-Orozco, Carola, and Marcelo Suarez-Orozco. 2009. "Educating Latino Immigrant Students in the Twenty-First Century: Principles for the Obama Administration." *Harvard Educational Review* 79 (2): 327–340.

Teachman, Jay, and Kathleen Paasch. 1998. "The Family and Educational Aspirations." *Journal of Marriage and the Family* 60 (3): 704–714.

Torres, Rebecca, Jeffery Popke, and Holly Hapke. 2006. "The South's Silent Bargain: Rural Restructuring, Latino Labor, and the Ambiguities of Migrant Experience." In *Latinos in the New South: Transformation of Place*, edited by Heather Smith and Owen Furuseth, 37–67. Burlington, VT: Ashgate Publishing.

UNC-GA. 2007. "Headcount Enrollment Total for UNC Total by Institution: Fall 2003 through Fall 2006." Report generated by Xiaoyun Yang, UNC General Administration.

US Census Bureau. 2010. "2010 Census Shows Nation's Hispanic Population Grew Four Times Faster Than Total U.S. Population." Accessed January 13, 2012. http://2010.census.gov/news/releases/operations/cb11-cn146.html.

US Citizenship and Immigration Services (USCIS). 2013a. "Consideration for Deferred Action for Childhood Arrivals Process." Last modified January 18, 2013. http://www.uscis.gov/portal/site/uscis/menuitem.eb1d4c2a3e5b9ac89243c6a7543f6d1a/?vgnextoid=f2ef2f19470f7310VgnVCM100000082ca60aRCRD&vgnextchannel=f2ef2f19470f7310VgnVCM100000082ca60aRCRD.

———. 2013b. "Deferred Action for Childhood Arrivals Process." USICS Office of Performance and Quality. Last modified March 14, 2013. http://www.uscis.gov/USCIS/Resources/Reports%20and%20Studies/Immigration%20Forms%20Data/All%20Form%20Types/DACA/daca-13-3-15.pdf.

Valencia, Elvia, and Valeria Johnson. 2006. "Latino Students in North Carolina: Acculturation, Perceptions of School Environment and Academic Aspirations." *Hispanic Journal of Behavioral Sciences* 28 (3): 350–367.

Villenas, Sofia. 2002. "Reinventing Educación in New Latino Communities: Pedagogies of Change and Continuity in North Carolina." In *Education in the New Latino Diaspora*, edited by Stanton Wortham, Enrique Murillo Jr., and Edmond Hamann, 17–36. Westport, CT: Ablex Publishing.

Wang, Margaret, Geneva Haertel, and Herbert Walberg. 1997. "Fostering Educational Resilience in Inner-City Schools." *Children and Youth* 7: 119–140.

8 The Neoliberal Turn in US Higher Education

Implications for Indian F-1 Students' Negotiations of Belonging

Susan Thomas

In recent decades, the influence of globalization on institutions of higher education can be clearly seen, most visibly in the growing numbers of students crossing national borders to pursue educational degrees. While the global migration of students is certainly not a new phenomenon, the scale of these migrations has undeniably grown, primarily as a result of universities' increased commitment to "internationalize" their campuses (Altbach and Knight 2006; De Wit 2002). Perceived as a necessity to survive in and reap the benefits of a globalized world (Altbach and Knight 2006), universities are enhancing their internationalization efforts, which involve various strategies including raising enrollments of students from abroad. A highly lucrative enterprise, the global market for educating overseas students is becoming more competitive, with some nations aggressively expanding their international programs and actively developing plans and strategies to promote foreign enrollment at their universities (Altbach 2004; Bevis and Lucas 2007; NAFSA 2006).

In the US, the provision of higher education to overseas students is a multibillion dollar industry and serves as the fifth-largest service-sector export according to the US Department of Commerce (2012). With 20% of the global population of student migrants (IIE, "Global Destinations"; OECD 2010), the US has become the most popular destination for students around the world seeking higher education (Clotfelter 2010), particularly from Asian countries. Globally, India is one of the largest target markets for the recruitment of overseas students, and the US is the leading receiving country for Indian students (IIE, "Project Atlas India"). In addition to creating revenue for the US economy, these students are also enrolling primarily in high-skill professional fields that are critical to the globally competitive edge the US boasts (Bevis and Lucas 2007; IIE 2010; Zakaria 2004), thus serving vital intellectual and technical needs in these areas, which are not being fulfilled sufficiently by domestic students. Moreover, many universities point to the presence of overseas students as a response to national demands for diversity on campuses.

Both the global market–driven trend to internationalize universities and the resulting increase in movement of young people from India across national borders to pursue opportunities for higher education are indicative of how the global expansion of a neoliberal order is affecting higher education. Although the neoliberal educational policies of internationalization are receiving attention by scholars and policymakers, we need more insights into how they are being lived by students themselves, as well as the institutions that host them.

In this chapter, I use ethnographic accounts collected at a public university in the New York City metropolitan area, to consider the strains internationalization places on the work of the international programs office in the post-9/11 era. Additionally, I address the complex raced and classed practices of housing and part-time work by which Indian overseas students are positioned while studying at the university, and how that positioning informs their everyday negotiations of community and belonging. Resisting an uncritical acceptance of internationalization, I seek to provide more nuanced insights into the implications of this neoliberal policy agenda for the practices and meaning making of those most directly affected by its implementation.

NEOLIBERAL TURN IN HIGHER EDUCATION

The expanding global market for university students is a result of neoliberalism's impact on higher education. Since the 1970s, the world has seen a shift toward a neoliberal political economic order, in which "an institutional framework characterized by strong private property rights, free markets, and free trade" reigns as the guiding force behind global relations (Harvey 2005, 2). With this shift, neoliberal logic now serves as a fundamental mode of governance in sites throughout the globe, particularly in nations that desire to participate in the global economy (see Ong 2006). Further, neoliberalism is transforming the relationship between nation-states, their populations, and key institutions such as those of higher education (see Ayers 2005; Giroux and Giroux 2004; Slaughter and Rhoades 2004). Although neoliberalism is purported to require minimal intervention on the part of the nation-state, in reality it involves extensive state intervention at different moments (Harvey 2005). When markets do not exist or are seen to require expansion, as has happened with the education market in many countries, the state often plays the critical role of creating the conditions necessary to facilitate this process.

The neoliberalization of higher education has led universities to adopt market-based strategies to compete for students from other parts of the world in an effort to tap into a crucial international source of revenue (Brooks and Waters 2011; Sidhu 2006). English-speaking countries and their universities tend to be the primary recruiters in the global competition for students, and the source of these migrant students tends to be the Global South, especially Asian countries (although this is not exclusively the case). India, in particular, has become a valuable supplier of consumers of US higher education. Since the 1990s, the liberalization of India's economy and the subsequent growth of its middle class are often portrayed as a significant instantiation of the success of neoliberal reforms (see Ablett et al. 2007; Friedman 2005; Panagariya 2008). Advocates assert that a key benefit of these reforms is the increased consumer choice they bring to India, a claim that is made in the area of higher education as well. In India, there has been a rising demand for higher education that the country is not currently meeting within its borders. The liberalization of India's economy, and the global expansion of the education market, has increased the choices available for middle-class youth seeking higher education. Furthermore, a university degree from a Western country, especially the US, serves as cultural capital for social and economic mobility, incentivizing young Indian students who can coordinate the necessary resources to move overseas and take advantage of these new educational opportunities.

While it is necessary to recognize the privileges of being able to do so, Fernandes (2006) challenges the discourse that portrays the "new" middle class as a "singular transnational elite" (xxviii) that is homogeneously benefiting from India's economic restructuring policies, and argues for the analytical significance of the differences existing within this socioeconomic group. Echoing Fernandes's point, my work reveals the importance of attending to the specific and varied social and economic circumstances that structure these students' trajectories, mediate their relationship to the university and the US, and form their social and cultural imaginaries as transnational students. Indian F-1 students' legal status, class backgrounds, and cultural differences position them in particular raced and classed ways at the university. The findings of my research reveal that many of these students live in segregated housing conditions and work in minimum-wage and, at times, exploitative part-time jobs on campus.

Additionally, during this study, there was growing pressure on the international programs office at the university to focus on compliance with national security regulations and retreat from providing social services and advising to overseas students. In contrast to the allies presented in Chen's study (this volume), the university administrators and policymakers in this study primarily seek to benefit from the neoliberal agenda of internationalization by increasing enrollments of overseas students. Like the structures discussed in research by Wicks-Asbun and Torres (this volume) and Monkman and Kamara (this volume), federal policies interlocked with university policies resulted in what Das Gupta (2006) calls place-taking, or institutionalized practices that lock immigrants out of spaces because of their citizenship or other identity category. The economic and social pressures resulting from place-taking forced Indian students to negotiate community and belonging within structures designed to exclude them. I explore these negotiations in this chapter.

METHODS

I began my ethnographic study in May 2011 at a public university in the New York City metropolitan region, which I refer to as Riverside University. There are over three thousand F-1 students at the university, making it one of the institutions with the highest number of students in the state of New York (IIE 2010).[1] With 20% of these students coming from South Asia, Riverside is a significant destination for South Asian F-1 students, the vast majority of whom enroll in the sciences, technology, engineering, and math fields,[2] which is representative of the national trend of South Asian F-1 student enrollment.

My primary methods of data collection were participant observation, semi-structured interviews, analysis of archival material, and discourse analysis of media sources; in this chapter, I draw exclusively from participant-observation fieldnotes and interviews. I met and recruited students as research participants primarily through snowball sampling that started with introductions at the international programs office and orientation events. I observed and engaged students at student group events, in study lounges, during social outings, and in their homes. I also conducted observations and interviews at the international programs office, speaking regularly with several of the staff members.

I was consistently introduced to individuals as a "researcher" and a PhD student attending another university who was studying students from South Asia. My own position as an Indian woman raised in the US led many students to express various attitudes toward me, including alternating perceptions of sameness and difference between us. At times, participants perceived my "Americanness" as interesting and different, whereas at other moments, it would create a distance. Some students had also conveyed to me that I was not American enough; one student, for instance, jokingly broke my identity down into percentages of "Indian" and "American," with the latter failing by a large margin. This positioning would become especially relevant during conversations regarding their social relationships to Americans.

FINDINGS

Changes at the Visa and Immigration Office

In the US, opening educational borders to overseas students has highlighted the tension between the global expansion of the neoliberal agenda and its relationship to practices of the nation-state. September 11, 2001 was a pivotal moment when the insecurities accompanying globalizing processes became especially apparent, raising the fundamental issue of national sovereignty and global power in the globalization era. "9/11," as the attack came to be known, brought particular attention to the repercussions of US imperial power (see Ahmad 2003; Harvey 2003; Maira 2009). While the US government used the events of 9/11 to justify wars abroad, it also used the opportunity to enhance domestic security to protect its borders from hostile forces, leading to the implementation of various policies including the Patriot Act of 2001 and the Visa and Entry Reform Act of 2002. Since at least one of the hijackers involved in the attacks on 9/11 arrived on a student visa, policies were developed after the attack to scrutinize the student visa process. These policies directly impacted institutions of higher education hosting overseas students, creating various security measures including visa restrictions, surveillance, and a tracking system, the Student and Exchange Visitor Information System (SEVIS), developed specifically for universities to monitor and report on their foreign student populations to federal government agencies.[3]

In the past decade, numerous members of the international education community criticized these security regulations, noting that such policies are potentially detrimental to US political and economic interests. For instance, Victor Johnson, the senior advisor for public policy at NAFSA: Association of International Educators, argued that these measures not only harm the position of the US in the global competition for overseas students, but may also damage diplomatic relationships, for which the international student community has always played a beneficial role (Johnson 2003). Despite these reactions, the policies have since become institutionalized, significantly affecting how overseas student populations at universities are managed.

The rapidly rising enrollments of overseas students at Riverside University, along with the elaborate documentation and reporting requirements that have accompanied post-9/11 federal regulations, have created tensions for the international programs office. Like other American public institutions, the state-run university has seen its government funding cut severely, a development that is the result of the neoliberal drive to withdraw government support for basic social services, such as education. Like other public universities that struggle to cover their costs, Riverside has turned to market-driven policies, including enrolling large numbers of overseas students who pay full out-of-state tuition. (Currently, Riverside's out-of-state tuition and fees are almost double the rate of in-state tuition.) With overseas students accounting for 13% of the total student enrollment and more than 20% of the total graduate student population, their fees contribute substantially to institutional revenue.

However, managing such large numbers of students in a post-9/11 policy climate that emphasizes regulating the entry and presence of transnational students is leading to important philosophical and operational shifts in the work of the office responsible for them. This is perhaps most symbolically captured in the decision by the new chair overseeing all of the international programs to change the name of the center: what used to be called "International Services" is now called the "Visa and Immigration Office." This change was a source of tension between the chair and the director of international student services, Sara, who had worked in the international education field for more than twenty years. For Sara, the name change disregarded the importance of the work of the center, which for her was not supposed to be focused on compliance; rather, she believed it was about the social and cultural aspects of hosting students from abroad. She explained:

> But for those of us who have been in the field for a long time, this work, it's almost like a calling, really, like a missionary. It's not just a job. . . . Many of us have done things like the Peace Corps, so we are accustomed to working without resources, or external support. But that means we end up doing a lot of extra work. So it has always been the case that you're behind in the work. . . . Even before SEVIS, there was compliance. But the office was a welcoming space that not only dealt with federal regulations but also served as a resource space for students. But now the office has been stripped down to that level. What are you trying to accomplish? To alienate [the students]? (Interview, October 14, 2011)

Sara felt the chair's decision to emphasize the university's role in compliance with federal regulations was eradicating the social significance of the relationship between the international programs office and the students. Once an internal mechanism for creating space for international students, the international center was turned into a place-taking body by the intersection of federal immigration policy and neoliberal institutionalized views of students as revenue sources.

Within a few months into the academic year, Sara was demoted, and the chair turned her work responsibilities as director of international student services over to the coordinator of the study abroad programs, Jenny. Sara was also forced to relinquish her office and move to an isolated space located on a lower floor, effectively erasing her role, presence, and views from the center (Fieldnotes, October 14, 2011). While this decision was partly a result of the individual personal conflicts between Sara and the chair, it was also indicative of the shift in the commitments of the center. In sharp contrast to Sara's emphasis on social services, Jenny stressed her efforts to improve the efficiency of the office, often describing in minute detail the procedural and administrative changes she was making to achieve this goal. One of these changes, for instance, included gutting the international student orientations, cutting them down from a three-day welcoming event to a three-hour information session focused on visa- and immigration-related issues and on processing students' documents (Fieldnotes, August 24, 2011). Jenny also hoped to manage some of the heavy documentation involved in the work by moving it into electronic format, and automating some of the communication with students. In one of our conversations, she pointed out that federal regulations required students to take responsibility for their own tracking, and that some of the changes she was attempting to make were meant to push students to do so (Fieldnotes, March 20, 2012). This emphasis on efficiency, procedure, and self-reliance is consistent with free-market values and reflects how neoliberal policy interests are transforming the everyday work climate of the international office from a space for students to a space designed to track, regulate, and, at times, exclude them.

Jenny explained that such procedural adjustments were designed to reduce the workload of the advisors, which is a concern as the international student numbers increase at the university and compliance with federal regulations has become more strictly monitored (Fieldnotes, March 20, 2012). However, conversations with two of the advisors at the Visa and Immigration Office revealed their sense of frustration at the changes these developments have imposed upon their work. Nicki, the international student advisor primarily responsible for the engineering students, spoke to me about the implications security regulations had for advisors' roles in the office. She stated:

Well, really, we end up . . . you know, doing [the government's] dirty work. We're the ones who have to track them. But it's hard because what do we represent? We represent the university and its regulations and we are supposed to be here for the students. We are not immigration officers. Not police officers—well, we try not to be that but you have to keep that balance. After 9/11, we did act like that though. We acted like police officers. Now, it has mellowed in some ways from that time . . . but there are other, new ways the tracking is getting expressed. They're working on it. The students are going to be tracked even better—all the holes, the gaps, they're going to be closed; that circle is going to be closed. . . . It will definitely affect us. We're [the government's] facilitators, right? (Interview, August 24, 2011)

Nicki's use of "immigration officer," "police officer," and "facilitator" illuminates the tensions that post-9/11 security measures are creating in advisors' sense of their own responsibilities. Her sentiments were also reflected in some of the comments made by her coworker, Sonia. For Sonia, 9/11 marked the creation of different categories of advisors. She described the differences:

There are those who are like me and have been doing this kind of work for a while. And then there are the "Past-SEVIS [*sic*] Advisors." That's what I call them. Yeah, the Past-SEVIS [*sic*] Advisors don't know any other system because they came after SEVIS was established. I had been working in this field for eleven and a half, twelve years so I have seen it the way it was before and there have been major changes. . . . Visa and Immigration—the name change occurred so that it was clear to the students that we were only here to deal with things related to their legal status and paperwork and then sending them away. I mean . . . there are only four advisors for over three thousand students . . . we're really understaffed. Yes, we can talk about security but there is no human touch, we are not actually helping anyone. (Interview, July 6, 2011)

Sonia's frustrations point to the particular ways the intersection of post-9/11 national security regulations and the university's market-driven practices influence the work of the office. The pressures linked with these concurrent processes are shifting the office's attention from the types of social and emotional support that both Sonia and Sara claimed was offered before 9/11, what Sonia referred to as the "human touch," and replacing it with the policing and bureaucratized work associated with immigration officers.

These findings also highlight the place of the university within a network of policies related to citizenship and security that directly affect higher education, even if they are not explicitly classified as education-related policies. Like the students in the chapter by Wicks-Asbun and Torres (this volume), the students at Riverside University were affected by place-taking policies that position them as subjects in need of surveillance due to their documentation status (or lack thereof). As will be described in the next section, the intersection of these policies narrowed students' possibilities for community and belonging, a reality that immigrants negotiated both within and outside campus.

Indian Students Navigate University Life Overseas

With such a shift to post-9/11 compliance at the university, how do Indian university students, one of the largest populations of overseas students at Riverside, make sense of their relationship to the university? For many of the participants, the Visa and Immigration Office represented precisely what its new name suggested: the university office they must approach to address the procedural and legal aspects of their F-1 status. For cultural and social experiences, and other forms of advising, students reported that they turned to one another. Informal student support networks formed in multiple ways. Students used social networking media, such as the highly successful website Facebook, to organize and prepare themselves even before they arrived in the US, including arranging their flight tickets together. The students who were at the university previously, referred to as their "seniors," maintained pages for the incoming classes, advising on various issues, including visa procedures, housing, courses, and even what kind of kitchenware to bring. Thus, in the face of place-taking practices,

Indian students produced organic forms of support networks and an underground culture of advising. Through such organizing, students made space for themselves and their peers within constrictive structures and institutions. However, they also faced numerous obstacles to negotiating space for themselves. The first—finding suitable housing—is discussed below.

Experiences with Housing

Several students expressed comfort in knowing that there were so many other students from India at the university with them, articulating a sense that it "felt like home" (Fieldnotes, August 25, 2011). Graduate students perceived their housing situation a key aspect of this familiarity of "home." Riverside University's housing options were too expensive for most of the participants. Although F-1 students, as middle-class youth from India, are able to mobilize the resources needed to enroll at a university in the US, for the vast majority of participants these resources consisted entirely of student loans they received in India. Additionally, most had applied solely to public institutions, where tuition fees were far less than at American private universities. Therefore, many of the students who arrived at Riverside from abroad, specifically India and China, needed low-cost housing options that would prevent them from plunging further into debt. This is how many ended up at Williams Apartments, the most affordable option in the area.

At Williams, most of the Indian students lived in two-bedroom apartments, with two students to each room, and a shared living space. Set apart at a considerable distance from the rest of the campus, Williams Apartments had basic amenities but was not well maintained, and the shared bedrooms were quite small. When the topic of Williams came up with a couple of the Visa and Immigration staff members, they would shake their heads. One staff member asked me, "You've seen Williams Apartments, right? It's nasty; I wouldn't want to live there" (Fieldnotes, March 20, 2012). Although some of the graduate students would sometimes complain about or laugh off the conditions of the complex, including the confined space and lack of privacy, some expressed the comfort they took in being able to live among other Indian students. This concentrated population made it easier to collectively handle cooking, grocery shopping, and holding Indian social and cultural gatherings. Furthermore, several students indicated that living with and among other Indian students at Williams Apartments helped create a buffer from the relative isolation of the campus.

Yet, as much as these students expressed comfort in their informal social networks, some students described feelings of segregation. A fundamental aspect of what they hoped would be part of their experience studying in the US was to have exposure to and build relationships with Americans, which they lacked because of the overwhelming enrollments of Indian and Chinese students in their fields and the economic constraints on their housing choices. Residency in Williams Apartments especially exacerbated this social distance they felt from Americans, a sentiment that was expressed by Karthik, a second-year engineering graduate student.

It was a late evening, and a few of the male students and I were sitting and talking in one of their rooms at Williams Apartments (Fieldnotes, March 5, 2012). The room had just enough space for two twin-size beds, which were placed a couple of feet from each other against the walls, and two student desks angled toward the back. The white walls were bare except for a single calendar placed over Jason's bed in defiance of management rules forbidding wall hangings. While we were sitting on the beds and talking, Karthik, a tall, dark-complexioned twenty-three-year-old student from Calcutta, came in to visit. Karthik often alternated between telling exaggerated and entertaining stories about his romantic pursuits and expressing his frustration with life in the US. That evening, he told me about how he was offered a decent job when he graduated from his undergraduate studies in India but that he had decided to turn it down because he wanted to see the US. "I wanted to experience American culture," Karthik shared with me, and after hesitating for a moment, continued:

> But it has been disappointing. . . . Because I stay at Williams. There's nothing to like about Williams. Here, it's just Chinese and Indians who stay here. I know a few of the Americans who stay here, I talk to them. They only stay because they can't afford it. If they could, they would stay somewhere else. But you know, they don't want to be around Asians. (Fieldnotes, March 5, 2012)

He then broke down for me which other apartment buildings he would have chosen if he had the resources. All of them housed Americans. When I asked him why he does not move to those buildings, he asked:

Karthik: Will you pay for it? Those apartments are too expensive, I can't afford them. I mean, I already pay $400 for this place; that should be enough.

Manu: Yeah, you should be able to get the "American" experience for the $400 you already pay. (Fieldnotes, March 5, 2012)

We all laughed at what Karthik was suggesting, and what Manu made explicit in his joke. Karthik found that his financial restrictions prevented him from engaging in an essential aspect of the "American experience," that is, to meet and build close social relationships with Americans.

On several occasions, Karthik expressed this wish, saying it was a crucial part of how he imagined life would be for him as a young student in the US. Grewal (2005) has argued that the imperial position of the US, and its neoliberal promises, make "Americanness" a significant global discourse in which many desire to invest, shaping the subjectivities of those outside American borders as well. Many of the students I met attached particular hopes to migrating to the US for higher education. For these students, "America" was an "experience" they only saw and heard of through film, media, and their networks of friends and relatives that visited or moved previously. These experiences produced a distinct aspiration for the American lifestyle. In addition to the opportunity to acquire degrees that would provide them with the cultural capital necessary to attain their career aspirations, for these young people, moving to the US held the promise of engaging with American life by socializing and building relationships with "real" Americans, a term I heard students use at times. In our discussion that evening, Karthik provided a glimpse of what "real" Americans meant for him when he switched from emphasizing his desire to know only Americans to know either Americans or Europeans. When I questioned him on this switch, asking him why he was including Europeans since it was "American" relationships he had so far been expressing a desire to have, Karthik responded, "Yeah, you know, whites. Chinese and Indians are basically the same culture, people who aren't Asian, you know what I mean?" (Fieldnotes, March 5, 2012).

Karthik's switch and explanation demonstrate a conflation of Americanness and whiteness, one that is reinforced and celebrated in American popular culture and has traveled to other locations through transnational channels. By attending a university in the US, Karthik expected to be engaged with white American social and cultural life, and thus be near this Americanness/whiteness; he was disappointed to learn, however, that he was socially distanced from it because his financial means kept him even from accessing the physical spaces where it is found.

Karthik's comments indicate how housing at Riverside informs F-1 Indian students' sense of belonging, as well as not belonging, through racialized and classed terms. While the university does not explicitly segregate students, the financial burden of tuition in combination with an emphasis on compliance rather than integration has limited the (actual) places students are able to inhabit. Although living with and among other Indian students served as a source of comfort and familiarity for many of the students I met, the undesirable conditions of Williams Apartments and its isolation from the rest of the campus produced a virtual ghettoization of Asian overseas students who could only afford this housing option. While raising enrollments of overseas students serves Riverside's interests, it is noteworthy that Indian F-1 students' sense of community—once they arrive—is being shaped by "othering," place-taking practices at the university, such as those emerging from its housing dynamics.

Experiences with Part-Time Work

Students' relationship with work also played an integral role in how they made sense of their everyday lives at Riverside. As students and their families went into debt for their education, participants felt tremendous pressure to find work and remain in the US after completing their degrees because it would be much more difficult to repay their loans if they returned home. While studying, these young people held part-time jobs in addition to their coursework to supplement their living expenses and, whenever possible, to save some money. Many students worked in more than one place, often taking up jobs at various vendors in Riverside's food courts, where they received minimum wage, or doing clerical work in the university's administrative offices.

Students regularly discussed their jobs with each other, sharing their experiences with different places of employment on campus, warning each other of different employers, and joking about their strained financial situations. Working is restricted for students on F-1 visas; they are only allowed to hold on-campus jobs, and are limited to twenty hours a week of paid work. If university personnel learn that a student has violated these restrictions, the student can be reported to the social security office and can lose legal immigration status. The students would sometimes make decisions about whether violating the work restrictions was worth the risk based on their own financial circumstances and the advice of other students. For instance, one afternoon, an engineering student from Tamil Nadu, Ani, and I had just climbed off the shuttle in front of Williams Apartments, along with many of the other Indian and Chinese students returning home from their classes and work, when Vivek, another Indian student in Ani's department, walked toward us. Vivek told him that he was looking for part-time work and was considering working at "Orchid," the campus's Asian fusion restaurant, which hired many Indian students. When he said he heard from his friend that Orchid would allow him to work more than twenty hours, Ani cautioned him about the owner:

> Yeah, they do . . . but I had a couple of friends who work there. They told me he cheated them. You see, what he'll do is he'll let you work over the twenty hours by paying you the extra hours in cash. But my friends said that after they worked, when it came time to pay them, he would pay less for those extra hours than what he owed. . . . Yeah, it's happened a few times. (Fieldnotes, September 19, 2011)

When I asked Ani what his friends did about this situation, he told me that they left their jobs there but never asked the owner about the underpayment. Orchid's willingness to pay under the table allowed students to maneuver around the twenty-hour restriction because those extra hours would not be documented. Yet, when a boss would decide not to pay what he promised, students like Ani's friends realized that their visa status left them little or no recourse; the restrictions placed on F-1 students positioned them to be vulnerable to exploitation in their jobs. On another occasion, two engineering students and employees of Orchid, Avni and Padma, noted that the owner would sometimes not pay the full amount owed them even when they did not work more than twenty hours (Fieldnotes, March 3, 2012). Although they expressed some frustration at this injustice, they quickly added that the owner, an Indian man himself, gave many of the Indian students' work, which allowed them to receive their social security numbers, something most F-1 students tried to secure as soon as possible to make navigating the various official aspects of residence in the US a little easier.[4] Therefore, while they were at times cheated in payment for their labor, they perceived that their employment and shared ethnic identity helped them secure the work and vital legal documentation that make life in the US more tenable.

Nikhil, an engineering student from Punjab, had struggled with his academic work in India. After finishing his bachelor's degree in engineering, he was not able to secure employment or acceptance into any Indian graduate programs. When Riverside accepted him, it was the opportunity he needed. Because Nikhil came from a more privileged background, his family had the resources to support him and, unlike his peers, he could attend Riverside without incurring student debt. However, he claimed he felt a sense of being a burden on his father, a sentiment shared by many of the young students. Having to go overseas to the US to pursue his educational goals, Nikhil referred to himself as his parents' "most expensive kid," and with a younger sister that they still had to support, he wished to alleviate the financial strain on his family as much as he could (Interview, October 24, 2011). In addition to full-time enrollment in coursework, Nikhil worked three jobs to help pay for his tuition and living expenses, save some money, and obtain some financial autonomy. For these reasons, being employed was important enough to him that he risked working more than twenty hours, as well as taking jobs off-campus, violating the terms of his visa.

Nikhil told me that he was working really hard in his graduate program and that his advisor promised to let him join the PhD program after the following semester. He was not certain of his prospects back in India and whether he would want to return home after the PhD program, but he knew that, for now, he had to work hard. As he explained:

> It's like how I do here . . . determines my value there. . . . I've done alright, even though I didn't do well back in India—here I am about to start a PhD program next year. I don't want to mess that up now. . . . I'm working really hard for my advisor now. (Interview, October 24, 2011)

For Nikhil, the lack of higher education options at home meant that studying overseas was necessary for him to secure an advanced degree, which, if received from an American university, would provide him with valuable cultural capital abroad. Because he was enrolled in the materials science branch, which had become notorious among overseas students at the university as the department where F-1 graduates could not secure work after graduation, his advisor's offer of paid work in her lab, and her promise to enroll him in the PhD program, provided Nikhil with some security in an otherwise precarious professional trajectory. Consequently, Nikhil was cautious when confronted with his advisor's delays in compensating him for his work, something that was a recurring issue:

> She hasn't paid me yet . . . I mean, I've asked her about it a couple of times, you know, just to remind her that I still hadn't gotten paid. But you know you have to be careful about what you say—I don't want to . . . you know, make her upset or anything. That'll mess things up. But yeah . . . if she doesn't pay me, I probably wouldn't be working as hard as I have been in the lab. . . . So . . . yeah but she told me that the check is on the way, so it's okay now. (Interview, October 24, 2011)

In another interview, Nikhil expressed confusion when discussing why his advisor would cause delays in paying him, and revealed the unevenness of their financial situations:

> I wasn't expecting that [delay in payment] because I'd been working well, everything went well. And I told her that I have health insurance for RU and if she delays it I have a gap then the health insurance goes away so, then she said okay. . . . I know how much money she has . . . she can afford it. . . . She does have a reputation . . . to minimize the payment. You know how much I earn in one week? I would say $200, $250 in one week. $250? Why would you want to save $250 if you have like $200,000 in your bank? $250 is nothing. . . . It's important to me, but it's not to her. (Interview, March, 1, 2012)

Financial constraints, visa restrictions, and anxieties over career prospects make Indian F-1 students vulnerable to various forms of exploitation, including being underpaid for the hours they work, which is what happened with students working at Orchid, or regularly receiving delayed payments, as was the case with Nikhil. Students like Nikhil, Avni, and Padma recognized the issues that arose for them at their jobs but made sense of their part-time work experiences in the context of the tangle of federal immigration policies designed to police noncitizens which directly affected their educational experiences.

Ani noted to me that he believed Americans perceived Indians predominantly as "poor cheap labor," a common racialized and classed image of Global South populations (Online chat, March 11, 2012). When I asked him why he believed this to be true, he replied, "From the movies, sitcoms, from Mildred's attitude" (Online chat, March 11, 2012; Mildred was one of the advisors at the Visa and Immigration office, where Ani worked). However, Ani also felt that in addition to his financial needs, his part-time work experiences were his only opportunity to engage with Americans and participate in the university community. For him, part-time work provided a sense of belonging to an American university, even if it may have perpetuated certain stereotypes of migrants from the Global South.

Priyanka, a student in the Mathematics Department, echoed Ani's sentiment about work and meeting Americans in one of our many online "chats" in which we discussed the challenges of being on an F-1 visa. Both Ani and Priyanka had questioned the twenty-hour work restriction associated with their F-1 status, as more hours would have helped them with their living expenses and cut down on how much of their student loans they used. Priyanka shared with me an incident in which she accidentally exceeded this limit by two hours and was chided for it by her manager. The manager warned her that it was her responsibility not to violate the restrictions on her visa, and that if the Department of Homeland Security questioned management, they would not lie for her. Priyanka could not understand why her need and willingness to work would be a matter of homeland security. As for Ani, working was not only a means for her to support herself, but it was also a valuable social activity that allowed her to have social exchanges and build relationships with "real Americans" (Online chat, March 11, 2012), an experience from which they were mostly excluded because of their housing and departmental situations. Whether it was through clerical work in the various offices of the university or food service on campus, it was by providing labor that these students felt they were included in the university community and the "America" they had come to experience.

CONCLUSION

I have explored how the current neoliberal drive in the US to internationalize higher education, which involves implementing various market-driven policies such as raising enrollments of overseas students, interacts with federal immigration policy to shape the day-to-day realities of a public university's relationship with its F-1 Indian student population, a growing presence on its campus. The concurrent marketization of higher education and more stringent national security measures are creating a more bureaucratized direction for the Visa and Immigration Office at Riverside University, pushing the center to retreat from the other types of social and cultural services that were an essential part of its work in the past. These types of services could play a valuable role in establishing ties between overseas students and the university, providing them with a sense of community that involved them with the social and cultural life of the institution in more enriching ways. Instead, students are left socially isolated and economically insecure, and, as a result, are made unwelcome in the university context. The space once created by an office dedicated to counseling and advising is rapidly narrowing through the activities (or lack thereof) of an office dedicated to security and policing.

As the purpose of the office changes, overseas Indian students' experiences with housing and part-time work reveal how they made sense of the social, economic, and legal circumstances attached to their presence as F-1 students from India. Rather than homogenously framing overseas middle-class Indian students as transnational elites, these experiences demonstrate that students' legal status, class backgrounds, and cultural differences position them in particular raced and classed ways at the university, and inform their ideas and practices of community and belonging as transnational students in the US.

University administrators and policymakers seek to benefit from higher enrollments of overseas Indian students, including profiting financially from their tuition fees and living expenses, raising enrollments in departments which face a stark absence of domestic students, and addressing national demands for diversifying their campuses. However, the perspectives of the students and staff I present here point to the importance of paying attention to how Indian F-1 students are included in and excluded from university life in the US once they are here. Doing so could encourage university policymakers to understand the everyday implications of their commitments to the internationalization agenda, and to critically examine their priorities in a globalized era.

Like the other work in this section, this chapter highlights how intersecting policies and practices create unwelcoming environments for students, dehumanizing them, segregating them, and treating them as security issues. The neoliberal agenda adds another dimension to this: treating students as revenue sources even when their class backgrounds make them financially insecure. While this chapter has demonstrated that students find ways to make sense of this reality, it also demonstrates the ways in which students and university allies refuse to accept it. By critiquing the purpose of the international office, segregated housing choices, and exploitative employment, and successfully skirting the restrictions imposed by work limitations both in terms of hours (in the case of students) and purpose (in terms of personnel at the international office), Indian students and their allies remake their educational spaces and, by extension, the policies that govern them.

NOTES

1. The New York City metropolitan area ranks as the leading city destination for foreign students in the US.
2. There are some variations to how the South Asian region is categorized, although the core countries include India, Pakistan, Bangladesh, Sri Lanka, Nepal, and Bhutan. In this paper, I focus solely on students from India.
3. By 2003, all universities hosting foreign students were required by the federal government to adopt the SEVIS protocol.
4. F-1 students must be offered a paying job in order to receive a social security number, but many places of work on campus would not hire F-1 students if they did not already have one.

REFERENCES

Ablett, Jonathan, Aadarsh Baijal, Eric Beinhocker, Anupam Bose, Diana Farrell, Ulrich Gersch, Ezra Greenberg, Shishir Gupta, Sumit Gupta. 2007. "The 'Bird of Gold': The Rise of India's Consumer Market (A Report from McKinsey Global Institute)." Accessed March 15, 2012 http://www.mckinsey.com/Insights/MGI/Research/Asia/The_bird_of_gold.
Ahmad, Aijaz. 2003. "Contextualizing Conflict: The US 'War on Terrorism.'" In *War and the Media: Reporting Conflict 24/7*, edited by Daya K. Thussu and Des Freedman, 15–27. London: Sage Publications Ltd.
Altbach, Philip G. 2004. "Higher Education Crosses Borders." *Change* 36 (March–April): 18–25.
Altbach, Philip G., and Jane Knight. 2006. "The Internationalization of Higher Education: Motivations and Realities." *The NEA 2006 Almanac of Higher Education*, 27–36. Washington, DC: National Education Association.
Ayers, David F. 2005. "Neoliberal Ideology in Community College Mission Statements: A Critical Discourse Analysis." *The Review of Higher Education* 28 (4): 527–549.
Beck, Ulrich. 2007. *World at Risk*. Cambridge, UK: Polity Press.
Brooks, Rachel, and Johanna Waters. 2011. *Student Mobilities, Migration, and the Internationalization of Higher Education*. Hampshire, UK: Palgrave MacMillan.
Clotfelter, Charles T., ed. 2010. *American Universities in a Global Market*. Chicago: University of Chicago Press.
De Wit, Hans. 2002. *Internationalization of Higher Education in the United States of America and Europe: A Historical, Comparative, and Conceptual Analysis*. Westport, CT: Greenwood Press.
Fernandes, Leela. 2006. *India's New Middle Class: Democratic Politics in an Era of Economic Reform*. Minneapolis: University of Minnesota Press.
Friedman, Thomas L. 2005. *The World Is Flat: A Brief History of the Twenty-First Century*. New York: Farrar, Straus and Giroux.
Giroux, Henry A., and Susan S. Giroux. 2004. *Take Back Higher Education: Race, Youth, and the Crisis of Democracy in the Post-Civil Rights Era*. New York: Palgrave Macmillan.
Grewal, Inderpal. 2005. *Transnational America: Feminisms, Diasporas, Neoliberalisms*. Durham, NC: Duke University Press.
Harvey, David. 2003. *The New Imperialism*. New York: Oxford University Press.
———. 2005. *A Brief History of Neoliberalism*. New York: Oxford University Press.
Institute of International Education (IIE). n.d. "Global Destinations for International Students at the Post-secondary (Tertiary) Level, 2001 and 2009 [graphic illustration pie charts of global market share of international students]." Accessed October 14, 2010. http://www.atlas.iienetwork.org/?p=48022.
———. n.d. "Project Atlas India: Atlas of Student Mobility [graphic illustration table of India's students overseas, 2009]." Accessed October 14, 2010. http://www.iie.org/en/Services/Project-Atlas/India/Indias-Students-Overseas.
———. 2010. "Open Doors." Accessed October 2, 2011. http://www.iie.org/en/Research-and-Publications/Open-Doors.
Johnson, Victor. 2003. "The Perils of Homeland Security." *Chronicle of Higher Education*, April 11.
Maira, Sunaina M. 2009. *Missing: Youth, Citizenship, and Empire after 9/11*. Durham, NC: Duke University Press.
NAFSA: Association of International Educators. 2006. "Restoring U.S. Competitiveness for International Students and Scholars." Accessed October 17, 2010. http://www.nafsa.org/resourcelibrary/default.aspx?id=9169.

144 *Susan Thomas*

Ong, Aihwa. 2006. *Neoliberalism as Exception: Mutations in Citizenship and Sovereignty.* Durham, NC: Duke University Press.
Organisation for Economic Co-operation and Development (OECD). 2010. "Education at a Glance [data file]." Accessed October 2, 2011. http://www.oecd.org/document/52/0,3746,en_2649_39263238_45897844_1_1_1_1,00.html.
Panagariya, Arvind. 2008. *India: The Emerging Giant.* New York: Oxford University Press.
Sidhu, Ravinder K. 2006. *Universities and Globalization: To Market to Market.* Mahwah, NJ: Laurence Erlbaum Associates Ltd.
Slaughter, Sheila, and Gary Rhoades. 2004. *Academic Capitalism and the New Economy: Markets, State, and Higher Education.* Baltimore: Johns Hopkins University Press.
US Department of Commerce. 2012. "Education Team Newsletter." Accessed March 15, 2012. http://export.gov/industry/education/eg_main_025977.asp.
Zakaria, Fareed. 2004. "Rejecting the Next Bill Gates." *The Washington Post,* November 23. Accessed October 20, 2010. http://www.washingtonpost.com/ac2/wp-dyn/A6008-2004Nov22?language=printer.

9 Misalignment of Teacher Outcomes and Student Goals

Transnational Migrants in an Adult ESL Program

Ronald Fuentes

In the US, community-based English as a second language (CESL) adult education programs have traditionally been aimed at assimilating immigrants into US society. CESL policies and practices are often rooted in a paradigm that assumes immigrants arrive in their new homes with the objectives of permanent settlement, severance with their home country, and assimilation of host country norms and values. Yet, increasingly, immigrants lead transnational lives, operating between two or more countries, retaining close links with their home country while becoming new members of another, and creating complex interrelated communities in multiple spaces (Basch, Glick Schiller, and Szanton Blanc 1994; Glick Schiller, Basch, and Blanc-Szanton 1992). Transnational migrants participate in and move among multiple sites through daily telephone and e-mail exchanges with family members and friends, contact with media sources, and interactions with home country nationals who frequently travel back and forth between such sites. The activities and social processes through which transnational migrants maintain links to their countries of origin impact the design of educational programs for adult English language learners (ELLs), such as open enrollment for transient and/or shifting populations, globally responsive curricula linked to geography and world cultures, and program design and aims.

This chapter focuses on how ELLs' transnational lives impact their English language education. Specifically, it examines three adult transnational students' experiences and perceptions of English as a second language (ESL) classes in an adult CESL program in the rural southeastern US. It also examines how initial migration goals, transnational ties, ambiguity of settlement, and concerns about the future condition students' views of language learning and contribute to a sense of displacement between home and host culture. I demonstrate that permanent settlement–oriented classroom practices aimed at integrating ELLs into American life clash with students' needs. Participants in this study expressed an interest in learning language that would enable them to successfully live in the US in their current sojourn while maintaining transnational ties; in contrast, the CESL program assumed that learners' goals centered on assimilation and permanent resettlement.

TRANSNATIONALISM AND EDUCATION

Globalization, a highly debated term, refers to "those processes, operating on a global scale, which cut across national boundaries, integrating and connecting communities and organizations in new space-time combinations, making the world in reality and in experience more interconnected" (Hall 1992, 299). Under the umbrella of globalization, the world is characterized by objects in motion, including people, technology, capital, images, and ideologies that traverse cultural, temporal, and spatial boundaries (Appadurai 1996). Globalization is also marked by the role of imagination in social life because it allows individuals to imagine themselves interacting and engaging in transnational processes that are no longer limited to a specific national territory but rather span national boundaries (Appadurai 2001). In these terms, individuals can continually (re)position and (re)define themselves in a mobile, fluid, and porous world. Globalization is rapidly reshaping and intensifying the interconnections and relations among nations, cultures, and economies. As the global movements of people, information, and capital become more pervasive and the access and use of communication technology continues to expand, migrants increasingly engage in transnational activities that link and widen their social, political, cultural, and educational networks across multiple nations.

Research on transnationalism has emphasized the political, economic, social, familial, and emotional connections and experiences of individuals whose movements, ties, and relationships span multiple countries (Aranda 2006; Burholt 2004; Guarnizo, Portes, and Haller 2003; Sánchez 2008). Scholars have examined migrant family members' construction and negotiation of identity and sense of belonging (Levitt 2001; Song 2010). Bartley and Spoonley (2008), for instance, found that young East Asian migrants' sense of displacement between home and host culture, adjustment experiences, and persistent social barriers resulted in a sense of "in-betweenness" (68). Pita and Utakis (2002) examined the transnational character of the Dominican community in New York City, and demonstrated that notions of immigration based on assimilation and permanent settlement provide an inadequate framework for analyzing the complexity of this fluid community. These studies reveal that narrow notions of permanent settlement and assimilation are inadequate means of describing the realities of transnational families who actively maintain multistranded relationships to both their host country and their country of origin.

Globalization and its resultant interconnectedness of trade and population movements also impacts schooling. Within the context of education, studies have tended to assume that students adopt one-way migration and permanent settlement (Menard-Warwick 2007; Peirce 1995) neglecting their fluid, mobile, and uprooted character (Burns and Roberts 2010; De Costa 2010). Transnational migrants do not necessarily establish rooted and fixed attachments to the culture, language, and belief systems of the host country. Their lives are situated in a constant flux of (dis)locations and (re)settlements in and between two or multiple spaces, a reality that the mainstream educational system neither recognizes nor (in some cases) values. For example, Rodríguez (2009) found that language learning plays a pivotal role in the transnational experiences of adolescents as they negotiate their subject positions in various Dominican and US schools. Fluency in Spanish and English was viewed as an asset in Dominican schools whereas only English was seen as an asset in US schools. Rodriguez's (2009) and Sánchez's (2007) studies on students with ties to the Dominican Republic and the US, and on transnational migrant youth shuttling between Mexico and California, provide evidence that schools have tended to ignore students' transnational lives.

Although scholars have examined migrant youth and education (Hamman, Zúñiga, and Sánchez García 2010; Martínez 2009), little research has focused on transnational adult migrants in ESL education programs. While several studies of adult ESL education document ELLs' needs, experiences, and educational trajectories, they do so using an assimilationist and permanent settlement lens (Cooke 2006; Menard-Warwick 2005; Warriner 2007). Furthermore, few studies are specific to transnational ELLs and to adult language education. The present study examines adult transnational students' experiences and perceptions of ESL education in a CESL program, and how their transnational character impacts their views of language learning.

THEORETICAL FRAMEWORK

Scholarship has increasingly adopted a transnational lens to examine migrants' settlement links, relations, and exchanges across national boundaries (Faist 2000; Kivisto 2001; Nieswand 2011). Scholars conceive transnationalism and transnational migration in multiple ways. Glick Schiller and Fouron (1999) define transnational migration as "a pattern of migration in which persons, although they move across international borders, settle, and establish relations in a new state, maintain ongoing social connections with the polity from which they originated" (344). Mahler (1998) discusses the different macrolevel and microlevel processes and activities involved in transnationalism "from above" and "from below." Drawing on previous scholarship, I define transnationalism as an ongoing relational system rooted in individuals' simultaneity of dispersed and interconnected social, ideological, religious, familial, economic, educational, and cultural relations and attachments that cross the physical and spatial boundaries of nation-states and shape individuals' visions of their present and future lives. With its myriad of interlocking connections and displacements, transnationalism necessitates an analysis that goes beyond perspectives embedded in the present-day rootedness of activities and relations within nation-state borders. Conceptualizing migrants within a transnational framework allows for a broader and more nuanced understanding of migrants' cross-border links and experiences. Migration cannot be analyzed solely in terms of unidirectional flows or the severance of links with country of origin; rather, it needs to encompass the complexity of migrants' willingness, desire, and ability to participate simultaneously in multiple cultures and spaces. A transnational lens can capture the complexity of migrants' cross-border lives and the ways they are intertwined in the processes of globalization.

This study adopts Ong's (1999) concept of *flexible citizenship*, which "refers to the cultural logics of capitalist accumulation, travel, and displacement that induce subjects to respond fluidly and opportunistically to changing political economic conditions" (6). While Ong uses it to describe the repositioning strategies that mobile managers, technocrats, and professionals use to acquire influence, financial gains, and social prestige, it is also possible for nonprofessional migrants to become flexible citizens. Transnational migrants can adopt a flexible citizenship stance not only to acquire capital but also to strategically navigate the multiple spaces of two or more countries and cultures. Whereas Ong situates flexible citizenship within Bourdieu's (1986) notion of symbolic capital (prestige, reputation, honor), arguing that it is principally economic capital (assets) that is converted into other forms of capital such as cultural capital (knowledge, skills, qualifications) and social capital (social networks and connections), I adopt the view that individuals can acquire and convert one form of capital for another. For instance, individuals may seek to acquire social capital in the form of a network of affiliations and influences rather than economic capital to obtain social promotion or other forms of capital. The notion of flexible citizenship and capital can provide valuable insights into the contestations between what capital adult ESL providers envision delivering and what capital adult ELLs find valuable. Like the other authors in this section, I critically analyze how program policies restrict spaces available for immigrants to adopt and explore multiple identities. Additionally, I document how immigrants maintain transnational lives despite the constraints imposed by policies blind to the realities of flexible citizenship.

METHODOLOGY

This study focuses on three transnational women, Angela, Somya, and Jenny, who are enrolled in a CESL program within an ESL program at a major public university in the rural southeastern US. They attended a free intermediate-level noncredit class two nights a week for ninety minutes every semester. Classes were comprised mostly of Latino students; however, they also included students from Sri Lanka, India, Ukraine, and Indonesia. The participants, who are part of a larger project examining transnational adults' lives both in and out of a university-sponsored ESL program, had been attending the intermediate-level class for one year. Angela, Somya, and Jenny were selected because of their unique and varied ethnic, socioeconomic, educational, migrant, and linguistic background. Additionally, more than the other participants, Angela, Somya, and Jenny provided, through their interviews, an extensive description of their transnational lives and how those lives impacted and shaped their views of and reasons for taking ESL classes.

I collected data over the course of an academic year starting in the fall of 2010. I interviewed ELL students and instructors, collected journal logs, conducted classroom observations and informal conversations, and read syllabi and classroom materials analyses. I triangulated interview transcripts, observation fieldnotes, and researcher journals. The recruitment procedure consisted of a brief survey, in Spanish and English, which I administered to approximately sixty students in the CESL program. Based on the information obtained from the survey, I recruited and interviewed ten student participants. I adopted the method of maximum variation sampling (Patton 2002) for participant selection, which details the unique characteristics of each participant while simultaneously identifying similar themes and patterns across participants. This approach allowed me to maximize the range and variety of perspectives. I also produced reflective journal entries throughout the data collection as well as the transcription process, subsequently adopting the stance that situates analysis as "a cyclical process and a reflexive activity" (Coffey and Atkinson 1996, 10).

The selection and recruitment of participants was based on the rapport I had developed with particular students as well as their background, including first language, ethnicity, gender, length of US residence, and educational level. My own transnational experiences allowed me to establish strong relationships with students in the CESL program. As a transnational migrant, I grew up in a Spanish/Catalan-speaking household that shuttled between Spain and Canada. My migration became an experience I commonly used to identify and interact with the students.

Furthermore, during the year prior to undertaking this study, I was assistant director of the university's ESL program and was responsible for the direction of the CESL classes. My principal CESL responsibilities included the recruitment of students and scheduling of classes. During my tenure, I developed trusting relationships with students, particularly Latinos. Because the majority of students in the CESL program were Latinos, my Spanish language skills and heritage were key factors in forging such close relationships. At the time of the study, budget cuts led to several program changes. Instructors were replaced with volunteer teachers, and general oversight of the program was mostly transferred to volunteer staff. Attracting uncompensated and qualified personnel became difficult. Although departmental restructuring led to the elimination of the assistant director of ESL position, I stayed on as the main administrator of the CESL program. My close relationship and ties to the local Latino community and CESL students was an important source of student recruitment and contributed to the CESL program's existence and continuity. In addition, I was interested in better understanding adult ELLs' transnational experiences and English language needs. For these reasons and for fear that the program would be eliminated, I decided to continue investing in the program and carrying out many of my previous responsibilities as it transitioned to a volunteer-based operation.

In situating my researcher positioning, I employ Sarangi and Candlin's (2003) categories of *researcher as outsider/insider* and *researcher as befriender*. I was involved in the participants' transnational lives beyond the CESL program, and through this involvement I embodied both of these categories. An insider can provide additional insights that are inaccessible to the outside researcher (Sarangi and Candlin 2003). As a transnational migrant I was able to claim insider status. My migration background was a common thread that allowed me to relate to both Spanish-speaking and non–Spanish speaking ELLs. A befriender can act as a friend, creating supportive opportunities and encounters that allow individuals to discuss their views openly and reflectively. I also adopted the role of researcher as befriender, creating rapport due to my continued involvement in the CESL program and in students' lives. I ate at their homes, attended ethnic community festivals, informed them about US customs and culture, and acted as a Spanish-English interpreter and translator.

I conceptualize interviews as a specific type of interaction (Cicourel 1964) where knowledge and meaning are socially co-constructed by the interviewer and the interviewee (Briggs 1986; Holstein and Gubrium 1995; Mishler 1986). As specific forms of interaction, interviews can shape the form and content of what is stated by speakers. In this type of interaction, interviewer and respondents construct themselves as certain types of people in relation to the interview and its topic, creating concomitant identities (Rapley 2001). In these terms, I recognize that my CESL involvement and status as both a native English/Spanish speaker and transnational migrant may have influenced students' perceptions of the CESL program. Certainly, my positionality could also have affected the way students responded to me because it gave them an outlet, in the form of an interested audience, for talking about their transnational lives. Without such a position and status I might not have been able to forge close relationships or access students' experiences and perceptions.

TRANSNATIONALISM AND LANGUAGE LEARNING

In this section, I present three transnational students' experience of and perceptions about language learning in a CESL program through excerpts from interviews and observations.

Angela

Angela is a forty-eight-year-old Sri Lankan housewife. She is Sinhalese, the largest ethnic group in Sri Lanka, and she describes her socioeconomic status as moderately high. Since 1986, Angela has lived in Canada, the US, and Sri Lanka intermittently. In 2008, she and her husband migrated to the southeastern US from Sri Lanka with their three children because her husband had accepted a position as a researcher at a public university and because Angela believed the US offered better educational opportunities for her children. Angela and her husband do not intend to settle in the US permanently. "When our kids finish their education, we'd like to go back to Sri Lanka," she stated. Angela and her husband plan to return to Sri Lanka once her children accrue cultural capital in the form of university credentials.

Angela interacts primarily with her husband and children and a few Sri Lankan friends. The Internet allows Angela to speak daily to Sri Lankan family members and friends and watch Sri Lankan television programs, thereby keeping her abreast of home country events. When asked why she spent so much time on the Internet, Angela responded:

> We listen Sri Lankan music. If not we are going to miss our music, also, everything. . . . We don't like to miss our movies. If we are in Sri Lanka we always watch same movies, tele-drama. If we watch those things here, we feel still we are in Sri Lanka. (Interview, September 21, 2010)

For Angela, the Internet is an important way of maintaining home country routines and transnational social networks.

Angela observes various Sri Lankan holidays such as Independence Day or New Year's Day. She said that celebrating these holidays is very important to her because it is a means of reasserting Sri Lankan culture and identity:

RF: Is it important for you to celebrate these [Sri Lankan holidays] here?
Angela: Yeah, we don't like to forget the special events and things.
RF: Why is it important for you to celebrate these events?
Angela: Because we are Sri Lankan. We have to keep our ceremonies and all those things.

(Interview, March 31, 2011)

These celebrations anchor Angela's life in two cultural spaces: the US and Sri Lanka. Angela said that, in addition to her connection to Sri Lanka, she has a strong attachment to the US. "I feel this is my country," she asserted. However, she does not consider herself to be American because she does not reside in the country "permanently." Her temporary status in the US and the eventuality of returning to Sri Lanka influences how she chooses to simultaneously acquire and maintain each culture. "If we are [in] America, we have to live like American. We go back to Sri Lanka, we must be a Sri Lankan. We have to keep Sri Lankan [culture]," she declared. Exercising flexible citizenship allows Angela to live in American and Sri Lankan spaces. To do so, it is important that she preserve Sri Lankan culture, both for herself and her family. Angela reminds her children to maintain their home country traditions as well as their language. "We tell them don't forget Sinhala. It is our mother tongue," she stated. Maintaining home country culture and language would facilitate home country reintegration.

Angela attends the CESL program because she wants to "communicate [with] other citizens." Angela's prior exposure to English in Sri Lanka and throughout her travels contributes to her perception that English is the global lingua franca. "English is important for international communication," she stated. "We can live around the world, like international people," she affirmed. Angela has a clear sense of her English language needs. "I need to learn grammar . . . grammar need for everything. When we speak, we need grammar. If we know very good grammar, we can easily speak or write anything," she declared. Angela connects her interest in grammar explicitly to her desire to return to Sri Lanka:

RF: You are only interested in grammar? Why?
Angela: This time I am stay here temporarily.
RF: So you only want grammar?
Angela: If he knows grammar, we can manage everything.

(Interview, March 31, 2011)

Because Angela has no intention of permanent settlement, she perceives that she needs specific English instruction that targets and parallels both her settlement status and her needs. It can be argued that her English language needs and migration goals are linked to her privileged position, granting her greater flexibility that might not be afforded to other migrants in determining US settlement status. However, less privileged individuals may have language learning and migration goals similar to those of more privileged individuals. Although socioeconomic status is important, transnational living can also affect language learning engagement.

Angela's instructor was unaware of her transnational character and impermanent status, and that it reflected her desire to gain different forms of capital to be used in Sri Lanka. The instructor stated, "They [students] are all permanent residents." She stated that students "need more content-based methods . . . to be able to apply this language . . . to real-life situations." Her lessons revolved primarily around topics or subject matter aimed at tasks related to permanent US settlement, such as seeking employment. However, Angela is not seeking employment, nor does she believe she needs to attain English to do so. Another reason for Angela's CESL attendance is that she needs to help her children and future grandchildren with English. "Someday we have to teach our children, grandchildren. If they ask something . . . maybe if we don't know, we have to suffer," she said.

Angela is aware of the status and importance that the English language holds worldwide. In Sri Lanka and throughout her travels, she has been exposed to English. Yet, instructors tend to view Angela and her classmates as having had little English language exposure. "Most of them were not taught English at all, hadn't been taught before they started taking this community class," her instructor stated. This assumption is inaccurate because Angela, Somya, and Jenny had already received English language instruction prior to their CESL enrollment. Additionally, globalization processes and communication advances have made exposure to or instruction in English a common feature of transnational migrants, as in the case of Angela and her classmates.

Angela's aims for and views about language learning clash with her instructor's views and practices. While her instructor assumes that Angela intends to transition from a Sri Lankan to an American identity, in reality, Angela sees learning English as part of a strategic decision to maintain a multifaceted transnational identity. Furthermore, although Angela's instructor describes her intention to design lessons that are relevant to immigrants' lives, in reality, she has done just the opposite: because Angela's instructor is not aware of Angela's goals, the lessons are not appropriate or relevant. By adopting a narrow view of citizenship, Angela's instructor has failed to provide her with the curriculum she needs.

Somya

Somya is a twenty-nine-year-old Indian housewife whose first language is Telugu. She describes her socioeconomic status as middle class. Somya holds a degree in computer science from an English-medium Indian higher education institution. In December 2003, she migrated to the US with her husband because a US firm had contracted him as a computer software engineer. Since her migration to the US, Somya has made frequent trips to India. The principle reason for her migration was to gain cultural and social capital, which Somya perceives as being highly valued in India. Returning to India with the accrued capital will in turn lead to social, economic, and educational opportunities. Somya explained:

Most of the people come [to the US] for [work] experience. If you
go outside of India, they would prefer [you] has some knowledge
of there [US]. So [they] would prefer that person that goes out. . . .
Now, most of the people they are going back [to India] permanently.
They are offered good job over there . . . and especially for kids their
education and everything. They got good opportunities. (Interview,
September 17, 2010)

Somya's initial goal for migration was the accumulation of capital, not permanent settlement. "After five, six years, we'll go back to India. . . . That is
the plan," she explained. "We are not permanent. We do not belong here.
Someday, we have to go back," Somya stated.

Somya experiences anxiety because of her transnational life. "I miss my
parents. I want to go back . . . I just have to go back," she explained. Maintaining a relationship with India helps Somya alleviate her homesickness.
The observation and celebration of Hindu festivals such as Diwali and Holi
play a key role in Somya's transnational life in that they allow her to retain
cultural links with her home country. The Internet is also instrumental
in maintaining Somya's home country ties: it allows her to communicate
with family and friends and keep up-to-date with home country events.
"If Internet is not there, I got nervous," she stated. Somya's social relations
with Indian migrants, involvement in Indian cultural associations, celebration of Indian festivals, and use of information technology are ways of
maintaining concurrent lives across two nations.

Somya attends the CESL program because she wants to improve her
oral English communication skills. "I want to communicate with people,
[become] more fluent English. Main thing [is] grammar," she remarked.
Like Angela, Somya believes that focusing on English grammar will result
in improved English oral skills. Somya's English language learning goals
are to attain a proficiency level that will allow her to help her son with
schoolwork and maintain simple conversational exchanges. "Because my
son is here, and I have to go to school, and I'm talking to teachers. . . .
Sometimes I don't understand what they speak actually," she explained.
Somya is focused on her son's education when she thinks about learning
English. Improving her English will allow Somya not only to understand
her son's teachers but also to assist and further her son's education.

Another reason that Somya wants to focus on speaking is that it is a
valued skill in India. "One more thing is I want to see [is] speaking in
front people . . . spoken English type of thing. In India they prefer for
that," she remarked. Somya perceives that acquiring this form of cultural capital will result in higher social and economic status upon returning. Somya commented that the CESL classes were "not fully" meeting
her needs. For instance, she seemed uninterested during a lesson about
US geography. Additionally, like Angela, Somya did not find the lesson
on employment relevant. When asked if she had been interested in that

lesson, she responded, "No. Not really. Because I'm not sure that kind of [lesson]."

Like Angela's, Somya's English language education views do not align with instructors' views. The program coordinator emphasized, "The absolute necessity for them [students] to learn English to be able to live here [US] long term." An instructor described his role as follows:

> Giving them the basic language skills to succeed in the community so they can go out and find other friends whether they are Americans or from other nationalities as well. . . . Get [them] out of their ethnic groups that they often live in, just as Americans. (Interview, April 26, 2011)

Instructors' goals are in conflict with Somya's English language aims, which are intimately tied to her intention to return to her home country. Rather than seek the skills necessary for permanent settlement, she is seeking the language skills that will allow her to navigate life in the US and attain higher social and economic status in India.

Contrary to her needs, in Somya's CESL class, little time was spent on oral language skills. An instructor wrote, "I could have done more activities involving speaking. But even when I tried to give them some speaking task, they were not active. . . . What is the problem with my students that prevents them from speaking?" The instructor dedicated little class time to oral skills because students did not speak during oral activities. She rationalized that students did not speak because they did not know grammar or linguistics; in addition, the class schedule made it difficult to teach the grammar needed to participate orally in classroom activities. Rather than informing herself about student's English language knowledge or considering other reasons for the lack of participation during such activities, the instructor had simply decided to spend less time on oral skills.

Instructors' views, curricula, and teaching practices seem to position students as permanent and low-income migrants. A former instructor praised CESL as one of the few programs that welcomed low-income students. "When you're coming in as a lower-income, lower-paid individual, there's not that many people with open arms for you," he stated. Another instructor noted, "Many of them have come all this way along to sit at a desk for the first time." This prevalent view among CESL instructors is an inaccurate depiction of all CESL students. Instructors do not seem to have a precise sense of students' socioeconomic, educational, and transnational status. For instance, like Angela, Somya's English language needs and migration goals can be linked to her privileged socioeconomic status. Her position can afford her greater freedom than other migrants might have in assessing language learning needs and US settlement status. This erasure of the intersection of class and ethnic identity leads to policies and program designs that position immigrants as a monolithic group with the common desire of achieving assimilation. Like Angela, Somya's example highlights the need to develop programs that are sensitive to variations in identities and intentions within immigrant groups.

Instructors do not seem to understand this class difference among their students, even though some students, like Jenny, do actually fit the lower socioeconomic model assumed by instructors.

Jenny

Jenny is a twenty-five-year-old working-class Mexican woman who is employed at a sweet potato farm. After years of shuttling between Mexico and the US as an undocumented worker, Jenny's father legalized his immigration status. Subsequently, he was able to bring his wife and children to the US. In 2001, Jenny, aged sixteen, migrated to South Carolina. Initially, Jenny was enthusiastic about migrating to the US. Yet, she quickly became disillusioned. Jenny was placed in mainstream ninth-grade classes with little ESL support. In contrast to Angela and Somya, Jenny said she experienced racial discrimination in the US. These experiences resulted in Jenny's discontinuing her studies and dropping out before she completed high school:

> I told my mother that I didn't want to continue going to school because I didn't understand anything. They didn't help us. I felt bad because in South Carolina the students would call us things. They called us Mexicans and other names. Now, I know the names they called us were bad. . . . I felt that it was a racist place because we were the only Hispanics . . . so I decided that I didn't want to go to school anymore. And then I started working in the sweet potato [farms].[1] (Interview, October 23, 2010)

A year later, Jenny migrated with her family to a small rural town in the southeastern US in search of better employment opportunities. Jenny has had some positive experiences in the US. She met and married her husband in the US. Her parents and younger sister live next door to her. She works with her mother, sister, and husband at the same sweet potato farm, and she travels two to three times a year to Mexico. Jenny watches television in Spanish and makes regular telephone calls to Mexico. She interacts mainly with immediate family members and other Latinos from her church. These transnational practices allow her to forge and maintain simultaneous lives in multiple spaces. Jenny's transnational life seems to produce an ambivalent sense of belonging. "Sometimes I feel I belong. Sometimes I don't," she affirmed. Jenny admitted that she didn't feel as strongly about returning to Mexico as she previously did: "At first, I did [want to return to Mexico] but now I think if I'm here I don't feel like, 'oh, I want to be there. I have to go back.'" Jenny does not discard the possibility of staying in the US even though she lacks the freedom to choose whether or not she can remain. Her low socioeconomic status and husband's citizenship status are obstacles that hinder her freedom of choice and contribute to her sense of uncertainty about the future:

> Right now, I have no definite plans. . . . My husband is illegal. I am legal. We started building a house in Mexico because the possibility exists that he may be deported. . . . At the beginning we thought let's do something and return and live over there. But now, there is little work. (Interview, October 23, 2010)

Her husband's immigration status weighs heavily on Jenny. "I don't think about it too much. I try not to but sometimes I'll start thinking about it," she stated. In contrast to Angela and Somya, Jenny has neither the freedom nor the socioeconomic resources to leave the US voluntarily.

Jenny is attempting to accumulate economic capital and cultural capital in the form of US citizenship: she wants to improve her English, particularly her vocabulary, in order to pass the US naturalization test. Obtaining such capital will give her more freedom of choice, thereby allowing her to choose the time and conditions of her return to Mexico. Once she obtains American citizenship, she can process her husband's immigration status.

> It's one of the reasons why I come to class to learn English. I have the questions but they are difficult. They come with the answers but they are difficult for me because I can't pronounce many of them, and I don't have anyone to tell me "this is the way you need to pronounce them." I need someone who can read them and then I can practice. (Interview, October 23, 2010)

Her goal in taking CESL classes is to focus on the English skills that will allow her to pass the US citizenship test, which will enable her to stabilize her husband's immigration status. But rather than seeing this as an opportunity to stay in the US, Jenny views this capital as a resource that will grant her more freedom in choosing when to return to Mexico.

Jenny's instructor does not have a well-defined sense of her background and language learning aims. Consequently, Jenny's transnational life and overall English language learning goals do not align with those of the instructor. While Jenny wants to improve her English vocabulary, her instructor does not prioritize vocabulary instruction. "I don't spend much time on vocabulary because they hear it," the instructor wrote. In her view, students' exposure to English from living in an English-speaking environment facilitates vocabulary acquisition. However, this assumption is inaccurate. Jenny rarely interacted with people in English; her interactions were primarily with Spanish speakers. She specifically indicated that gaining a wider range of vocabulary was critical to her ability to pass a citizenship test, as was improved pronunciation. The instructor recognizes that students need to improve their English pronunciation; yet, she believes if students have not already improved their pronunciation it is unlikely to occur, particularly given the limited class time and students' unfamiliarity with linguistics. According to the instructor, not knowing how to do phonetic transcriptions of speech hindered their ability to improve pronunciation. She notes:

> They've been here for years, and if they haven't acquired the pronunciation yet, it's not very likely to happen during [a] ninety-minute class twice a week. . . . The situation could be better if they had any idea of transcription.

Furthermore, while the instructor expresses her desire to help students gain skills necessary to navigate authentic, real-life situations, she does not know that for Jenny, this means passing a citizenship test. The instructor writes in her journal, "My goal is to teach them general language aspects with the emphasis on the surviving skills." The instructor believes that "if they're here, if they came to the US, they really need that language." For the instructor, migrating to and living in the US necessitates acquiring language skills for participating in US society without necessarily gaining citizenship. Hence, the instruction frequently did not match Jenny's reality or target her language education goals. For instance, Jenny remarked on the irrelevance of a lesson on travel. For Jenny, air travel to distant locations was implausible because of her social and economic position; she principally traveled to Mexico by car or bus with her family.

Like Angela and Somya, Jenny's transnational ties, sense of displacement, and uncertainty about future settlement and plans shaped her English language learning aims. However, the instructor principally viewed Jenny and her classmates as permanent residents who needed to integrate into society rather than as transnationals who needed to gain the skills necessary to be competitive economically in their home country, or as people who lacked the language skills necessary to create choices for themselves through obtaining citizenship or other forms of capital without the intention of permanent settlement. Perhaps most tellingly, when asked if she was aware of the transnational character of her students, she responded, "I haven't come across such kinds of students." Yet, as the data from this study shows, this is not the case.

DISCUSSION

Curricula and instructional practices at the CESL program are principally permanent settlement–oriented and aimed at integrating students into US society by helping them develop the necessary language skills to navigate daily life in the US. Instructors falsely positioned students as permanent settlers with low socioeconomic status whose principle goal was to assimilate into US society. In contrast, the participants in this study reported that their reasons for migration were the accumulation of social, economic, and cultural capital that they could use upon their return to their home countries. They did not perceive themselves as permanent settlers severing links with a home country; rather they perceived themselves as highly mobile individuals adapting to changing environments. They fashioned a cross-border existence that engaged them in the life of both their home and host countries. For some, this was a consequence of economic privilege; for others, it was due to a lack of options arising from a lack of financial stability.

Students' perceptions of migration reflected notions of flexible citizenship (Ong 1999), particularly the ways in which they acquired capital. They wanted skills they could take back to their home country, or the ability to access the capital they needed to create stability. The web of transnational ties, the ambiguity of settlement, and the general concern about the future shaped participants' experiences and perceptions of language learning. Educational background and socioeconomic class granted Angela and Somya more control over their English language education needs and migration status. Jenny's limited education and access to resources affected her English language needs and migration status. Whereas Angela and Somya could call upon the resources to return to their home country whenever they wished, Jenny could not freely do so. However, learning English was a key component of Jenny's strategy for creating transnational choices for herself and her family.

Instructors held an inaccurate sense of students' background, and their classroom aims and practices clashed with students' transnational character and language learning needs. Students' English language goals did not align themselves with instructors' goals and practices, which tended to be based on a narrow view of immigrants' alternatives for identity and belonging. Participants' mobility, impermanent status, and future return to their home countries impacted their perceptions of the degree and type of English language competence they required. Because they frequently articulated that they were in the US temporarily, they were uninterested in developing the types of language skills emphasized in the course, which was designed on the assumption that students needed English for permanent settlement. Students often questioned the utility of particular lessons because they were irrelevant to their needs.

Like the other chapters in this section, this chapter demonstrates how policies can either expand or limit the spaces available for immigrants to maintain multiple aspects of their identities. Unlike the other chapters in this section, this study focuses on a program explicitly designed to widen students' access to capital, not restrict it. However, because instructors were unaware of students' lived realities, the program unintentionally became a limiting space where immigrants were exposed to curricula and instruction based on a narrow view of their citizenship possibilities. The increase in global movement and interconnectedness and transnational ties raises questions about transnational migrants and their educational needs throughout their lives, something that we, as educators and administrators, must seek to understand before, rather than after, we design programs. Additionally, we must be cognizant of students' transnational character, experiences, future directions, and lives beyond the classroom, as well as how multiple aspects of their identities intersect to shape their goals, assets, and needs. Adult ESL programs such as the one in this study cannot base instruction on the assumptions that students' main goal is permanent residency and integration into US society, and that students have a shared class background just because they may have a shared citizenship status. Even though most adult ESL programs are not required to collect information about students' home language use, socioeconomic status, cultural background, social and professional interactions, education and employment history, length of residence in the US, reason for migration, or future aspirations, it is vital that instructors obtain such information to better meet the language learning needs of their students. Collecting this data allows teachers not only to identify the capital that students have but also to help students access the capital they desire. The intensity and regularity of contact with the home country as well as the simultaneity of living across multiple nations, languages, and cultures affects not only transnational migrants' positioning within such spaces but also their language learning aims.

To meet such aims, preservice training, in-service and teacher education programs, adult education program policies, curricula, and practices need to take into account students' transnational life experiences, migration trajectories, and adaptation processes. Furthermore, federal, state, and local areas should invest in contextualized adult education classes that provide more specialized language needs, including classes aimed at building the language skills necessary to navigate situations encountered in children's schools (such as registration, parent teacher conferences, etc.) and citizenship goals (such as the citizenship test). Finally, policymakers must value bilingualism, both in K–12 and adult education settings, seeing it as an asset rather than a disadvantage. Doing so not only helps learners understand the skills they bring to their classes, but also validates the experiences of adults and young people who may have limited exposure to English at home because they live in families or communities where speaking another language is necessary and valuable. In short, educators, administrators, and policymakers must realize that in an increasingly transnational world, language learning serves a variety of different—but equally important—functions in the lives of immigrants. Quality programs must recognize and address these functions for all learners.

NOTES

1. Interview was conducted in Spanish and translated by the researcher.

REFERENCES

Appadurai, Arjun. 1996. *Modernity at Large: Cultural Dimensions of Globalization.* Minneapolis: University of Minnesota Press.
———. 2001. "Grassroots Globalization and the Research Imagination." In *Globalization,* edited by Arjun Appadurai, 1–21. Durham, NC: Duke University Press.
Aranda, Elizabeth M. 2006. *Emotional Bridges to Puerto Rico: Migration, Return Migration, and the Struggles of Incorporation.* Lanham, MD: Rowman & Littlefield.
Bartley, Allen J., and Paul Spoonley. 2008. "Intergenerational Transnationalism: 1.5 Generation Asian Migrants in New Zealand." *International Migration* 46 (4): 63–84.
Basch, Linda, Nina Glick Schiller, and Christina Szanton Blanc. 1994. *Nations Unbound: Transnational Projects, Postcolonial Predicaments, and Deterritorialized Nation-States.* New York: Routledge.
Bourdieu, Pierre. 1986. "The Forms of Capital." In *Handbook of Theory and Research for the Sociology of Education,* edited by John G. Richardson, 241–258. Westport, CT: Greenwood Press.
Briggs, Charles L. 1986. *Learning How to Ask: A Sociolinguistic Appraisal of the Role of the Interview in Social Research.* Cambridge: Cambridge University Press.
Burholt, Vanessa. 2004. "Transnationalism, Economic Transfers and Families' Ties: Intercontinental Contacts of Older Gujaratis, Punjabis and Sylhetis in Birmingham with Families Abroad." *Ethnic and Racial Studies* 27 (5): 800–829.
Burns, Anne, and Celia Roberts. 2010. "Migration and Adult Language Learning: Global Flows and Local Transpositions." *TESOL Quarterly* 44 (3): 409–419.
Castles, Stephen. 2004. "Migration, Citizenship and Education." In *Diversity and Citizenship Education,* edited by James A. Banks, 17–48. San Francisco: Jossey-Bass.
Cicourel, Aaron V. 1964. *Method and Measurement in Sociology.* New York: Free Press.
Coffey, Amanda, and Paul Atkinson. 1996. *Making Sense of Qualitative Data: Complementary Research Strategies.* Thousand Oaks, CA: Sage Publications.
Cooke, Melanie. 2006. "'When I Wake Up I Dream of Electricity': The Lives, Aspirations and 'Needs' of Adult ESOL Learners." *Linguistics and Education* 17: 56–73.
De Costa, Peter. 2010. "From Refugee to Transformer: A Bourdieusian Take on a Hmong Learner's Trajectory." *TESOL Quarterly* 44 (3): 517–541.
Faist, Thomas. 2000. *The Volume and Dynamics of International Migration.* New York: Oxford University Press.
Glick Schiller, Nina, Linda Basch, and Christina Blanc-Szanton, eds. 1992. *Towards a Transnational Perspective on Migration: Race, Class, Ethnicity, and Nationalism Reconsidered.* New York: New York Academy of Sciences.
Glick Schiller, Nina, and Georges E. Fouron. 1999. "Terrains of Blood and Nation: Haitian Transnational Social Fields." *Ethnic and Racial Studies* 22 (2): 340–366.
Guarnizo, Luis E., Alejandro Portes, and William Haller. 2003. "Assimilation and Transnationalism: Determinants of Political Action among Contemporary Migrants." *American Journal of Sociology* 108 (6): 1211–1248.

Hall, Stuart. 1992. "The Question of Cultural Identity." In *Modernity and Its Futures*, edited by Stuart Hall, David Held, and Tony McGrew, 273–326. Cambridge: Polity Press.

Hamman, Edmund T., Víctor Zúñiga, and Juan Sánchez García. 2010. "Transnational Students' Perspectives on Schooling in the United States and Mexico: The Salience of School Experience and Country of Birth." In *Children and Migration: At the Crossroads of Resiliency and Vulnerability*, edited by Marisa O. Ensor and Elźbieta Gozdziak, 230–254. London: Palgrave Macmillan.

Holstein, James A., and Jaber Gubrium. 1995. *The Active Interview*. Thousand Oaks, CA: Sage.

Kivisto, Peter. 2001. "Theorizing Transnational Immigration: A Critical Review of Current Efforts." *Ethnic and Racial Studies* 24 (4): 549–578.

Levitt, Peggy. 2001. *The Transnational Villagers*. Berkeley: University of California Press.

Mahler, Sarah J. 1998. "Theoretical and Empirical Contributions toward a Research Agenda for Transnationalism." In *Transnationalism from Below*, edited by Michael P. Smith and Luis E. Guarnizo, 64–100. New Brunswick, NJ: Transaction Publishers.

Martínez, Isabel. 2009. "What's Age Gotta Do with It? Understanding the Age-Identities and School-Going Practices of Mexican Immigrant Youth in New York City." *High School Journal* 92 (4): 34–48.

Menard-Warwick, Julia. 2005. "Intergenerational Trajectories and Sociopolitical Context: Latina Immigrants in Adult ESL." *TESOL Quarterly* 39 (2): 165–185.

———. 2007. "'Because She Made Beds. Every Day': Social Positioning, Classroom Discourse, and Language Learning." *Applied Linguistics* 29 (2): 267–289.

Mishler, Elliot G. 1986. *Research Interviewing*. Cambridge, MA: Harvard University Press.

Nieswand, Boris. 2011. *Theorising Transnational Migration: The Status Paradox of Migration*. New York: Routledge.

Ong, Aihwa. 1999. *Flexible Citizenship: The Cultural Logics of Transnationality*. Durham, NC: Duke University Press.

Patton, Michael Q. 2002. *Qualitative Research and Evaluation Methods*. 3rd ed. Newbury Park, CA: Sage.

Peirce, Bonny N. 1995. "Social Identity, Investment, and Language Learning." *TESOL Quarterly* 23 (1): 589–618.

Pita, Marianne D., and Sharon Utakis. 2002. "Educational Policy for the Transnational Dominican Community." *Journal of Language, Identity, and Education* 1 (4): 317–328.

Portes, Alejandro, and Min Zhou. 1993. "The New Second Generation: Segmented Assimilation and Its Variants." *Annals of the American Academy of Political and Social Science* 530: 74–96.

Rapley, Timothy J. 2001. "The Art(fulness) of Open-Ended Interviewing: Some Considerations on Analyzing Interviews." *Qualitative Research* 1 (3): 303–323.

Rodríguez, Tracy. 2009. "Dominicans entre La Gran Manzana y Quisqueya: Family, Schooling, and Language Learning in a Transnational Context." *High School Journal* 92 (4): 16–33.

Sánchez, Patricia. 2007. "Urban Immigrant Students: How Transnationalism Shapes Their World Learning." *The Urban Review* 39 (5): 489–517.

———. 2008. "Coming of Age across Borders: Family, Gender, and Place in the Lives of Second-Generation Transnational Mexicanas." In *Transformations of la Familia on the U.S.-México Border*, edited by Raquel Márquez and Harriett Romo, 185–208. Notre Dame, IN: University of Notre Dame Press.

Sarangi, Srikant, and Christopher T. Candlin. 2003. "Trading between Reflexivity and Relevance: New Challenges for Applied Linguistics." *Applied Linguistics* 23 (3): 271–285.
Song, Juyoung. 2010. "Language Ideology and Identity in Transnational Space: Globalization, Migration, and Bilingualism among Korean Families in the USA." *International Journal of Bilingual Education and Bilingualism* 13 (1): 23–42.
Warriner, Doris S. 2007. "Language Learning and the Politics of Belonging: Sudanese Women Refugees Becoming and Being 'American.'"*Anthropology & Education Quarterly* 38 (4): 343–359.

10 Internationally Recruited Teachers and Migration

Structures of Instability and Tenuous Settlement

Omar Kamara and Karen Monkman

Between 1999 and 2002 one of the nation's largest school districts recruited more than one hundred teachers from all over the world through their Global Educators Recruitment (GER) program. (GER is a pseudonym, as are all names of individuals, local entities, and locations.) The main purpose of the recruitment was to address teacher shortages. This qualitative study examines the experiences of GER teachers recruited from African countries to work in the Metro School District (MSD). In this chapter, we situate the recruitment of the teachers within the context of international labor migration and the social processes of migration. Like the other chapters in this section, we examine how multiple policies in the areas of citizenship, security, and education intersect to affect the lived experiences—educational and otherwise—of the immigrants participating in this study.

Our findings demonstrate that the GER program facilitates labor migration yet undermines teachers' stability, which, in turn, affects settlement processes. The program's structure lacks sufficient focus on how to support educators through their settlement processes, and all but ignores the impact this has on teachers, their work, and their families. Our findings reveal how unstable employment, struggles to understand the US school system and therefore teach effectively, and the precariousness related to immigration status, coupled with unmet expectations and the district's missed opportunities to promote cultural understanding, compromise the settlement process. We end with implications related to migration theory and educational policy.

MIGRATION SCHOLARSHIP

Migration as a Social Process

Recently, scholars have begun to reject the long-held notion that the social process of migration is linear, and that people move from one country to another in response to push and pull factors (conditions that pushed people out of their home countries, or that pulled them to other countries). In contesting these simplistic notions, Chavez (1992) and Massey et al. (1987)

argue that migration is a long-term process that encompasses phases of separation (decisions to migrate, leaving), transition (moving and initial settlement), and integration or incorporation (long-term settlement processes). The boundaries between these phases are fluid and blurred. Return migration and cyclical or temporary migration suggest that migration is far from linear: migrants return home, go elsewhere, or move back and forth, often facilitated by social networks that span national boundaries (Massey et al. 1987). This literature calls into question static notions of borders and citizenship, revealing the inadequacies of these fixed definitions.

Since the early 1990s, scholars have begun describing migration in transnational terms, exploring how individuals frame their lives in multiple locations simultaneously (Levitt 2001); diminishing the salience of borders (Glick Schiller, Basch, and Blanc-Szanton 1992); recognizing the integral role of social relations that span national boundaries (Grewal 2005; Smith and Guarznizo 1998); and acknowledging the transnational nature of identity (Smith 2006). These studies also identify transnational structural linkages related to economic and political processes (Ong 1999), and embed the global flows of people (Appadurai 1996) and various influences of globalization in their analysis.

In this chapter, we present data that reflects a linear model of migration. This is because none of the participants have returned to Africa and their primary goal, at this point, is establishing themselves in the US. However, employment conditions that affect settlement stability may lead to long-term experiences that reflect a circulatory form, or a transnational orientation of migration, as some participants may be forced to return.

Migration research is often focused on children (e.g., Igoa 1995; Suárez-Orozco, Suárez-Orozco, and Todorova 2008), or on families or adults (e.g., Levitt 2001; Foner 2005; Arthur 2010), but rarely on teachers. Furthermore, migration research that involves the US focuses primarily on Latin America or Asia. Our research addresses these gaps in the literature by focusing on the experiences of African educators now teaching in the US.

African Migration

Wide-scale migration between African countries and the US is relatively recent, with noticeable increases after the 1964 changes in US immigration laws that reversed exclusionary policies barring non-Western immigrants from entrance into the US (Ngai 2005). These changes coincided with a variety of independence movements in African countries, which resulted in a drastic decrease in European colonization on the continent.

Almost fifty years later, relatively little is known about the social processes of African migration to the US. Between 1960 and 1987, at least thirty percent of Africa's skilled professionals left the continent for industrialized countries of the Global North (Robertson 2006, 2). The Immigration Act of 1990, which sought to increase immigration to the US from underrepresented countries, resulted in an increase in the annual number of legally admitted African immigrants from less than 40,000 in 1999 to almost 120,000 in 2006 (Arthur 2010, 84). Most migrants have college degrees and a few years of professional experience (Arthur 2010). Teachers are among these educated African émigrés, although the active recruitment of teachers from African countries is a fairly unusual phenomenon for US school districts: in this study, only seven out of 120 recruited teachers are from African countries.

Global Recruitment of Teachers

US school districts recruited teachers internationally to fill positions in subjects such as foreign languages, mathematics, science, and special education that were open as a result of a nationwide teacher shortage, which the US Department of Education estimated at 50,000 per year in the early 2000s (Omanio 2005). MSD's GER program is one such program.

In her report to the National Education Association on Trends in Foreign Teacher Recruitment, Barber (2003) reported that "public school systems throughout the country are utilizing the services of perhaps as many as 10,000 foreign teachers in primary and secondary schools on 'nonimmigrant' work [H-1B] or cultural exchange [J-1] visas" (1). The H-1B visa is a temporary (three-year term) work visa, renewable once for a total of six years; it is for nonimmigrants who work in jobs where there is a shortage of US workers. They must be sponsored by an employer and can work only for that employer. The J-1 visa, intended for individuals participating in exchange programs, is issued for an initial one-year term, renewable twice for a total of three years. Whereas some teacher recruitment programs are exchange programs, the GER program is not: it was designed primarily to address a teacher shortage. H-4 visas were provided to the dependent family members of the GER teachers in this study; these visas do not permit work and have other restrictions, discussed in more detail through our findings. In short, the visa situation plays a place-taking role (see A. Chin, herein).

The global recruitment process lacks regulation and oversight. As the American Federation of Teachers (2009) reports, "Currently, there are absolutely no standards, whether voluntary or mandatory, establishing acceptable practices for recruiting teachers from abroad for our public schools" (26). Furthermore, as Barber (2003) points out, foreign teachers are "at will employees . . . who can be subject to a range of abuses and pressures" (2). Their "at will" status renders foreign teachers unable to access many protections, leaving them vulnerable to exploitation, and at the mercy of their recruiters or employers (Dunn 2011).

Despite these issues, even after a decade of recruiting teachers for US schools, very few empirical studies examine the experiences of international educators through their settlement experiences. Because most of what we know about international teacher recruitment programs tends to be from policy reports and media coverage about incidents (e.g., Toppo and Fernandez 2009; SPLC 2011), and because of the policy implications for this practice (Dunn 2011), research on this subject is necessary and timely.

RESEARCH DESIGN

MSD recruited about 120 foreign teachers from all over the world between 1999 and 2002. Of the 120 GER teachers, seven came from sub-Saharan African countries. One of the seven returned to Africa before the study was conducted, one is the lead author, and the remaining five were invited to take part in the study. This chapter examines the stories of the three who consented to participate; their experiences are not unlike those of the lead author. Kamara interviewed participants in 2009 for about ninety minutes each. He focused on the recruitment process, participants' motivation for participating in the GER program, their teacher training background and experience teaching in other countries, their migration experience, and their teaching experience in the US. As an educator recruited through the program, Kamara had close relationships with the participants. His motivation for the study stems in part from his curiosity about the experiences of teachers in situations similar to his own. Because they had these experiences in common, Kamara conducted this research from an insider perspective, asking the participants for information in ways that an outsider may not have considered and eliciting more openness than an outsider may have been able to. Monkman supervised Kamara's thesis research and helped to develop this chapter.

In addition to interviews, documents that teachers received from the program were also analyzed. These include letters and memos from the school district, contracts, and agendas from the training and induction sessions. The information in the documents was triangulated with data from the interviews for consistency.

FINDINGS

Teacher Profiles and Background

All teachers in the study originate from African countries, and came to the US with college degrees and teaching experience. Joseph Masela came from Cameroon with an MS degree in computer design and programming. A technology company had already hired him to work in the US before MSD approached him. In Cameroon he had been a computing technology teacher at a vocational school for three years. Makela Narre', born in Uganda, was recruited from Tanzania, where he was a refugee after he fled from a rebel war in his native country. At the time of his recruitment, he had a BS degree in science and mathematics, and was head of the science department at an international school. Lamrana Othabu is Nigerian but was recruited from the Gambia, where he had taught secondary school mathematics for five years prior to arriving in the US. He had a BS degree in mathematics education. Unlike Joseph and Makela, who still teach in MSD, Lamrana now teaches in a school district in another state. MSD authorities suspended the GER program after Lamrana was recruited and arrived in the US, but before he actually took up appointment, so he left the area. Although Lamrana did not teach in the city of Metropolis, he is included in this research because he was recruited through the GER program.

Recruitment

The GER recruitment process was structured such that it was available only to individuals with sufficient economic resources. For example, most participants reported that they learned about and applied to GER online, thereby implying that the applicant pool was limited to those with access to the Internet. Additionally, applicants invited for interviews by MSD had to make their own travel arrangements and secure visas to be at the interviews in Metropolis, which presented another financial investment. MSD supported applications for US work permits and for H-1B visas for successful candidates. Reasons for participating in the program ranged from Lamrana's "desire to work abroad and enjoy better conditions of work" to Makela's "escape from unpleasant life experiences" caused by a civil conflict in Uganda, followed by discrimination in Tanzania, where he lived as a refugee. All of the study's participants stated that the city where they would be located was immaterial, because their primary goal was to migrate to the US.

The Structural Underpinnings of Instability

We turn now to data related to the instability embedded in employment, cultural knowledge, and visa status. Participants felt that their status was precarious because of instability in structures and processes in the work environment, missed opportunities by the school district to more fully support the teachers' understanding of US schooling, and delays in processing their visas and permanent residency.

Getting Acclimated

While they were afforded some support from the school district, there was little evidence that the district or the schools in which they worked were equipped to help them make cultural sense of the US schools. While this is not unlike the experience of most new teachers in urban school districts, it is made more complex by the international dimension. Job instability, along with inadequate training for cultural understanding, made for challenges in settlement in MSD and Metropolis.

MSD implemented several strategies intended to support the teachers' transitions and develop their knowledge of education in Metropolis. MSD planned an intensive three-week orientation program followed by a four-month Mentoring and Induction of New Teachers (MINT) program where participants worked in schools with veteran teachers who served as their mentors. Guest speakers from city agencies spoke to the teachers on issues such as public transportation, housing options, and applying for social security numbers. In lectures on teaching in an urban setting, they learned about classroom management, curriculum and lesson plan preparation, district policies and procedures, employee benefits, legal issues, standards-based instruction and planning, learning theories, and evaluation. Participants presented demonstration lessons, and also took a general education course in US history to provide them with an understanding of their new country. While this staff development was useful in many ways, participants felt it was too general and basic, falling short of engaging the GER teachers in developing a nuanced understanding of the culture of teaching, classrooms, and students in US urban schools.

Also during these early weeks, MSD required teachers to sign a document entitled "Conditions for Participation" that outlines the requirements of the GER program: they were required to accept school assignments and/or reassignments; complete all coursework necessary for, and obtain, the State's Standard Teacher certificate within a four-year time frame; and receive satisfactory annual performance evaluations. The document states that failure to meet those conditions "will result to [*sic*] loss of the district's sponsorship of your H-1B visa. Loss of the district's sponsorship may result in your return to your last place of residence abroad." In addition to these explicit mandates, the Conditions for Participation document points out emphatically that "*this document shall not be considered all inclusive and shall not be considered as an employment contract*" (emphasis in the original). Thus, much was required of the teachers with little assurance of job security. At the time of making the commitment, the teachers did not fully understand the implications of signing the documents; in hindsight Joseph confessed that he felt "trapped in the program."

Employment Instability

After orientation, MINT classes, and the initial mentoring, the GER teachers were on their own. Makela left the school in which he was mentored at the end of the first semester for what he described as his "most rewarding assignment," a position in a small center within a large school teaching refugee students who came mostly from African countries. After two years, the center closed, and Makela was assigned to "support refugee students in five schools on the north side of the city." He left that job after only two months because he was spending more time traveling from school to school than working with students: he didn't feel he was "having any meaningful impact on students' learning." His next job was at a school with a population that was over 90% white. His teaching position was eliminated after one very challenging year during which he felt "a lack of support." He explained, "I failed to establish meaningful relationships with both students and the adults in the building."

Makela's experiences were not unique in terms of the job insecurity and the adjustment challenges the teachers had to deal with in their first few years teaching in the US. Like Makela, Joseph was forced to change schools after just one year. In fact, according to them, by the second year of the program, rumors were rife among GER participants about other participants "quitting the program and returning to their countries" of recruitment or origin, or simply "leaving the teaching profession."

Simultaneously, budgets became tight in the school district, resulting in the elimination of administrative positions. Subsequent district staff knew little or nothing about the program. Makela believed that, with the exception of one administrator in the human resource department, the recruited teachers were "all but forgotten."

In 2002, following the 9/11 terrorist attacks, and shortly after the fourth cohort was recruited but before the teachers were invited to take up appointments, the program was officially suspended. Lamrana was one of the candidates who was interviewed and accepted by MSD for cohort four. After spending what he described as "a fortune" for an average African teacher on "travel to the US for the interview," he was disappointed that the program was abruptly discontinued. Luckily for him, he got a job teaching (and H-1B sponsorship) in another state. At about this time, the district renamed the GER teachers "visiting teachers" in their letters and memos, with no explanation provided. This recategorization added to participants' feelings that their positions were precarious.

Frequent school changes meant that the teachers didn't have time to get to know their colleagues and students well enough to develop rapport and to make sense of the cultural nuances embedded in American education. This cultural knowledge was not included in the orientation and initial professional development offered by the district.

Cultural Sensemaking: Knowledge as Structures of Instability

The district's orientation missed opportunities to support teachers' acquisition of necessary cultural knowledge about US schooling. Consequently, participants struggled in their new environments. Lamrana's experience, markedly similar to that of the other teachers, has been fraught with challenges related to this lack of cultural knowledge: the inner-city students whom he teaches, he lamented, "appear completely unmotivated to learn." Similar to what Joseph and Makela said about MSD's students, he feels they come to his classroom "unprepared and unwilling to learn." As a math teacher, he said he is "constantly battling to keep them interested" in the curriculum. The students' "lack of discipline and mastery of basic mathematics skills" overwhelms him. Comparing them to the students he taught in Nigeria and the Gambia, he couldn't understand how the American students got to high school with so little mastery of basic concepts and skills in mathematics. Similarly, comparing teaching in Cameroon to teaching in the US, Joseph explained:

> In my country it is the teacher's responsibility to provide the knowledge expecting . . . students and parents to make sure that the students put the necessary effort to master the skills and concepts, with the support of the teacher. Here the teacher is held responsible for both the teaching and the learning process with little or no responsibility or accountability on the parts of the students and their parents.

Coming from a country where students have to pass national exams to be promoted to the next class, Lamrana said he is still "baffled by the social promotion" that is practiced in many US school districts. The other teachers expressed similar sentiments, along with disappointment about inadequate science labs and lack of materials in their MSD classrooms. When Lamrana left Africa, he expected "highly motivated students in well equipped classrooms in US schools"; these expectations have remained "dreams" that he is not sure he will ever realize. He has not lost hope but he thinks the road to realizing his ideal classroom remains "a challenge" not only at his school district but nationwide because of the sociocultural dynamics of US society, about which he agreed he "still ha[s] a lot to learn." He realizes that the settings are completely different, but still he cannot stop comparing his experiences in the US to those in Africa. In contrast, Makela found his first job with refugee students from Africa (mentioned earlier) "rewarding" because he could make sense of his students and figure out how to teach them effectively. Makela's experience demonstrates that cultural context is an important factor in teachers' abilities to succeed in their jobs as well as achieve professional satisfaction, both of which contribute to a feeling of stability.

GER teachers were trying to make sense of the students in their classrooms, but they were struggling without support or context. These deficit perspectives could have been actively countered in the orientation and courses provided by MSD by providing teachers with a better understanding of structural and historical influences on US urban schools and their students. This would have enabled foreign teachers to recognize the power structures in which their students are expected to learn. It is likely that MSD and mentor teachers' lack of knowledge about education outside the US results in staff development that fails to cover what newly arrived teachers from abroad would most need to learn, and to critically examine differential academic achievement across race, class, and gender lines. These challenges in comprehending classroom dynamics accentuate the teachers' sense of instability. The lack of time to develop meaningful relationships with colleagues and students from whom they could learn further—a direct result of frequent transfers between schools and assignments—made it difficult for teachers to find allies to help them process this information outside of formal professional development settings.

Adjusting to work and to life in any new place can be complicated. The lack of secure and consistent jobs, meaningful rapport with colleagues, and relationships with students is further complicated by delays in processing visas and stabilizing immigration status.

Immigration Status, Migration Decisions, and Settlement Instability

Teachers in this study were deeply affected by policies relating to citizenship and stability (see also A. Chen, Thomas, and Wicks-Asbun and Torres in this volume). As holders of H-1B visas, the teachers have legal authorization to work only for the sponsor of their visas, a requirement that infringes upon teachers' abilities to choose their employers and where and how they live. Furthermore, educators' family members initially did not have permission to work because of their visas. Consequently, teachers saw changing their immigration status as a pathway for stability for themselves and their families. Unfortunately, the process was challenging, if not impossible.

Makela explained that to be in his visa status indefinitely "is deeply troubling." As a holder of an H-4 visa tied to Makela's H-1B visa, Makela's wife was not allowed to work for several years. She enrolled in a community college but did not have access to student loans or grants, so "we paid all expenses out of my single salary," Makela explained. At first, she could not get a driver's license, because she was not allowed to obtain a social security number until seven years after arriving in the US. Such restrictions, Makela said, "caused us economic and psychological hardship," which he thinks may have compromised his effectiveness as a classroom teacher during his transition from one school to the other. "How can you give off your best in such circumstances?" he asked. The spouses of the other teachers were similarly restricted.

Additionally, Makela's daughter is almost ready to graduate from high school, and he is worried that she may not be able to go to college because they cannot afford the fees. "Unless our immigration situation changes, my daughter, like my wife, will not have access to financial assistance or a driver's license or any employment," he lamented.

Makela's family applied for a change of residency status from nonimmigrant (H-1B) visa status to permanent residency status. At the time of this study—two years after submitting the application—no progress had been made. Makela said, "What I found difficult to understand is why it takes so long to process our papers when we see that friends and relatives coming to the country with different visas have their papers processed within weeks."

He spoke about a friend who came as a refugee and another who won the Diversity Visa Lottery; they both received permanent residency status in less than six weeks. The US Citizenship and Immigration Services (USCIS) has repeatedly told Makela that there is a backlog of cases. The question he said his family continues to ask is: "What is inherently so complicated about processing H-1B cases that they should take so long?" He also wondered, "Whose best interest is served in keeping us from becoming an integral part of society in spite of our service?" Makela pointed out that although most of the GER teachers in his cohort have met the school district's conditions for participation in the program, a cloud of uncertainty still hangs over them: they continue to be at the mercy of the school district and the US government.

The GER teachers were given substitute teachers' certificates at the start of their employment and, subsequently, when they completed the state certification requirements and were awarded the initial probationary teaching certificates, on which was written: "To maintain the validity of this certificate, the holder must become a United States citizen [within four years]." This citizenship requirement for obtaining a standard teaching certificate "raised our hopes even more," Makela said. The teachers felt this should motivate the district to assertively support teachers' visa adjustment processes, because it would also be in the best interest of the district to maintain its teaching workforce and to comply with state regulations.

The governor eliminated the citizenship requirement for receiving a teaching certificate before the four years were up, but teachers were still required to pursue citizenship. Makela, like other GER teachers, complied with that requirement, but eight years after his recruitment by MSD, he remained unsuccessful. He said he has "paid hefty amounts to government in application and processing fees, [an] immigration attorney, and we have done everything we have been asked to do, but we continue to face seemingly bureaucratic obstacles in reaching our goal of becoming US citizens." Makela's experience illustrates the divide between the State's expectations and the reality of federal policy, as well as the ways in which expectations for teachers shift depending on the political climate and agenda of elected officials.

Given his situation, Makela said, he was amazed by the arguments he frequently hears in the media from anti-immigrant activists in regard to the nearly twelve million undocumented immigrants currently said to reside in the US. The argument goes like this, Makela said: "If only they had joined the line and waited for their turn, it should have been okay. We have no problem with welcoming immigrants if only they come the right way." That does not seem to agree with the experience of Makela and other GER teachers who have been waiting, some for more than ten years, while they serve in some of the most challenging schools in America.

Lamrana considers himself to have been "fortunate" not to have been stuck with the GER program and caught up in the same immigration debacle as the GER teachers. He now has permanent residency, which he pursued independently, even though he came to the US nearly four years after the first cohort of GER teachers were recruited. Joseph recently had to renew his H-1B visa again for another three years. And most likely, Makela and his family will have to go through a similar process before their visas expire. In the meantime, Makela said, "we just have to wait and hope for the best but there is nothing we can do. If we renew them, it will be our fourth time for a total of twelve years, even though the visa category initially set a limit of six years."

As the above findings demonstrate, GER teachers frame their migration experiences as a linear process, while also struggling with potentialities that are more circulatory or transnational in nature. They are clearly committed to settling in the US, gaining citizenship and raising their families here without leaving their pasts behind. They nurture dreams of returning home with the knowledge and skills that could benefit those communities, but wonder if this will ever happen. Although they recognize the potential of "brain circulation" (Robertson 2006), their immigration and employment status restricts travel home. This precarious state deeply affects the teachers' economic, social, and professional lives and the life experiences of their family members, rendering them pawns in the global labor force rather than agents of their own life choices. Makela asked, "What guarantee is there that at some point in the future, maybe very close to our retirement age, we will not, for some flimsy reason, be shipped back to our countries to die?" If they are able or forced to return home, at an age young enough to meaningfully contribute to schools there, we wonder how the conditions of their return—as voluntary or forced—might shape the particulars of "brain circulation." We cannot say at this point, because none of the GER teachers in this study have returned home, even for a visit. They are conflicted, due in large part to the inconsistent support from MSD and USCIS's failure to process visas in a timely manner, both of which place them and their families in insecure positions in their attempts to contribute meaningfully to US society, settle here, and, in the future, return home and help reverse the effects of brain drain. While they would like to meaningfully contribute to "brain circulation," their current situation has served to dampen their dreams of returning home.

The instability the teachers experience is embedded in the structures of insecure work, inadequate access to knowledge about US schools, and requirements related to processing legal status. Woven through this state of instability is another story of the teachers' expectations and the district's missed opportunities, deepening educators' instability and compromising their settlement.

DISCUSSION

Expectations and Missed Opportunities: Instability and Tenuous Settlement

In this section we unpack teachers' expectations relative to their experiences (relying mostly on the stories already presented) in the policy context of the GER program, and show that the challenges they experienced negatively influence their ability to become more fully integrated into their schools, communities, and US society. The GER teachers all expressed hope that their employment by one of the nation's largest public school districts would lead to a path to citizenship, job security, and a better life for their families. Unfortunately, immigration status was not the only barrier to creating safe and stable homes.

One of the district's requirements is that all teachers reside within the city. An unexpected consequence of this rule was that the majority of teachers' children lived and attended public schools in inner-city neighborhoods where safety is a concern. Makela describes this residency rule as "unfair" as it exempts some employees who lived in suburbs before the rule was enacted, and it also allows waivers to be granted to new employees who are designated "special needs employees," a group that includes new teachers of mathematics and science. The GER teachers are not categorized this way, even though some of them teach science or math. To Makela, it is not only a question of fairness, but also a security issue.

Before coming to the US, Makela and his family fled from violence in a war-torn country. One of his reasons for jumping at the opportunity to come to the US was, as he put it, "to bring my family to a safe and more secure environment." For them, living in the inner city in unsafe neighborhoods where gang wars claimed the lives of more than thirty teens during the first few months of the 2008–2009 academic school year is what Makela characterized as a "disturbing" and constant reminder of the very violence they fled.

The violence is particularly challenging because Makela and his family are in a new and unfamiliar environment, where they anticipated better security than what they experienced in the conflict situation they left behind. In addition to filing several police reports, Makela encountered situations he did not anticipate being a part of his life in the US. For example, he said, "I had to accompany my teenage daughter to the local library because she was having trouble with other girls in the neighborhood." It is these kinds of unanticipated challenges that complicate the experiences of situating oneself in a new job, community, and country. School districts, as employers, rarely recognize, let alone get involved with, the life issues that affect their teachers' job performance and satisfaction, even when the challenges arise due to school policy and practice. The district fell short in helping the teachers to understand urban violence, or community or neighborhood issues, either in the initial orientation or when helping them to find housing.

These conditions are, again, symptomatic of policies outside the realm of education that affect the economies of inner-city neighborhoods and their residences. The web of policies that have led to decades of neglect of urban low-income communities in turn affects the lives of immigrant educators, further demonstrating how immigrants' access to work and education are influenced by policies that, at first glance, would not appear to be related to citizenship or schools.

In addition to physical insecurity, the teachers and their families face job insecurity. Professionally, the teachers anticipated better work conditions in the US, and with stronger labor unions, they expected that they would be holding more stable jobs compared to what they left behind. But, to their disappointment, the GER teachers found their jobs to be less secure in the US. When asked about how secure he felt about his job here in the US compared to that in his native country, Joseph replied, "Job security? Teachers generally in Cameroon are employed just as civil servants. Once you get a job you can hardly be fired unless you downright do something very unprofessional or not perform, but generally your job is secure." Joseph's words imply that the US system does not provide the type of professional stability he expected upon migrating.

Makela lamented the restrictions imposed on them by the conditions of the H-1B visas. The educators could work only for the sponsoring employer, which he said limits "our ability to freely choose who we want to work for like other teachers can." He explained that to be in such a condition indefinitely is "deeply troubling"; he believes "it infringes on our international labor rights," which he understands as granting workers the right to equal opportunities and equal treatment without discrimination. The use of an expendable work force, in turn, undermines some of the original aims of recruiting teachers from abroad. Teachers are forced to independently make sense of a new culture and its school system, and, individually, to ameliorate their precarious situations. All this detracts from their potential as strong teachers who contribute meaningfully to the school system.

Implications for Classroom Practice

All of the participants expressed disappointment in the school and/or classroom environments, not only in regard to students' lack of discipline and intrinsic motivation, but also in regard to the underresourced environments in which they were expected to achieve prescribed learning outcomes (as discussed previously). Contrary to their expectations, teachers' classrooms were not well equipped, nor were supplies available. As Makela observed, "materials and equipment are less accessible to some students and teachers than others." Such experiences, in direct contradiction to the teachers' high expectations, negatively affect teachers professionally. Makela pointed out how these conditions affect their "effectiveness in the classroom" and, consequently, "students' learning." Both Joseph and Lamrana expressed disappointment in their daily realities compared to their expectations before migrating. When asked which experiences, if any, affect the performance of his job as a teacher in the US, Joseph replied:

> I would say the uncertainty from year to year as to not knowing whether or not the position I hold will remain open at the end of the year or even whether the whole school will be open because new schools are

being opened every year and there are new policies coming up, and so it's a worry that affect[s] long-term instructional planning—not knowing exactly what to expect.

Dozens of schools have been and continue to be closed in this district as a strategy to address poor performance and low enrollments. The closings affect mostly African American schools, where most of the GER teachers work.

CONCLUSION

Coming from African countries to teach in what Joseph described as "the world's most advanced country," the teachers met with considerable challenges relating to their visa status, job security, community violence, poor school conditions, and students they struggle to understand, all of which contribute to settlement instabilities. Von Kirchenheim and Richardson (2005) argue that the "difference between expectations and reality" is an important influence on adjustment processes, suggesting that "negative surprises detracted from successful socialization or adjustment" (408). This is clearly the situation here. Teachers' experiences of insecurity and lack of support hindered their ability to fully incorporate themselves and their families into their new schools and communities. These feelings are derived from a variety of state and federal policies, many of which are not directly related to education. This study demonstrates how intersecting policies come together to determine outcomes for immigrant educators and students alike. (See also A. Chen, Thomas, and Wicks-Asbun and Torres in this volume, for discussions of similar dynamics.)

Migration comes with challenges, some more predictable than others (Massey et al. 1987). It is in the best interest of school systems and employers that encourage migration to facilitate a smoother process of adaptation for their teachers, who are more likely to excel and remain rooted in their communities if they receive the proper support. The shortsightedness of MSD in failing to more aggressively obtain visa adjustment and to aid teachers in finding ways to meaningfully adapt to their new environments undermines the potential of internationally recruited teachers to successfully integrate themselves into schools and communities. This limits the ability of educators to adequately serve MSD students, and constrains long-term educational improvement in the district. Dunn (2011) makes the same point in relation to Indian teachers recruited through a third-party, for-profit agency. While teachers like the ones in this study may be motivated to take on the challenges of becoming part of a new nation, poorly designed policies and institutionalized neglect severely curtail—if not eliminate—their ability to do so. Furthermore, in school districts' search for trained and experienced but inexpensive labor, it seems that concerns with improving the educational experience of children through full, more comprehensive support has been all but lost.

This study reveals a variety of issues that are central to education policy. We end with a few points that would be useful for school districts to consider when engaging in global labor recruitment, which entails the migration of not only teachers but also their families.

Teacher recruitment is never *only* about addressing a teacher shortage: it cannot be divorced from broader concerns like school improvement. The district missed opportunities to place teachers in positions that they could grow into over time, to educate the newly arrived teachers about US schooling so they could interact with students and communities more effectively, and to more actively support the processing of visa applications so their families could be more secure in the US. These missed opportunities jeopardize the success of our schools overall. Furthermore, a program that is structured to rely on an expendable workforce will discourage long-term planning and teacher development and undermine a sense of community within a school, all of which are necessary for optimal learning environments. Moving teachers from school to school weakens the ability of teachers to know their students, the communities from which they come, and their colleagues, and as a result, limits their ability to develop meaningful and coordinated instruction.

Helping the recruited teachers to better understand the new environment will keep teachers in classrooms and support positive student experience. To do this well requires a deeper understanding of cultural process and meaning systems (Levinson and Holland 1996); programs like GER should include explicit support for learning more about schools and districts as culturally constructed spaces. While the initial orientation provided some very basic information, it fell short of supporting the teachers' deeper understanding of their new work environment. This missed opportunity resulted in a much longer process of settlement in the teachers' schools, classrooms, and communities than might have been possible.

Additionally, in the case of teacher recruitment, immigration and citizenship policy directly influences the outcomes of teachers and the students they serve. The district should have more aggressively supported the processing of the teachers' visas and permanent residency status. This would have created more stability within the teachers' families, and enabled them to more fully engage with their jobs, by reducing their concerns and time spent with USCIS. Further, the district should have been more transparent about the immigration process from the beginning, and included more coordination between the state and federal governments throughout the process of granting contracts and explaining the risks inherent in taking a job under the given visa status. Perhaps most importantly, immigration policies should be reassessed as to their effectiveness in creating paths to citizenship for valuable persons like educators filling positions in underresourced schools.

Recruiting teachers internationally has an ethical component that cannot be ignored. School districts should be more fully aware of the ways that their programs can create, or reduce, job insecurities that create precarious life conditions. Bringing people from afar to work in an environment that they do not fully understand compromises their ability to succeed pedagogically. Districts must commit more fully to teachers and their families by improving their understanding of schooling and life in other parts of the world and of issues surrounding immigration status, so that they can better anticipate teacher needs and the shortcomings of their own programs.

School districts would do well to recognize the underlying influences that shape their policy agendas. Understanding the influence of globalization, for example, would require a more critical analysis of the powers and forces in the market, politics, and culture (such as that conducted in Stromquist and Monkman [in press] or Arnove and Torres 2013), including how the global recruitment of teachers is theoretically constituted. Is the teacher recruitment policy of the district defined by a neoliberal agenda, or another orientation? What other global policy agendas might the school district consider?

Awareness of the relationships among culture, migration, transnationalism, and globalization processes is a worthwhile focus of analysis for school districts, in relation not only to internationally recruited teachers, but also to international and immigrant students. How do school district practices integrate (or marginalize) not only their students but also teachers and their families? What would it take to more fully follow through on these policy initiatives?

The GER teachers came to the US to teach American students, to enhance their own professional skills, and to support their families in pursuing their versions of the American dream. While they are struggling to reach these goals, the limitations in their ability to do so are clearly linked to the precarious nature of their legal status and working conditions in the US, over both of which the school district has some control. This situation is conditioned by the global nature of international labor recruiting, where motivations (conditioned by neoliberal agendas) are often about getting quality labor for cheap, and which creates situations where jobs are not stable and workers are expendable (AFT 2009). Can school districts become more enlightened about their participation in these processes? While they are pressured with shrinking budgets and increasing public and media scorn, they are also a product of our globalizing world, and pressured to become more competitive and effective in ways that are often more about an economic bottom line and a narrow notion of accountability and less about the educational well-being of students, which requires committed and supported teachers, a coherent vision of education, and support of schools and school districts. We hope that global teacher recruitment programs in the future will prioritize goals beyond fulfilling a teacher shortage, strive to more fully understand the cultural and global dynamics inherent in such initiatives, and more fully commit to supporting the recruited teachers so that they can more easily become contributing members of society and serve our students and educational systems.

REFERENCES

American Federation of Teachers (AFT). 2009. *Importing Educators: Causes and Consequences of International Teacher Recruitment.* Washington, DC: AFT. Accessed February 3, 2012. www.aft.org/pdfs/international/ importingeducators0609.pdf.

Appadurai, Arjun. 1996. *Modernity at Large: Cultural Dimensions of Globalization.* Minneapolis: University of Minnesota Press.

Arnove, Robert F., and Carlos Alberto Torres, eds. 2013. *Comparative Education: The Dialectic of the Global and the Local.* 4th ed. Lanham, MD: Rowman and Littlefield.

Arthur, John A. 2010. *African Diaspora Identities: Negotiating Culture in Transnational Migration.* Lanham, MD: Lexington Books.

Barber, Randy. 2003. *Report to the National Education Association on Trends in Foreign Teacher Recruitment.* Washington DC: Center for Economic Organizing.

Chavez, Leo R. 1992. *Shadowed Lives: Undocumented Immigrants in American Society.* Fort Worth, TX: Harcourt Brace Jovanovich.

Dunn, Alyssa Hadley. 2011. "Global Village versus Culture Shock: The Recruitment and Preparation of Foreign Teachers for U.S. Urban Schools." *Urban Education* 46 (6): 1379–1410.

Foner, Nancy. 2005. *In a New Land: A Comparative View of Immigration.* New York: NYU Press.

Glick Schiller, Nina, Linda Basch, and Cristina Blanc-Szanton. 1992. "Transnationalism: A New Analytic Framework for Understanding Migration." In *Towards a Transnational Perspective on Migration: Race, Class, Ethnicity, and Nationalism Reconsidered,* edited by Nina Glick Schiller, Linda Basch, and Cristina Blanc-Szanton, 1–24. Vol. 645 of *Annals of the New York Academy of Sciences.* New York: New York Academy of Sciences.

Grewal, Inderpal. 2005. *Transnational America: Feminism, Diasporas, Neoliberalisms.* Durham, NC: Duke University Press.

Igoa, Cristina. 1995. *The Inner World of the Immigrant Child.* New York: Routledge.

Levinson, Bradley A., and Dorothy Holland. 1996. "The Cultural Production of the Educated Person: An Introduction." In *The Cultural Production of the Educated Person: Critical Ethnographies of Schooling and Local Practice,* edited by Bradley A. Levinson, Douglas E. Foley and Dorothy C. Holland, 1–54. Albany, NY: SUNY Press.

Levitt, Peggy. 2001. *The Transnational Villagers.* Berkeley: University of California Press.

Massey, Douglas, Rafael Alarcón, Jorge Durand, and Humberto González. 1987. *Return to Aztlan: The Social Process of International Migration from Western Mexico.* Berkeley and Los Angeles: University of California Press.

Ngai, Mae. 2005. *Impossible Subjects: Illegal Aliens and the Making of Modern America.* Princeton, NJ: Princeton University Press.

Omanio, Roque Glenn. 2005. "10,000 Foreign Teachers a Year Asked to Fill Gap in U.S. Schools." *Chicago Sun-Times,* March 27.

Ong, Aihwa. 1999. *Flexible Citizenship: The Cultural Logics of Transnationality.* Durham, NC: Duke University Press.

Robertson, Susan L. 2006. "Brain Drain, Brain Gain and Brain Circulation." *Globalisation, Society, and Education* 4 (1): 1–5.
Smith, Michael Peter, and Luis Eduardo Guarnizo, eds. 1998. *Transnationalism from Below*. New Brunswick, NJ: Transaction Publishers.
Smith, Robert Courtney. 2006. *Mexican New York: Transnational Lives of New Immigrants*. Berkeley: University of California Press.
Southern Poverty Law Center (SPLC). 2011. "Precedent-Setting Decision Issued in SPLC Teacher Trafficking Case." Southern Poverty Law Center website, December 20. Accessed February 1, 2012. http://www.splcenter.org/get-informed/news/precedent-setting-decision-issued-in-splc-teacher-trafficking-case-0.
Stromquist, Nelly P., and Karen Monkman, eds. In press. *Globalization and Education: Integration and Contestation across Cultures*. 2nd ed. Lanham, MD: Rowman and Littlefield.
Suárez-Orozco, Carola, Marcelo M. Suárez-Orozco, and Irina Todarova. 2008. *Learning in a New Land: Immigrant Students in American Society*. Cambridge, MA: Belknap Press of Harvard University Press.
Toppo, Greg, and Icess Fernandez. 2009. "Federal Complaint: Filipino Teachers Held in 'Servitude.'" *USA Today*, October 27. Accessed February 3, 2012. http://www.usatoday.com/news/education/2009–10–27-filipino-teachers_N.htm.
Von Kirchenheim, Clement, and Warnie Richardson. 2005. "Teachers and Their International Relocation: The Effect of Self-Efficacy and Flexibility on Adjustment and Outcome Variables." *International Education Journal* 6 (3): 407–416.

Part III

Space-Making

11 Why Bother to Continue Learning a Heritage Language?

Mainstream Policies and the Politics of Heritage Language Maintenance

Neriko Musha Doerr and Kiri Lee

What makes a child want to keep learning his/her heritage language? What learning environments are conducive to children learning heritage languages? These are questions this chapter addresses. A "heritage language" is a language spoken at home while another language is spoken in mainstream society. The "heritage language speaker" has been broadly defined in the US as one "who is raised in a home where a non-English language is spoken, who speaks or at least understands the language, and who is to some degree bilingual in that language and in English" (Valdés 2001, 38).

Since the 1990s, both the view that minority heritage language education raises the self-esteem of the language learners while nurturing the cultural autonomy of the heritage language community (Campbell 2003; Carreira 2004; Wright and Taylor 1995) and the growing public recognition of non-English speakers as a resource for the country as a whole (Peyton, Ranard, and McGinnis 2001) have bolstered support for minority language education in the US. Much research has focused on how communities support heritage language education outside "mainstream" education systems[1] (Chinen 2004; Curdt-Christiansen 2008). In this chapter, we shift the focus to the mainstream educational system and highlight how changes in federal policy gave students, families, and institutions the opportunity to make space for heritage language learning. That is, the new government policy and resultant moves by mainstream institutions created space for particular ethnic identifications and practice, which students capitalized on by continuing to study their heritage language. We show this through illustrating how shifting institutionalized attitudes in mainstream US education toward a particular minority language—Japanese—affected students' motivation to continue their studies at a part-time community Japanese language school.

Drawing on our ethnographic research at a weekend Japanese language school in the northeastern US, we demonstrate that the government policy that identified Japanese as a critical language, and the US College Board's subsequent adoption of Japanese as an Advanced Placement (AP) subject for high schools, helped make space for learning environments that motivate middle-school children to continue learning their heritage language.[2]

Our four-year study revealed that the middle school years are a critical period during which students tended to abandon heritage language schooling as a result of intensified schoolwork, extracurricular activities, and social lives in mainstream day schools. Students who recognized the possibility of leveraging their knowledge of the heritage language to strategically navigate mainstream schooling—most commonly by using their knowledge to get high scores on an AP exam—were more likely to continue.

To investigate changing motivations and perceptions about learning a heritage language, we conducted a four-year ethnographic study of a group of Japanese students in the same grade at Jackson Japanese Language School (JJLS; all names are pseudonyms), a weekend Japanese language school. The changing motivations of students correspond to three stages in their education: (1) the need to communicate with extended family in Japan (preschool–early elementary stage), (2) sense of self as a bilingual/bicultural person (late elementary–middle school stage), and (3) the desire for leverage in college applications and future career (high school stage). Earlier motivations may continue to exist in later stages, although with different intensity.

Our focus in this chapter is the transition from the second to the third stage. In the second stage, general recognition in mainstream schooling of the value of being bilingual and bicultural allots cultural capital (Bourdieu and Passeron 1977) to students' knowledge of their own heritage language and culture. However, our data show that when the workload increases in mainstream American middle schools, students' perception of the importance of the cultural capital of being bilingual/bicultural gives way to their perception of the importance of educational capital gained by succeeding in mainstream schooling. Consequently, they prioritize mainstream schoolwork over learning Japanese unless they recognize that knowledge of Japanese will soon become educational capital directly linked to college admissions via the AP test and as an extracurricular activity on their curriculum vitae. That is, the value of the cultural capital of knowing Japanese is not, by itself, enough to keep some students at JJLS: they chose to stay only upon recognizing that it will become educational capital soon after.

Students in high school (the third stage) perceived JJLS's preparatory instruction for the AP Japanese test as beneficial, as it allowed students to take an AP test without taking the official high school AP courses. For the first time, the mainstream educational system explicitly assigned value to learning Japanese. Furthermore, students had a clear path for using their knowledge to gain educational capital.

We argue that educational language policies play significant roles in creating a sociocultural context that provides individuals with various ethnic backgrounds the space for heritage language maintenance—a space-making practice which helped motivate students to continue learning the language. Federal policies designate particular languages as critical for the nation. The College Board highlights the need to learn these languages by including them as AP subjects, high schools offer the AP courses, and college policies allow students to receive college credit for AP achievement. Furthermore, we suggest a need for mainstream US schools to value Japanese language academically as educational capital at various critical stages, especially middle school. Although we focus on Japanese in this chapter, our argument could be extended to other heritage languages as well. As our findings show, heritage language speakers are adept at taking advantage of educational policies that open up space for their heritage language.

Various factors influence the ways language as heritage is passed on. Elsewhere we (2009, 2010, 2012, 2013) have analyzed peer dynamics in classroom contexts, perceptions of what constitutes "heritage language learners" and "native speakers" of Japanese, the stance of speakers of Japanese dialects in relation to heritage language education abroad, and so on at JJLS. Whereas our previous work focused on the dynamic interconnections among language proficiency, subject positions, and national belonging, in this chapter we examine the link between the shift in motivation and the position of the Japanese language in the mainstream US educational system.

HERITAGE LANGUAGE EDUCATION AND THE MAINSTREAM EDUCATIONAL SYSTEM

"Minority issues" are less about the minority than about the mainstream society that marginalizes minority groups (Baldwin 1985; hooks 1992). Relations of dominance in society are often reflected in the school culture, which subordinates the experience, knowledge, and beliefs of minority cultures (Bourdieu and Passeron 1977; Cummins 1996/2001). Even when the minority language is taught, language practices often reinforce the hegemonic understanding of the minority language as inferior, overriding the overt support for the minority language and perpetuating the hierarchy between languages as well as their speakers (Meek and Messing 2007). It is not only the practice of education but also the wider sociocultural and educational environment in which the language skills are acknowledged and valued that supports minority language education. Policies at various levels are an important part of this wider educational environment.

In the 1990s the study of whiteness and dominant groups' politics of invisibility emerged as studies of race relations that sought to understand the marginalization of minorities (Doerr 2004; Frankenberg 1997; Spoonley 1991). However, this approach was not as prevalent in heritage language research. Existing research on social aspects of heritage language education tends to focus on heritage language learners (Krashen 1998; Wright and Taylor 1995). The mainstream context's importance for heritage language education has been examined only tangentially, mainly in relation to English as a second language (ESL) education (e.g., Wiley and Wright 2004). On the other hand, research that examines how the (lack of) cultural sensitivity in mainstream schools affects minority students' self-esteem devotes little attention to how it also affects heritage language maintenance (Meek and Messing 2007; Niyozov and Pluim 2009; Valdés 1996). While this chapter does not investigate mainstream society's reception of heritage language as whiteness studies proponents would urge, it does shed light on the influence of the mainstream social and educational context and suggests possible policy initiatives to support heritage language education.

JAPANESE AS A HERITAGE LANGUAGE IN MAINSTREAM US EDUCATION

Heritage language learning was not actively encouraged after World War I because of concerns about national unity and security: at the time, individuals who spoke languages other than English were seen as potentially disloyal to the US, and therefore a threat (Pavlenko 2002). Only since the 1990s have heritage language research and instruction gained much ground (Brinton, Kagan, and Bauckus 2008). Peyton, Ranard, and McGinnis (2001) argue that heritage language education owes this advancement to three changes dating from that decade: (1) before the 1990s, language preservation efforts were community initiated and remained outside the public school system; in contrast, recent initiatives integrate language learning into formal educational systems; (2) scholars know more about language maintenance and teaching than ever before; and (3) for the first time in American history, globalization, democratization, and the position of the US as a world power have resulted in the growing recognition that non-English speakers are resources rather than threats.

Changing attitudes to heritage languages led to the establishment of the Heritage Languages Initiative by the National Foreign Language Center (NFLC) and the Center for Applied Linguistics in 1998. The initiative aims to build an education system that supports heritage language communities with the end goal of developing a greater number of bilingual citizens. The Alliance for the Advancement of Heritage Languages was also established within the NFLC to connect individuals with organizations that support maintenance of heritage languages for the benefit of individuals, communities, and society.

Meanwhile, in 2006, the National Security Language Initiative (NSLI) was established to increase the number of advanced-level speakers of non-English languages, particularly "critical need" languages, identified as Arabic, Chinese, Korean, Japanese, and Russian[3]. In conjunction with the NSLI, the secretaries of state, education, and defense and the director of national intelligence allocated funding to expand US critical foreign language education from kindergarten to postsecondary education and into the workforce.

Once a language is identified as a "critical need" language, the government devotes increased resources to relevant education, thus encouraging individuals to study that language. This "critical need" designation is reserved for languages associated with societies and countries thought of as economic and security concerns—much as the regions promoted through the development of area studies in US higher education in the 1960s were those seen as potential threats. While the motivation behind the designation is problematic, identification as a "critical need" language has resulted in increased attention and resource allocation to minority language communities, and has raised the desirability of learning these languages.

Most importantly, critical language status was crucial to making Japanese an AP test subject in 2006.[4] While only the College Board–certified schools can offer AP courses, students may take any AP exam without taking an official course at their high school. Acknowledging this, some weekend heritage Japanese language schools began offering classes geared toward preparing students for the AP Japanese test. Thus, although the government policy of increasing the number of advanced-level speakers of "critical need" languages through mainstream schooling did not directly recognize or encourage heritage language learning, it created opportunities for heritage speakers to tie what they learned in their community schools to the mainstream educational system.

However, explicit recognition of knowledge of Japanese as valuable in the mainstream educational system remained restricted to the high school level. In what follows, we show how the government policy aimed at mainstream education created an added incentive for high school students learning Japanese as a heritage language. Conversely, lack of a similar structure at the middle school level led some students to stop coming to the weekend Japanese language school.

WEEKEND JAPANESE LANGUAGE SCHOOLS

As of October 2012, there were seventy eight *hoshūkō* (weekend supplemental Japanese language schools approved by the Japanese government) in the US[5]. These schools are designed to provide children in the first to ninth grade (ages six to fifteen) of (mainly) Japanese expatriates with the same education they would have received in Japan's compulsory educational system, so that they can continue in the Japanese school system upon their return. The schools compress five days of general instruction into one school day, focusing on language arts. *Hoshūkō* sometimes include a preschool, a kindergarten, and a high school. They receive grants from the Japanese government that partially cover teachers' salaries and the cost of renting classrooms. The Japanese government sends a senior teacher from Japan to schools with a student body of one hundred or more.

These inputs by the Japanese government reflect its perceived responsibility to provide children of Japanese citizens overseas with access to Japanese education. This policy is based on Article 26 of the Japanese Constitution, which guarantees free compulsory education for Japanese children between the ages of six and fifteen (MEXT 2008). The Japanese government's contributions to weekend Japanese language schools in the US suggest that it regards this arrangement as education of Japanese children abroad, rather than heritage language maintenance. That is, it shares Japanese society's perspective—that Japanese citizens should be educated in Japanese ways to prepare them for their return—rather than regarding Japanese children as minority language speaking children and adopting the increasingly common point of view in American society that heritage language education should raise the self-esteem of minority Japanese students (Sato 1997).

Since the 2000s, however, *hoshūkō* have enrolled increasing numbers of children whose Japanese parents migrated to the US to attend universities and stayed to work and/or marry an American, and therefore had no intention of returning. To cater to these students, whose desire to study Japanese differs from that of *hoshūkō* students, a new type of program called *keishōgo* (Japanese as a heritage language) program was developed within, and to a lesser degree outside, *hoshūkō* in some US cities (Chinen 2004). *Hoshūkō* programs follow the national language/language arts curriculum known as *kokugo*, which is based on Japanese government guidelines and uses government-certified textbooks. As *hoshūkō* must fit five days' instruction into a single day, the workload is heavy. *Keishōgo* programs, by contrast, provide locally produced curricula created by the given institution's teachers and approved by its administrators, and need not adhere to the guidelines set by the Japanese government (see Doerr and Lee 2009, 2010, 2012, 2013). JJLS, the site of this research, included components of both types of schooling.

METHODS: FIELDWORK AT JJLS

Our research site, Jackson Japanese Language School, was established in 1980 in a suburb of a major metropolitan area in the northeastern US. It caters to students, from preschoolers to adults, who wish to learn Japanese. JJLS is a private nonprofit organization overseen by a board of trustees. Its funding comes from tuition, Japanese government grants, and donations from local businesses whose employees' children are JJLS students; these sources anchor JJLS in the Japanese community. The school is in session from 1:00 p.m. to 4:20 p.m., forty-two Sundays a year (following the Japanese school calendar, which starts in April), and is located in a rented building at a local university.

As of April 2011, JJLS had two education divisions: a first division comprising solely *hoshūkō-bu* and a second division comprising a *keishōgo* program called the Jackson Course along with other Japanese language programs. The Jackson Course offered flexible multiage classes and also prepared high school students to take the AP Japanese test in their mainstream schools. JJLS students could not attend courses in both divisions: they had to choose between *hoshūkō-bu* and the Jackson Course.

JJLS's students fall roughly into three groups according to the length of their intended stay in the US, following conventional categories used at *hoshūkō* (Sato and Kataoka 2008): (1) *chūzai* (short-term resident) students, who live in the US for the three to five years, often because of a parent's intracompany transfer; (2) *chōki-taizai* (long-term resident) students, who plan to stay in the US for more than five years, usually owing to a parent's long-term transfer within the company; and (3) *eijū* (permanent resident) students, who have no plans to live in Japan.[6] In this chapter, we focus on *eijū* students because their educational goals are situated in the American context and their need to study (in) Japanese is less urgent than that of *chūzai* students, who plan to return.

This chapter is part of a wider project investigating how different types of language classes influence students' sense of national belonging (Doerr and Lee 2009, 2010, 2012, 2013). Doerr performed the participant observation, conducted most of the interviews, and analyzed the data; Lee handled permissions, conducted interviews, provided information on JJLS, and provided the analysis with critical feedback. We have been part of the JJLS community as parents, and Lee was the principal of the second JJLS division from April 2004 to March 2012 and became a board member in April 2012 to present (December, 2013). While these relationships allowed us to gain the trust of participants, they also situated us in particular power dynamics within the school. For example, we suspect that students and parents were less likely to frankly express negative views about the Jackson Course to Lee because she was the administrator in charge of Jackson Course, whereas they might have been more frank with Doerr, considering her a fellow parent. Also, because we are both part of the JJLS community, parents probably were less likely to discuss negative social relationships among parents with us than they would have been with researchers outside the JJLS community.

Our fieldwork involved four years of observation of a group of students who, as of the 2006–2007 academic year, were in the sixth grade in *hoshūkō-bu* and Level 3 in the Jackson Course. Altogether, we carried out participant observation in twenty-eight sessions of *hoshūkō-bu* and twenty-six sessions of Jackson Course classes. Of seventeen sixth-grade *hoshūkō-bu* students, we interviewed ten students (three once, five twice, two three times) and ten of their parents (four once, four twice, two three times). We also interviewed all five Jackson Course Level 3 students (one once, four twice) and parents of all five (one once, four twice), as well as one new Level 4 student and his parent (both twice). We interviewed eight teachers of the classes we observed and three JJLS administrators.

Interviewees were asked a set of standard questions about their family background, how they came to live in the US, their experiences at JJLS, dialects of Japanese they spoke and how they felt about them, their views on *hoshūkō* and the Jackson Course, and the interviewees' and their family members' ethnic identities. Most interviews were conducted before or after classes at school; some interviews of parents and teachers were done outside of school or on the phone. Interviewees were asked to choose the interview language (English or Japanese). For this chapter, we translated the Japanese-language interviews into English. We are fluent in both English and Japanese, but research was conducted mainly in Japanese.

We analyzed our data using case study method in which we focused on particular students and traced their changing motivations within the context of their family and sociocultural background. To build the case studies, we triangulated semistructured interviews of students and parents conducted at the beginning and end of our four-year research period, as well as participant observation.

STUDENTS' AND PARENTS' EXPERIENCES

Jake

Jake was born and raised in the US. His Japanese mother had married an American, and they lived in Japan for three years before Jake's father's work brought them to the US in 1991. Jake began attending JJLS in preschool and stayed in *hoshūkō-bu* until he left JJLS in eighth grade.

Jake saw studying Japanese at JJLS as personally, rather than educationally, beneficial. He never considered joining the Jackson Course, explaining, "It's for the kids who don't really speak Japanese" (Interview, March 4, 2007). Jake said he attended JJLS during the first two stages "because it makes my mom happy." In her first interview, Jake's mother said she had sent Jake to JJLS because she was Japanese and her parents in Japan spoke only Japanese (Interview, February 18, 2007).

In our second interview, conducted after he had left JJLS, Jake explained that he had left JJLS because the "homework load at American school was too much" (Interview, February 13, 2011).When he had made the decision to leave JJLS, he was looking forward to "having Sunday off. More time to do my American school's homework. Watch the Jets game." At the same time, he was worried about "not being able to speak as well, not just to Mom but to other Japanese relatives and friends." After he left, "time management got worse. More time, but I'd think I'll do it on Sunday," he said with a laugh. In her second interview, Jake's mother also said Jake had left JJLS because of "the increased amount of homework in American school and busy schedule of his sports. He could not finish homework and he needed Sundays to work on his homework. Also, "because he will be going away for college, we wanted family time before he does," she said, and she and her husband were looking forward to having more time with their son. But she also worried that Jake might forget Japanese.

In his second interview, Jake recalled the impact the JJLS experience had on him:

> As a kid, it felt like it was a chore. It's weekend, all day, and homework. Once I left, I felt that JJLS was important in helping me speak Japanese and it teaches you how important Japanese is to you. [Now] I use it every day with mom and dad. Basic . . . "What's for dinner?" (Interview, February 13, 2011)

In terms of his sense of self, JJLS "helped me feel unique and lucky to speak Japanese well." At the end of the interview he added, "As I got older, I realized that it is a great community." The reason he would want to speak Japanese was that "Mom is Japanese and she speaks it." In her second interview, Jake's mother said she felt that the impact of JJLS on Jake was that "he became bilingual, although not perfectly. He should feel proud that he can speak a language other than English. He could also learn about Japanese culture, so that was good experience. . . . It also made him open to other cultures." In terms of his sense of self, she said, "he was always aware that he has half Japanese blood. But, if he hadn't come to JJLS, he would have thought he is American but his mother is Japanese. By coming to JJLS, he felt he is half Japanese more."

Here, Jake's and Jake's mother's responses show the importance of Japanese to his ethnic identification. Although he felt this, his decision to leave JJLS to pursue mainstream schoolwork reveals that he did not feel that the pursuit of this community space and ethnic identification was enough to continue his studies. Further, he gives no indication that he recognized how mainstream schooling might make space to value his Japanese language education. Originally, his motivation for coming to JJLS was to make his mother happy. It involved family obligation, the search for affection, sharing the same language, and possibly gaining a sense of heritage. After he left, he missed the ability to speak Japanese well, as well as the JJLS community. It is important to note that Jake felt the loss of these benefits only retrospectively, indicating that they were not strong enough to keep him at JJLS.

Both Jake and his mother mentioned a wish to have more free time. Jake wanted to spend more time on things rooted in American life rather than coming to JJLS—doing homework for American school and watching Jets games. His mother linked more free time to the enrichment of family life. Here the earlier link JJLS provided between JJLS and family life by enabling communication in Japanese was reversed as JJLS came to be viewed as something that robbed the family of time together.

Jake did not seem to bridge his JJLS life with his American life. For example, he did not take AP Japanese or see advantages to bilingualism.

Had he stayed at JJLS, he would have had more opportunities to consider taking AP Japanese and to figure out how to bridge his Japanese language study to mainstream American education. He did not consider switching from *hoshūkō-bu* to the Jackson Course, whose curriculum incorporates students' bilingualism and links students' learning Japanese and their knowledge to school life in the US. Making this switch would have made it easier for Jake to bridge the two schools. Jake's case was not unique: several *hoshūkō-bu* students left JJLS during or after seventh grade because of the stepped-up workload in their mainstream American school: one student in seventh grade; two students in eighth grade; and two students in ninth grade (not counting those who moved away).

One benefit of the Jackson Course was that as a program, it raised awareness among students of federal policies that made space for Japanese language in mainstream education. Unlike the *hoshūkō-bu,* the Jackson Course gave students and families strategies for leveraging their heritage language for more than just personal identification practices, strategies that made heritage language learning more attractive.

Before the Japanese AP examination was introduced in mainstream schooling, and the JJLS administrators and teachers started incorporating it into curriculum, Jake's case was more typical of JJLS students, in that it was difficult for them to build connections between mainstream and JJLS education by themselves. The introduction of the AP examination and the school's effort to help them prepare for it, however, provided a way for students like Mayumi, described next, to find value in learning Japanese that could be translated to benefits for their future as Japanese Americans.

Mayumi

Mayumi said she was "half Japanese, half Russian" (Interview, February 25, 2007). She explained what influenced the Japanese aspect of her sense of self: "Parents . . . Japanese language school, definitely. And going to Japan. Having a kimono." When asked what makes a person Japanese, she answered, "One of the parents is any portion Japanese," and then added, "I feel I am more Japanese [than Russian] because I speak it [Japanese]." Like Jake, Mayumi saw language as central to her ethnic identification, although she later came to see it as a resource to increase educational capital in mainstream US education. Mayumi moved from *hoshūkō-bu* to the Jackson Course starting in seventh grade because, she explained, the slower pace of the class helped her understand the content better and keep up with her work (for details see Doerr and Lee 2012).

Mayumi's mother came to the US in the 1980s to attend a university, she told Lee in her interview (Interview, June 10, 2007). She married "a [Russian-] American" and stayed in the US. "I might have forgotten about Japan if I hadn't had Mayumi," she said. She felt that coming to JJLS and learning Japanese language and culture had helped Mayumi realize she was

"Japanese." Mayumi explained that she had begun attending JJLS in pre-school (the first stage) because her mother wanted her to be able to speak Japanese to her grandparents. Mayumi's mother's answer to the same question in her first interview was very similar: "Because I am Japanese, I wanted her to speak in Japanese with my family in Japan."

Mayumi stated in her first interview that during the second stage, she had come to enjoy learning about her "own culture" and wanted to be bilingual. Asked how JJLS had influenced her, she mentioned that it "gives me a sense of being Japanese." Mayumi's mother said in her first interview that at this stage, Mayumi "herself wants to study Japanese. She has begun to feel that it is cool to be bilingual. She has begun to feel proud of that." Mayumi's mother said that by coming to JJLS, Mayumi was learning Japanese culture and customs by learning Japanese language. "If she had not come to JJLS, she would not have felt she is Japanese this clearly." At this stage, Mayumi's mother encouraged Mayumi to join the Jackson Course because it would prepare her for AP Japanese, indicating that at this point, Mayumi's mother already saw the value of Japanese within the mainstream educational system, rather than solely within a family context.

In her second interview, carried out while she was in the third stage—high school—Mayumi described her reason for studying Japanese as follows:

> I have been studying Japanese since I was three. So, I want to continue that. It's also so that when I graduate from college, I can use it for my career. Also, for AP Japanese. I have the AP Japanese test in May. It's once a year . . . When I was in elementary school and middle school, I studied Japanese because I wanted to talk to my grandma. My mom wanted me to talk to my grandma, too. (Interview, January 1, 2011)

Mayumi's response is particularly important because it shows her own strategic thought process about maintaining contact with JJLS and her heritage language. Similar to the students in Bangura's (this volume) and Subramanian's (this volume) studies, Mayumi did not rely solely on adults to make decisions for her. She engaged in using resources and paths that she became aware of, the help of her mother notwithstanding, to maintain her own connection with her language. Mayumi's mother was supportive, saying in her second interview that she was still sending Mayumi to JJLS at this third stage because the Jackson Course would prepare her for the AP exam and she thought Mayumi should stick with it until she graduated from high school. But, she added, it had become very difficult to continue as Mayumi was busy with schoolwork from her high school (Interview, March 9, 2011). Along with her mother, Mayumi had understood how to use her JJLS experience to complement her high school work, thereby overcoming this challenge by recognizing opportunities available as a result of federal policies.

Mayumi left JJLS in September 2011 after taking an AP Japanese test in May 2011. She reported to Lee that she had received a five, the highest possible score. Lee suggested that once Mayumi was done with her college application process she should come back to JJLS to finish the academic year that ended in March 2012. That way, she could receive the graduation certificate, a symbolic recognition of her Japanese schooling—symbolic, because it is not officially recognized for school credit in Japan. Mayumi did not answer, but her eyes filled with tears. Her mother, standing next to her, told Lee that she would be too busy at her high school. Mayumi's statement from her earlier interview—that she wanted to finish off what she had begun at age three—suggests that her tears indicated ambivalence about leaving before the end of the academic year. Such ambivalence reflects the difficulty of balancing the sentimental value of a symbolic recognition with practical management of a busy daily schedule centered on the mainstream American educational system.

Mayumi's case shows how her motivation and her family's support of her desire to learn Japanese shifted through three stages. First, when she was in preschool and early elementary school, her mother wanted her to learn Japanese so that she could talk to her Japanese grandmother. This was a family-related, practical, communicative reason focused on the relationship with family in Japan. Second, as a sixth grader (late elementary–middle school stage), she came to JJLS to be Japanese-English bilingual and Japanese-American bicultural. JJLS gave her a sense of being Japanese while living in the US, and contributed to the development of her ethnic identification. At this point Mayumi's sense of self derived from linguistic proficiency and cultural competence. Third, as a tenth grader (high school stage), she viewed JJLS as an educational investment in her future in the US (for her college preparation—AP Japanese—and for her career) and for its sentimental value (to continue what she had been doing since she was three years old). Giving these two reasons for continuing to attend JJLS does not imply that they had replaced her valuing her sense of being Japanese and being a bilingual/bicultural individual. Rather, these latest reasons for coming to JJLS built on her already being bilingual/bicultural by this time: Mayumi took advantage of the Japanese AP exam to gain mainstream recognition for her bilingualism. The question then was the merit of continuing to attend JJLS at this stage to finish off what she had started after her proficiency in Japanese had already gained recognition (her AP score) in the mainstream schooling.

Some other students reported a similar trajectory of shifting reasons for attending JJLS. For example, April, who began attending JJLS in preschool and moved from *hoshūkō-bu* to the Jackson Course in third grade, attended JJLS because of her parents' desire that she learn Japanese (sixth grade). By tenth grade, this shifted to attending "for college credits . . . AP test" and to be with her friends. Martin, who enrolled in the Jackson Course in fourth grade (the second stage), said he originally attended because his parents wanted him to learn to read and write in Japanese. He also felt that coming to JJLS made him feel more "Japanese" (sixth grade). But in the interview he gave in tenth grade (the third stage), he explained his reason for attending JJLS differently: "Because my mother is Japanese, she advised me to study Japanese. And, because if I can speak two languages, it's easier to find a job . . . I began thinking about the job after I entered high school." His mother also modified the reason from learning to read and write in Japanese, making Japanese-speaking friends, and boosting his confidence (sixth grade) to "excellent extracurricular activity for his resume," his college application, and his career (tenth grade).

Not all students saw the connection between mainstream education and heritage language learning as reason enough to keep learning Japanese.[7] Some students left JJLS despite the fact that they connected their Japanese language studies to the mainstream American education system.

Anne

Anne's Japanese father and American mother met in Japan. In 1995 they came to the US, where Anne's father attended business school. Anne, who was born and raised in the US, said she is a "mixture of Japanese and American" (Interview, March 18, 2007). Anne began her education at JJLS in preschool. She attended *hoshūkō-bu* and left JJLS upon graduating middle school at the end of ninth grade.

Anne's parents said they sent Anne to JJLS during the first stage because they wanted her to be bilingual. In the late elementary–middle school stage, Anne said that what she wanted from JJLS was to learn Japanese language and culture so that she could say "I can speak Japanese" and "I have two cultures" (Interview, March 18, 2007). She further commented, "When I go somewhere and say I am Japanese . . . if I didn't go to Japanese-language school, it would feel strange. It's strange to say I cannot speak Japanese but I am Japanese." She also wanted to talk with her grandmother in Japanese. As a student of *hoshūkō-bu*, Anne never thought about joining JJLS's alternative Jackson Course program because she felt "people mix Japanese and English in the Jackson Course. It is a little too easy."

In their first interview, Anne's parents said that at this stage, they would leave it up to Anne to continue at JJLS. However, upon finding out that Anne had an interest in Japanese culture, they did not encourage her to join the Jackson Course. This is because they felt Anne could handle the Japanese government-sanctioned curriculum alongside *chūzai* students, and that this rigorous Japanese education would prove useful in the future. Although Anne's father thought that Anne would probably identify herself as American, coming to JJLS reminded her that she was also Japanese, he said (Interview, March 18, 2007).

On the verge of high school, Anne said that she decided to leave JJLS that year because "the regular school became too difficult. A lot of homework and it just got too much" (Interview, March 14, 2010). In response

198   *Neriko Musha Doerr and Kiri Lee*

to the interview question about the benefits of attending JJLS, she mentioned four advantages: learning to speak Japanese; doing something different from what her friends in the mainstream American school did; learning Japanese culture; and learning Japanese with other Japanese kids, which she saw as very different from learning Japanese as a foreign language in a mainstream American school.

She mentioned that one negative aspect of coming to JJLS was that some teachers treated her and her fellow students differently. "Because I am not 100% Japanese," she said, "some teachers used English only to me. That's a bit prejudiced. Not much, but sometimes" (Interview, March 14, 2010). When asked if she was made to feel a minority in class, she answered, "Only sometimes," and explained that only four students in the entire class were born and raised in the US and only three, including herself, were "half Japanese." However, nobody really talked about it and everyone was friendly to everyone else, she said.[8] When asked about her plan for studying Japanese after leaving JJLS, she said, "I will be taking the AP Japanese exam, so I need to keep up with my Japanese." She did not plan to study Japanese formally at JJLS but would watch Japanese television and speak Japanese at home to keep it up, she added (Interview, March 14, 2010).

She looked forward to going out on Sundays after leaving JJLS, but she felt that she would miss her friends and the weekly routine when she quit. In response to the question about JJLS's influence on her sense of self, she related an episode that took place when she was in sixth grade. At a YMCA camp she attended, a girl told her, "Oh, you are a half" (Interview, March 14, 2010). She did not mind this, but when she told her parents about the incident, they did. They told her she was not a half but "both" because she was both Japanese and American. She said that although she had not understood the meaning of this incident at the time, her experience at JJLS helped her appreciate the benefit of being biracial. Now, whenever she has to check a box for her race on the SAT or other tests, she chooses "Other," not "Asian" or "Asian-Caucasian," she said, because she is neither American nor Asian but both: "If I hadn't come to JJLS, I wouldn't know Japanese language and, when I see the box, I'd choose 'American.' . . . Because I attended JJLS, I can speak to my family in Japan. That's why I choose 'other.'"

In the interview a month before Anne left JJLS, Anne's father said that Anne was planning to study for AP Japanese with him at home. He was not worried about her Japanese skills deteriorating after she left JJLS. He said she enjoyed JJLS, especially school events, and had gained basic proficiency in Japanese by interacting with people in Japanese outside the home; however, the workload in her mainstream American school as well as social life on weekends had pushed her to decide to leave JJLS. Because some students who were "half Japanese" had moved to the Jackson Course, he mentioned, Anne had become a minority in *hoshūkō-bu*, which made her feel that teachers treated her differently because she was not "pure" Japanese (Interview, February 28, 2010).

In contrast to Mayumi, Anne's reasons for coming to JJLS did not change: she wanted to learn Japanese language and culture so that she could say she is "Japanese," and to talk with her Japanese grandmother. That is, her needs to stake her ethnic identification and to communicate with extended family were the two main reasons. She did not want anything less than the Japanese education provided in Japan. Her sense of self was the reason she did not join the Jackson Course, a *keishōgo* program. It is worth noting here that Anne's idea of what constitutes "knowing Japanese" (i.e., being able to follow the *hoshūkō-bu* curriculum) differed from Mayumi's (i.e., obtaining knowledge in the Jackson Course, which does not follow the *hoshūkō-bu* curriculum). Ironically, however, Anne's perception led her to leave JJLS altogether because the workload in *hoshūkō-bu* proved too much, combined with the mainstream American school workload.

That is, Anne prioritized her mainstream American school over the value she placed on JJLS; faced with a heavy workload in both schools, she chose the mainstream American school over JJLS. Here, Anne did not view continuous attendance at JJLS as necessary for either maintaining her heritage language or using her knowledge to garner educational capital from the mainstream system. She thus differed from Mayumi, who valued her continued attendance at JJLS because it was helping her stake her ethnic identification as well as preparing her for AP Japanese: Anne saw the possibility of gaining both of these benefits without attending language school. Anne's case also contrasts with that of Jake, who also left during middle school but did not see Japanese language proficiency as advantageous in the mainstream US educational system. Anne's case was rare in that she left JJLS but still used her Japanese skills in the mainstream American system. Her case illustrates how policy can motivate students to continue to shape their ethnic and linguistic identifications outside institutions like JJLS because they see possibilities of garnering educational capital.

STUDYING JAPANESE AND THE MAINSTREAM AMERICAN EDUCATION SYSTEM

The cases discussed in this chapter concern how the Japanese language's status and the potential benefits of knowing it within the mainstream American educational system affected students' motivation to continue their language study during middle and high school years. While all of the students in this study saw Japanese language learning as central to staking their ethnic identifications and gaining connections to Japanese culture through being bilingual/bicultural, those who chose to continue with their studies did so only when they saw space for leveraging their knowledge to gain educational capital through mainstream channels developed as a result of federal policy. Ultimately, at the high school level, the continuation of Japanese language studies—both through formal channels like JJLS and informal channels like studying at home with family—depended on the educational capital that knowledge of the language conferred in mainstream American schooling.

The cases of Mayumi and April show a common trajectory of motivation to attend JJLS. In the earliest stage, the motivation was their practical need for communication with families in Japan. In the late elementary–middle school stage, the primary motivation became sense of self—being bilingual and bicultural—as these qualities gave them cultural capital in mainstream American life.

By the high school stage, students tended to continue with language studies when they saw the opportunity to parlay their language skills into educational capital in the mainstream American education system as well as future career opportunities. By the end of the second stage, sense of self and knowledge of Japanese as cultural capital alone were often insufficient motivation to continue attending JJLS, but seeing knowledge of Japanese as educational capital could tip the scale in favor of keeping on.

The federal policy on critical languages that led to the creation of an AP Japanese language exam played a significant role in helping students who valued bilingualism and their ethnic identification as Japanese remain in a heritage language program that provided both socio-emotional and intellectual benefits. Students who attended JJLS developed a community of peers, a greater sense of self, and a stronger connection to their ethnic identification. The examples show the potential of mainstream language policies to positively affect the educational and emotional lives of language minority youth by giving them strategies to justify to themselves and their families the need to continue with learning a heritage language that is central to their ethnic identifications.

However, motivation to take the AP exam was not enough to keep all students at JJLS, as Anne's case shows. The key factor helping students recognize the value of Japanese proficiency appears to have been the Jackson Course program, in that it encouraged students to link their Japanese language skills to the mainstream American education system. In the group of observed students, only one *eijū* Jackson Course student left the school during the transition from the second to the third stage, whereas four *eijū hoshūkō-bu* students left.[9]

These case studies also indicate the importance of making linkages between heritage language schools and the mainstream educational system earlier in students' lives, particularly in middle school, when students like Jake are likely to stop attending. As Jake's case shows, once a student leaves JJLS, it is difficult to maintain Japanese language study. For some students, like Anne, the potential for educational capital may help motivate students to continue studying at home. Whereas this maintains their ability to learn a heritage language, it disconnects them from their community of peers, and therefore may not be ideal for every student.

For these reasons, we argue that language policies that position knowledge of minority languages as an important part of the mainstream educational system are crucial to inspiring heritage learners to continue learning these languages. Inclusion of Japanese as one of the critical languages, which led to its inclusion in AP test subjects, as discussed in this study, is an example of such a policy. On the other hand, we argue that having a program like Jackson Course that links the study of a heritage language to the mainstream US education system is also important.

A final, and equally important, implication of this chapter is the fact that policies are not static, but are constantly remade in a way that reflects the government's current needs and repurposed, sometimes counter to the government's intention, by individuals seeking to take advantage of the space opened up for themselves within the mainstream educational system. As the cases of Mayumi and Anne show, such practices are not limited to adults: in fact, students are adept at recognizing and taking advantage of policies that offer even the smallest space for their ethnic identifications. As the remaining chapters in this section show, minority Americans of all ages and their allies treat policies as avenues of possibility, rather than a defining set of boundaries for their world.

ACKNOWLEDGEMENTS

We would like to express our gratitude to all the research participants in the Jackson Japanese Language School for sharing their views and allowing us to observe the classes. We thank the editors, Jill Koyama and Mathangi Subramanian, and anonymous reviewers for their constructive comments. All responsibility for the material discussed here remains our own.

NOTES

1. We use "mainstream education" and "mainstream educational institutions" to refer to the US education system that is in session on weekdays and "heritage language education" to refer to education at a part-time weekend or after-school heritage language school.
2. What constitutes a speaker's heritage language is not always "objectively" given but can be socially constructed, decided through negotiations of the speaker's sense of belonging and obligation, future aspirations, peer relations, availability of school programs, and family dynamics as well as others' positioning of him/her in regimes of difference in a given society (see Doerr and Lee 2013). However, in this chapter, for readability, we treat Japanese as the heritage language of all the students attending the weekend Japanese language school where we conducted ethnographic fieldwork.
3. http://www.thelanguageflagship.org/students-a-parents/critical-languages. Accessed November 11, 2013.
4. www.collegeboard.com. Accessed January 6, 2012.
5. http://www.joes.or.jp/g-kaigai/gaikoku03.html. Accessed November 11, 2013.
6. Another group of students—those who study Japanese as a foreign language—are beyond the scope of our research.

7. One student left because of the workload as well as a scheduling conflict with his sport activities. We do not know why the others left because they did not participate in this research.
8. *Eijū* and *chūzai* students were divided in that the former viewed the latter as "Japanese," as though they themselves were not. Occasions of open conflict decreased as students matured. However, as Anne's comments show, teachers and students acted on the basis of this categorization (for details see Doerr and Lee 2012, 2013).
9. See Doerr and Lee (2012) for detailed analysis of the difference between these programs.

REFERENCES

Baldwin, James. 1985. *Price of the Ticket: Collected Nonfiction, 1948–1985.* New York: St. Martin's Press.
Bourdieu, Pierre, and Jean-Claude Passeron. 1977. *Reproduction in Education, Society and Culture.* London: Sage.
Brinton, Donna M., Olga Kagan, and Susan Bauckus, eds. 2008. *Heritage Language Education: A New Field Emerging.* New York: Routledge.
Campbell, Russell N. 2003. "Directions in Research: Intergenerational Transmission of Heritage Languages." *Heritage Language Journal* 1 (1): 1–44. Accessed August 29, 2013. http://hlj.ucla.edu/Journal.aspx.
Carreira, Maria. 2004. "Seeking Explanatory Adequacy: A Dual Approach to Understanding the Term 'Heritage Language Learner.'" *Heritage Language Journal* 2 (1): 1–25. Accessed August 29, 2013. http://www.international.ucla.edu/media/files/carreira.pdf.
Chinen, Kiyomi. 2004. "Heritage Language Development: Understanding the Roles of Ethnic Identity, Attitudes, Motivation, Schooling, Family Support and Community Factors." PhD diss., Carnegie Mellon University.
Cummins, Jim. 2001 (1996). *Negotiating Identities: Education for Empowerment in a Diverse Society.* Los Angeles: California Association for Bilingual Education.
Curdt-Christiansen, Xiao Lan. 2008. "Reading the World through Words: Cultural Themes in Heritage Chinese Language Textbooks." *Language and Education* 22: 95–113.
Doerr, Neriko. 2004. "Desired Division, Disavowed Division: An Analysis of the Labeling of the Bilingual Unit as Separatist in an Aotearoa/New Zealand School." *Anthropology and Education Quarterly* 35: 233–254.
Doerr, Neriko, and Kiri Lee. 2009. "Contesting Heritage: Language, Legitimacy, and Schooling at a Weekend Japanese Language School in the United States." *Language and Education* 235: 425–441.
———. 2010. "Inheriting 'Japaneseness' Diversely: Heritage Practices at a Weekend Japanese Language School in the United States." *Critical Asian Studies* 42: 191–216.
———. 2012. "'Drop-Outs' or 'Heritage Learners'? Competing Mentalities of Governmentality and Invested Meanings at a Japanese Language School in the United States." *Discourse: Studies in the Cultural Politics of Education* 33: 1–13.
———. 2013. *Constructing the Heritage Language Learner: Knowledge, Power, and New Subjectivities.* Berlin: Mouton de Gruyter.
Frankenberg, Ruth, ed. 1997. *Displacing Whiteness: Essays in Social and Cultural Criticism.* Durham, NC: Duke University Press.
hooks, bell. 1992. *Black Looks: Race and Representation.* Boston: South End Press.
Krashen, Stephen D. 1998. "Language Shyness and Heritage Language Development." In *Heritage Language Development,* edited by Stephen D. Krashen, Lucy Tse, and Jeff McQuillan, 41–49. Culver City: Language Education Associates.

Meek, Barbra, and Jacqueline Messing. 2007. "Framing Indigenous Languages as Secondary to Matrix Languages." *Anthropology and Education Quarterly* 38: 99–118.

MEXT. 2008. *Kaigai de Manabu Nihon no Kodomotachi—Wagakuni no Kaigaishijyo Kyōuiku no Genjyō* [Japanese children overseas: Present situation in our country]. Tokyo: MEXT.

Niyozov, Sarfaroz, and Gary Pluim. 2009. "Teachers' Perspectives on the Education of Muslim Students: A Missing Voice in Muslim Education Research." *Curriculum Inquiry* 39: 637–677.

Pavlenko, Aneta. 2002. "'We Have Room for but One Language Here': Language and National Identity in the US at the Turn of the 20th Century." *Multilingual* 21: 163–196.

Peyton, Joy Kreeft, Donald A. Ranard, and Scott McGinnis. 2001. "Charting a New Course: Heritage Language Education in the United States." In *Heritage Languages in America: Preserving a National Resource*, edited by Joy Kreeft Peyton, Donald. A. Ranard, and Scott McGinnis, 3–28. McHenry: Delta Systems Co.

Sato, Gun-ei. 1997. *Kaigai/kikoku Shijokyōiku no Saikōchiku* [Reconstruction of education of overseas/returnee children: From the perspective of cross-cultural education]. Tokyo: Tamagawa University Press.

Sato, Gun-ei, and Hiroko Kataoka. 2008. *Amerika de Sodatsu Nihon no Kodomotachi* [Japanese children growing up in America]. Tokyo: Akashi Shoten.

Spoonley, Paul. 1991. "Pakeha Ethnicity: A Response to Maori Sovereignty." In *Nga Take: Ethnic Relations and Racism in Aotearoa/New Zealand*, edited by Paul Spoonley, David Pearson, and Cluny Macpherson, 154–170. Palmerston North: Dunmore Press.

Valdés, Guadalupe. 1996. *Con Respeto: Bridging the Distances between Culturally Diverse Families and Schools*. New York: Teachers College Press.

———. 2001. "Heritage Language Students: Profiles and Possibilities." In *Heritage Languages in America: Preserving a National Resource*, edited by Joy Kreeft Peyton, Donald A. Ranard, and Scott McGinnis, 37–77. McHenry, IL: Center for Applied Linguistics & Delta Systems Co., Inc.

Wiley, Terrence, and Wayne E. Wright. 2004. "Against the Undertow: Language-Minority Education Policy and Politics in the 'Age of Accountability.'" *Education Policy* 18: 142–168.

Wright, Stephen C., and Donald M. Taylor. 1995. "Identity and the Language of the Classroom: Investigating the Impact of Heritage versus Second Language Instruction on Personal and Collective Self-Esteem." *Journal of Educational Psychology* 87: 241–252.

12 In Search of Success

Where School and Marriage Meet in the Educational Lives of Immigrant African Girls with Limited Formal Schooling

Ramatu T. Bangura

On the African continent, the story of African girls and their schooling has been an evolving one. However, the stories of their schooling once they emigrate are less often told. According to the 2010 US Census, 1.5 million Africans are living in the US, making up 4% of the immigrant population (Capps et al. 2005; Capps, McCabe, and Fix 2011). Although Africans have migrated extensively between countries on the African continent and to former colonizing powers such as England and France, migration to the US is relatively recent, spurred initially by the 1965 Immigration Act, which abolished national quotas and made it legal to migrate to the US from the Global South, and more recently by family reunification visas and refugee visas for conflict areas and the Diversity Visa program. The US is now the third most likely emigration destination, after England and France, for Africans (Capps, McCabe, and Fix 2011). Forty percent of these Africans live in just four states: New York, California, Texas, and Maryland (Wilson 2003). Washington, DC, Maryland, and Rhode Island have the highest proportions of Africans. For example, in Silver Spring, Maryland, 35.2% of the foreign-born population is African immigrants. Given the rapid growth of these communities and the limited research about African populations, it is becoming essential for educators to learn more about how best to serve the children of these immigrants.

One of the challenges many newly arriving African immigrants face is interrupted schooling. In New York State, these young people are given the designation of students with interrupted formal education (SIFE). SIFE are a subset of the English language learner (ELL) population who come from a home where a language other than English is spoken, who have had two fewer years of schooling than their peers, who function at least two years below expected grade level in reading and in mathematics, and who may be preliterate in their first language (Klein and Martohardjono 2006). SIFE who have had sporadic or no formal schooling prior to emigrating are most often older high school students requiring significant remediation. Most SIFE are Spanish speakers (64%), with more than half coming from the Dominican Republic. However, New York City (NYC) schools are increasingly enrolling SIFE from African countries speaking languages such as Fulani and Bambara (Capps, McCabe, and Fix 2011; Office of English Language Learners 2009). The cultural and linguistic diversity of the SIFE population poses the most significant challenge to developing policies and practices that meet the needs of these students.

This chapter centers on the voices and the meaning making of African girls to understand how three African immigrant girls—Bintou, Fanta, and Djenebou—negotiate and utilize marriage in support of their educational goals. These young women share cultural expectations about the appropriate age for marriage, as well as the SIFE designation of low literacy ELLs. Consequently, they simultaneously encounter expectations associated with adolescence and adulthood in the space of high school. Given the limited time they have to make up lost educational ground before facing the impending socioeconomic realities of adulthood with severely truncated educations, the stakes for these students are high (Fine et al. 2007). For these young women, early marriage is a form of what Das Gupta (2006) calls space-making, or the process of finding ways to broaden possibilities for identity and power within institutions and structures that may be oppressive. Sometimes space-making practices address the strictures imposed by the coethnics in a diasporic community. Other times, they push against the boundaries imposed by outsiders. As the findings in this chapter demonstrate, SIFE African girls strategically use marriage as a way to address constraints imposed by both insiders and outsiders from their communities.

IMMIGRANT GIRLS, SCHOOLING, AND "TRADITION"

The challenges of education in sub-Saharan Africa become exponentially more numerous and complicated when the gaze is turned solely to girls (UNESCO and UNICEF 2005). Poor and low-income girls living in rural areas are significantly disadvantaged with regard to school access and quality. For example, the Forum of African Women Educationists (Shabaya and Konadu-Agyemang 2004) reports that in areas where equal numbers of girls are enrolled in the first grade, only half of the female students are still in school by the fourth grade; nearly two-thirds will leave school before they have acquired full literacy; and only 34% will complete primary school. By age 16, fewer girls than boys are in school in nearly every country in sub-Saharan Africa (Shabaya and Konadu-Agyemang 2004). Although gains have been made in ensuring access to primary schooling for children in sub-Saharan Africa, the quality of their education is tested when they enter secondary school or when they migrate abroad and attempt to make use of their educations; often, their preparation is revealed to be inadequate.

Despite the increased migration of young women from the Global South to more industrialized nations, the research concerned with their schooling experiences has been limited. Existing studies tend to either compare immigrant adolescent females to males from their same communities (Qin-Hilliard 2003) or offer a comparison to the experiences of their American-born female peers (Olsen 1997; Suárez-Orozco 1999). The research that does exist on immigrant young women within their ethnic groups suggests that immigrant young women are passive adherents of their more restrictive home cultures and these oppressive norms may offer a shield of ethnicity that protects them from social risk factors that might negatively impact their grades and career aspirations (Suárez-Orozco 1999; Subramanian, this volume; Baolian Qin 2009). Further, Lee's (2005) ethnography documents how Hmong girls who exhibit more traditional characteristics of being quiet, passive, and obedient were more likely to be classified as successful students than those who were framed as more American. While being labeled traditional can be helpful for girls to be considered successful students by Western standards, it becomes problematic in the context of early marriage, in which school staff want young women to stand up to their families and defy expectations of tradition (Olsen 1997). The refusal to stand up for themselves ("Youth Voices Stand Up" 2011) reinforces perceptions of traditional girls as helpless sympathetic characters (Lee 2005) faced with oppressive cultural demands (Monekosso 2001).

High schools where students marry become negotiated spaces where young women's decisions about marriage are viewed as an expression of their opposition to or collusion with positive educational outcomes (Ngo 2009). However, Ngo (2009) questions whether a young woman's decision to enter into an early marriage can easily be translated into a desire for or rejection of school success, or whether the decision-making process is more complex. Lee (2005) cautions educators to give girls the opportunity to balance "multiple worlds and consider a range of life choices" (Lee 2005, 6), without automatically condemning early marriage or other such politicized points of cultural difference. Ngo (2009) warns that excessive concern with these narratives of generational and cultural conflict serves to deflect attention from the "politics of exclusion and differentiation prevalent in immigrants' lives" (Ngo 2009, 203). Rather than depending on constructions of immigrant girls as ethnically shielded from social ills and unable to exercise their agency, the work of Ngo (2002, 2009) and Lee (2005) portrays young women as actively engaging their life choices in unfamiliar and inequitable racial, gendered, and socioeconomic contexts. In fact, using Das Gupta's (2006) terminology, the authors consider these young women to be space-makers who see marriage as tool for expanding their possibilities, educational or otherwise. This study contributes to this body of work, demonstrating how West African immigrant young women make choices that render marriage and education mutually beneficial, rather than mutually exclusive, categories.

METHODOLOGY

The three young women featured in this chapter—Bintou (age twenty), Fanta (age nineteen), and Djenebou (age eighteen)—share experiences that are representative of the perspectives of the fourteen African immigrant girls who participated in this study. I recruited them using snowball sampling: as I encountered participants through outreach to schools and community agencies, I asked them to suggest other potential participants. I chose participants based on their consistency with SIFE characteristics, identification as African, and their age. The semistructured interviews covered their backgrounds in both the US and Africa; their insights into their schooling experiences; their hopes and expectations for their educational, professional, and family lives; and the assets and the challenges they encounter. I also spent three to six hours observing the participants in their school settings and/or while they were interacting with their peers. In addition, I invited participants to keep journals documenting the time they spent seeking help and support in their educational pursuits. All interviews were tape-recorded and transcribed. Names have been changed to pseudonyms.

I coded each line of the transcripts and journals for emergent themes of education, decision making, and family planning. Codes were identified based on the number of times they occurred across the participants, their omission despite my expectation that they might arise, and those that participants explicitly identified (LeCompte 2000). I then reevaluated themes to combine some, diminish the importance of others, and confirm the primacy of others (Charmaz 2006). I identified three themes relating to marriage and schooling: marriage as facilitative, marriage as prohibitive, and the wait-and-see approach. The participants' attitudes shifted throughout the course of this study, as their life circumstances changed and as their academic prospects evolved. I mapped each participant's evolving perspectives on marriage over time as well as onto their evolving notions of their educational outlook to understand how the two impacted each other.

Most of the young women in this study hid their marital status and/ or the pressures to marry in their lives from the school staff because they were "particularly sensitive to what mainstream Americans think about early marriage" (Lee 2005, 98). I attribute their willingness to talk to me about marriage to a perceived shared cultural and religious background (I am a second generation Sierra Leonean immigrant and a Muslim), as well as to their understanding of my role as the director of a youth program serving African immigrant girls in NYC. However, I do not come from a community that practices early marriage and am not married myself. The combination of these factors created both opportunities and blind spots in data collection and analysis. For example, I found that I needed to call participants following our earlier meetings to clarify their interpretations of events to ensure that I did not impose my own. Further, I found that the participants used the fact that I was unmarried as a point of comparison between myself and the women in their lives. For example, the participants would describe women in their lives as being "like you (me)" or not. Finally, I found that I had access to resources and information that the girls did not; I chose to share them. Wherever possible, I documented those interactions and included them in the data.

These interviews, observations, and journals produced an intimate documentation of the participants' deliberations on their futures and their families. The stories that follow shed light on a complex process in which education, family challenges, and beliefs about future life prospects mediate gendered and age-specific expectations of marriage. These young women are struggling to control the circumstances under which they marry and find that marriage both limits and enables their efforts to further their education.

MARRIAGE AS FACILITATIVE: BINTOU'S STORY

Bintou is a wife, mother, and nursing student in her first year at a community college. During her sophomore year of high school, she entered into a marriage that her mother and stepmother[1] arranged with her consultation. She explained, "I wanted someone who was nice and wasn't too old and who went to school" (Interview, January 4, 2011). She explained that a husband with these characteristics would understand the struggles of a student. When I asked her husband's age, she refused to answer specifically but indicated that he was in his thirties.

Bintou is Fulani and from Labé, Guinea's second-largest city, where she farmed with her mother and her four siblings before coming to the US. In Guinea, Bintou's family allowed her to attend school because they saw her as a particularly hardworking student. However, her mother struggled to pay for her and her siblings' schooling: "The financial thing wasn't easy. I love my mom. She did a lot of things for us. She take care of us and she advise us to go to school and study so she don't want us to be like her because she never went to school" (Interview, January 4, 2011). Her financial struggles meant that Bintou could only attend school irregularly. She said that missing so much school was "very difficult. Your friend is going to school and you—you staying home."

She joined her father and his current wife in NYC at age fifteen. Despite reading at what she was told was a fourth-grade level, Bintou was placed in the ninth grade because of her age. She was not placed in any literacy or ESL classes although she was officially designated as SIFE. Bintou enjoyed high school and was considered a leader among many of the students, especially the African female students. For example, when a new African girl arrived at her school, both teachers and students connected her with Bintou as a first step. Teachers and other students also utilized her leadership skills to help orient and encourage other students:

Bintou: I was good student because, by the end [of the school year], I get awards. . . . Sometimes I get two or three. That's the way like, you know, all the teachers they will show how you care for them.

Ramatu: So you think your teachers would describe you also as a good student?

Bintou: Yeah, actually they talk to me about it. They always talk to me cause sometimes they always ask me, OK so you should give some of your friends advice. You know, they should do this, they should do that cause they always see me put in lot of effort, all my studying and they always try to tell all my friends to do the same thing. (Interview, January 4, 2011)

Given this role among the African students, her choice to marry was particularly troubling to her high school teachers, school counselors, and social workers. They responded to her marriage by advising her on how to "deal" with her husband. Bintou explained:

People like in America, they felt like to get married young it's not good. . . . But I don't like when I was in—in high school they was—some teachers they always tell me, "OK, when you go home don't cook—don't tell your husband—don't cook for your husband. Don't this, don't do that." I say, "OK, fine." "Don't have children now." But I wanted to have a kid. So I always say, "OK, OK" but I know what I want. (Interview, January 4, 2011)

Their advice reflected an assumption that Bintou's husband would not want her to do well in school and that Bintou would have little say in the dynamics of the relationship. In reality, Bintou's husband encouraged her to do well in school, and provided her with the economic stability she needed to focus on her studies.

Bintou dismissed her teachers' warnings about marriage by saying that they "just didn't understand my culture" (Interview, January 4, 2011). While she had a positive view of her teachers' ability to help her with academic questions, Bintou did not trust them with "cultural" questions. She knew of several young women who felt this way and simply tolerated the advice of school staff and hid their marital status. Bintou refused to do so: "Some people ask me, 'We heard that you got married.' I tell them yes!" Her candidness about her marriage and her subsequent pregnancy also elicited unwanted concern from the hospital social worker. She recounted:

When I was pregnant, I went to the hospital and I was seventeen and there was like a social worker. She wanted to talk to me. She say, "Are you married?" I said, "Yes." She say, "Did your parents force you?" I tell them, "No." They say, "So, why you get married so early?" I say, "Because that was my choice." (Interview, January 4, 2011)

Bintou became a mother in her junior year of high school. She only missed four weeks of school and she was able to return in time for her Regents Exams, tests which are required to earn a diploma in New York State. She noticed that her teachers no longer utilized her to orient new students, a trend she attributed to her marriage and pregnancy. This attitude presents a stark contrast to that of the administrators that A. Chen (this volume) interviewed in her chapter, who saw themselves as allies who wanted to understand the realities of undocumented immigrants and help them navigate institutional obstacles with their support. Bintou characterized her interactions with adults as based in a lack of understanding or willingness to help her negotiate educational spaces given her choices and constraints.

However, Bintou's ability to secure a husband who supported her education, provided for her and her family financially, and allowed her to have a child with minimal interruption to her education raised her status among her peers, who still asked her to help newcomers. Bintou seemed to relish how her marriage affirmed her strong identification with her Fulani culture, a fact she shared with her peers when discussing the benefits of getting married sooner rather than later. When advising other immigrant African young women, she would say:

You have to think what is your—what is your best thing to do. Have to think of your own life. You know like don't just come from Africa and say OK I'm going to take American style. Think about your home culture too. (Interview, January 4, 2011)

As young women continued to come to her for advice, she would also warn them that it was not easy to be a mother and wife and still be a student. She would tell them, "You can do it but you have to be very strong and very organized. You can't just go out to parties and say you're going to do well [in school]" (Interview, January 4, 2011). Bintou passed her Regents Exams and graduated high school on time, in large part due to the support of her husband and her stepmother.

As a high school student, she took advantage of the childcare provided in her school building by the New York City Department of Education. However, as a college student, Bintou was prompted by the lack of childcare and her intense work and class schedule to send her daughter to her mother in Guinea. She planned to have her daughter return during the summer. Bintou saw her relationship with her husband and their marriage as a way to facilitate her college-going. She did not have to worry financially: "My husband, he supports me 'cause he's the one who pays all the bills" (Interview, January 4, 2011). With the money she earned at her job, she was able to financially support her mother and siblings back home.

I'm working and I'm—for myself I support my parents. He always tell me to help my parents because he's taking care of the bills. . . . I pay for my siblings. I have like, one of my mom's siblings and one of my cousins and I have my sister and my brother. I pay for those three kids to go to school. And this year, I send my mom to Hajj (Interview, January 4, 2011).

Bintou and I shared the recent achievement of sending our parents on the Islamic pilgrimage at least once in their lives. This was a major financial accomplishment for Bintou. She also discussed how her husband's reasonable domestic expectations enabled her to focus more time on her studies:

My husband is an easy guy. Easy, easy! He don't tell you, you know, "cook this, cook that." No. 'Cause sometimes there's times I ask him "What do you want me to cook for us?" He say, "Cook whatever you like." If I go home and see that I like it, OK, I'm going to eat it if I'm hungry. On that side I don't have any problems like with housework (Interview, January 4, 2011).

Bintou's studies are going relatively well. She has been able to pass most of the remedial classes her college required her to take and expects to start the courses for her major the following year. She has a job as a nurse's aide and a clear plan for transitioning to a career in nursing. She had originally wanted to become a doctor, but given her time restraints and the money she had already spent on remediation, she felt nursing was a better way for her to achieve her goal of helping people.

Bintou is happy with her choices and feels that she picked her husband well. She admitted that her experience is not widely replicated across her community. Although Bintou warned other girls that "it's not easy," her adoption of these expectations in the face of discouragement from teachers and hospital social workers facilitated significant support from her family in the US and enabled financial support for her family in Guinea.

Marriage facilitated Bintou's transition to college as it allowed her to continue with her studies and to provide for her mother in Guinea. While Bintou was the clearest example among the participants of marriage facilitating schooling, six of the other participants discussed the possibility that marriage could facilitate their education, such as by enabling them to get more financial aid by filing independently and allowing them more freedom of movement to work and study. They also discussed the ways that getting married might free them from the gossip associated with trying to be a normal (Lesko 2001) teenager. While Bintou's story suggests that marriage is relatively uncomplicated and possibly facilitative, Bintou's clarity in her decision making was not shared across all of the participants, especially when their educational aspirations did not align with the expectations of their families.

FANTA: WAIT AND SEE

Fanta is a nineteen-year-old high school senior from Conakry, Guinea, who was raised by her grandmother. She said, "We was raised in a huge family because my grandfather had four wives and I was raised with my grand-mother and my two step-grandmothers"[2] (Interview, November 10, 2010). Fanta's parents were able to send money to her grandmother to pay for Fanta to go to a good school in Guinea. She experienced gaps in schooling due to one year in Senegal preparing her visa to come to the US and an extended ill-ness that caused her to miss eighteen months of school, during which time she spent four months in the hospital and then the rest of the time at home with her mother utilizing "African medicines" (Interview, November 10, 2010).

Fanta described herself as a pretty good student. She is literate in French, reading at a sixth-grade level. While Fanta did not find high school to be too difficult, she struggled with the Regents Exams: "When I take the prac-tice tests I do so good, like eighty-five and ninety. But when it's time for Regents I fail it so bad" (Interview, March 14, 2011).

She joined her parents and three younger siblings in Brooklyn five years ago. Fanta spoke frequently of missing her grandmother and her sense of freedom in Guinea: "I had so much freedom then like to do what I want, to make my own choice. Now they control me too much. Now that I'm here, like, sometimes I feel like I'm not loved enough like I was before" (Inter-view, February 3, 2011). Several of the research participants described how their freedom of movement diminished when they came to the US because of their parents' safety concerns.

The reunification with her family has been difficult for Fanta. She said, "They don't know me at all. My dad accuses me of some terrible things that make me think, 'you don't know me. I would never do those type of things'" (Interview, November 10, 2010). His accusations generally center on her interaction with boys at school and her refusal to wear the *hijab*, the head covering traditionally worn by some Muslim women. So as not to upset her father, she wears the *hijab* on her way to school, takes it off only after she gets into the school building, and puts it back on when she goes home.

The conflicts with her father and the challenges of family reunification after nearly a decade of separation factored significantly into Fanta's college plans. During our first interview, Fanta shared that she and her mother's youngest sister have devised a strategy for Fanta to go to college in Ohio, where the sister lives, as an appropriate way for her to leave her parents' home. She explained:

> First of all, I want to go to college. You know how getting married is important in my culture? I want to get away from hearing that word first. And that will happen by me going away for college. I'm applying to go away for school. I have a family there . . . so I think they're [her parents] OK (Interview, November 10, 2010).

In May, Fanta and I met to check the university's online system for the status of her application. We learned that the school had not received a recommendation letter. Fanta was surprised by this and visibly upset. She had submitted the request to her guidance counselor for a recommendation early in the process. Before calling the admissions office, we discussed what she should say. When she called, she was told that she could still submit the forms and that if she was accepted she would be placed on the waiting list. Fanta was distraught. She had not applied to any other school out of state because her parents would not allow her to go anywhere else:

> If I stay here, my dad will say he has to drive me to school. I won't be able to go to the library. Only go to class and go home. It's too much stress. If I get married then he can't tell me nothing if my husband say it's OK. (Interview, March 14, 2011)

Fanta had been cultivating a relationship with a young man in France whose family was connected to hers. He seemed to be a good prospect because he is a graduate student, Fulani, and a Muslim. However, she would probably need to move to France to be with him: "He says he don't want to come to America. I told him my French is not that good anymore. He says I can learn it again and then go to college, but I don't know" (Interview, March 14, 2011). She also liked that he is "still young. I can talk to him about current stuff."

In the midst of all of this decision making, Fanta still had to take Regents Exams. In late June, I expected to hear from Fanta that she would be graduating. However, she called to tell me that she had not passed her Global Studies exam. She earned a sixty-three when she needed a sixty-five and thus would not be able to graduate with her class. She planned to take a Regents prep course in July and retake the exam. She said that she would make no plans about her future until she passed the exam.

After I completed data collection, I learned she graduated in August after taking a Regents prep summer course. She went to visit the young man and his family in France for one week. She said that the visit went well, but that she wanted to wait one year to see if she could get into college in Ohio, where her parents would permit her to attend college. Her parents were hopeful that she would choose to marry the young man in France. Fanta was determined to go to school and seemed ambivalent about getting married. However, marriage was an option if schooling in Ohio did not materialize. Fanta believed that if she adamantly refused to get married, then her parents might physically force her and she would lose all say in choosing her future husband. In our last conversation, she was not sure how long her family would wait, but she planned to keep a good relationship with the young man in France just in case.

For Fanta, marriage felt inevitable. At that moment in her life, it might not have been the most desirable option, but it felt like a strategic possibility if she was not able to make schooling work in a way that was acceptable to her family. Not getting into college in Ohio, where she could live with her extended family, closed off an acceptable route to an education and made marriage less avoidable in the short run. Marriage, although not her first choice, might allow Fanta to attend school, albeit in France, with some control over the circumstances.

DJENEBOU: MARRIAGE AS PROHIBITIVE

Djenebou was an expressive eighteen-year-old from Mali. She and her mother came to the US to join her father. When they arrived, they learned that her father had taken another wife, although Djenebou believes her mother knew before they arrived. Her father, the new wife, and their two children live in a two-bedroom apartment in the Bronx. Djenebou shared a room with her mother in the crowded apartment. Tensions were high in the household. "My mother don't say nothing. My stepmother don't like me at all. Anytime my father buys me something, she complains and he have to buy something for her kids" (Interview, December 21, 2010).

Despite the challenges she faced here, Djenebou was glad she came to the US because "I have more opportunities here than in Mali. Being poor here is different than being poor in Mali. At least here I can be somebody" (Interview, November 10, 2010). She and her mother shuttled between the residences of different family members because her father was inconsistent in sending enough money for them to pay the rent and eat. She did not always get along with the extended family members:

> I was always fighting because they want me to come in their house like a slave. Their own kids don't have to clean all day and take care of their own brothers and sisters. But, me, they want me to do it. The last time my father's sister told me to leave school to take care of her child we argue and I called my Dad in America. He told me and my mother to go to his brother in the village. (Interview, November 10, 2010)

In all of this moving around, Djenebou attended school sporadically and had to drop out often due to unpaid school fees or because she and her mother moved. Djenebou's father, now a US citizen, sent for her and her mother two years ago, when Djenebou was sixteen years old. Djenebou was immediately placed in the ninth grade. She did not know what her reading level was, but she was placed in a SIFE class that she called her literacy class; I confirmed her SIFE designation through visits to her school. During this study, Djenebou was in the eleventh grade and had just graduated from the SIFE class. She still received regular literacy tutoring after school from the SIFE teacher. Despite the significant gaps in her schooling, she described her grades as strong. During my observation of one of her before-school math tutoring sessions, her teacher described her as "extremely gifted" in math. Djenebou attributed her good grades to her hard work and hoped to become an engineer. The journal she kept for this study indicated that she spent every morning before and after school in tutoring or Regents prep. She did not get home most nights until after 8:00 p.m. because she would go to the library to do homework. When asked why she spent so much time out of the house, she answered that her home life had become unbearable. She explained, "Miss, I can't go back to that house. I can't even think. The noise is too much. My stepmother can't see me sitting down. She has to tell me to do something" (Interview, December 21, 2010).

In the late winter, her relationship with her family deteriorated to the point that Djenebou left home and stayed with friends for two weeks. Her father eventually insisted that she come home with promises that the relationship with her stepmother would improve. Upon her return, her mother told her that her father was planning a marriage for her within the next six months. According to Djenebou, her mother was supposed to keep the marriage secret, but decided not to because she knew that any surprise would not go well for the family because of Djenebou's fiery temper. Djenebou said that she knew the plans were underway because her father made comments like, "'If you were married, we wouldn't be going through this right now.' And then sometimes they say, 'Girls your age in Mali already have four kids. If you were there, you'd already be having your third child right now' (Interview, December 21, 2010)"

The impending marriage weighed heavily on Djenebou and she felt that there were few people she could talk to. Despite all of these challenges, Djenebou's attendance was among the best at her school. She rarely missed a day and wanted to attend a four-year university. Although her father had no issue with her desire to go to college, he would rather she marry first. Djenebou explained, "They don't want me to go to college in their house. That way if anything happens then, it's not their problem" (Interview, March 11, 2011). Like many of the young women in this study, the "anything" their families referred to was mainly out-of-wedlock pregnancy. Djenebou had a boyfriend who was in college, but she did not believe her father knew about the boyfriend. She also did not factor him into her future decisions: "He is nice now but you don't know what's in the future" (Interview, December 21, 2010). The fact that he was from Nigeria also seemed to make her uncertain about any future together: "His family want him to marry somebody from his culture, so I don't think we can get married."

When I asked Djenebou if her mother could be supportive, she said, "She's not a strong lady like you, Miss. She just keeps quiet and don't say nothing" (Interview, May 12, 2011). She also said that her mother knew of the boyfriend and was afraid that Djenebou's father would find out, or worse, that Djenebou would get pregnant. Any evidence of sexual activity, whether or not it resulted in pregnancy, might make it more difficult for her father to find Djenebou a husband.

Djenebou's friends did not support her either. She said that most of them thought she should just get married:

> When I say I want to get married at twenty-five and they're like twenty-five is too old to get married. They're like, it's better to get married early because all your friends are getting married and you're gonna be the one like out there by yourself . . . they think marriage is like the only place for women. (Interview, March 11, 2011)

Djenebou exhibited several symptoms of depression, including difficulty sleeping and concentrating. She reached out to a few of her teachers, but they seemed unsure of what to do and often asked me how they should handle the situation. While her teachers and guidance counselor were supportive of her decision not to marry, they offered her little in the way of support that would help her deal with the consequences of defying her father, such as alternative housing or schooling options if she was forced to leave her father's home. Further, Djenebou worried that they would call the police on her father. Consequently, she felt she could not tell them too much. During the course of our relationship, I helped Djenebou complete employment applications and we practiced interviewing for different jobs. Over the course of the school year, she got two jobs in retail, but the hours became too demanding and it was difficult for her to do her schoolwork.

As the data collection phase of this study came to a close, Djenebou and I spent much time discussing her dreams, her concerns about marriage, and my work with African girls, partly because Djenebou often tried to avoid going home, but also because I found her to be an extremely engaging person. While she felt responsible for her mother, Djenebou feared becoming too much like her. Her model of marriage was an abusive one in which her mother's inability to provide financially for herself and her children forced her to tolerate the disrespect of her husband and the second wife. I questioned her on how she believed young women get into such relationships:

> I don't know. And like they don't have so much confidence in themselves and I feel like so many girls they are very smart more than they think they are but . . . I don't know. I used to be like that. I don't know what got me here but I think they need to be pushed to realize and to be trained to be able to make better choices. (Interview, March 11, 2011)

By the end of the school year, things had calmed. Her father continued to invite prospective husbands that he called "friends" over to eat with the family on Fridays after the Islamic congregational prayer. Djenebou tried to ignore them and often aimed to be out of the house when she thought they might be coming to visit. She and her stepmother had reached a stalemate, with neither one talking to the other. Djenebou braided hair on weekends for extra money and is still looking for a job that will enable her to rent a room for her and her mother. She knows that she will eventually have to leave her father's home when he decides it is time for her to get married. Also, like Bintou, Djenebou knew that she would eventually be responsible for financially supporting her mother. She considered dropping out of school to get her high school equivalency because of the flexibility in the class schedule; however, her school guidance counselor told her that it might take her more time to finish the high school equivalency than it would to get her high school diploma. Given the stress that Djenebou was under and the limited resources afforded her by the school guidance team, I referred her to services at my agency. Due to the agency's confidentiality guidelines, I do not know the outcome of that intervention. Djenebou passed two of her five Regents Exams at the end of the school year and planned to return in the fall.

THE COMPLEXITIES OF MARRIAGE AND SCHOOLING

The stories of Bintou, Fanta, and Djenebou offer glimpses into the complexity of future planning and decision making for immigrant young women who may have little control over the circumstances of their schooling or marriage. The young women's words reveal the maneuverings and the compromises they make in the face of educational uncertainties. Bintou's case demonstrates how early marriage can facilitate continued schooling; in contrast, Djenebou's case illustrates how marrying early can threaten to derail a young woman's educational trajectory. For Fanta, marriage was something in between—an option if her plans for attending college did not materialize. Despite holding differing perspectives on when to marry, each of these young women hoped for husbands who would be supportive of her schooling. Rather than a foregone conclusion, schooling after high school was a privilege dependent upon the decisions they made regarding their spouse and their marriage.

Postcolonial feminists have offered insight into the ways in which women in the Global South have resisted binary-laden proposals for their lives— traditional or modern, African or Western, and wife or student. Rather than accept messages that schooling and marriage are incompatible, these young women are creating a third way to simultaneously achieve the ideal their families have for them and their personal goals of leaving their family home in an appropriate way while reaching their academic goals. Because early marriage and motherhood run contrary to the hegemonic notions of Western youth femininity, they create a point of intervention for educators and social workers seeking to help, armed with Western feminist beliefs that education is a necessary passage en route to freedom from the confines of culture (Narayan 1997). However, as evidenced by Bintou's encounters with her teachers and the hospital social worker, narrow constructions of acceptable studenthood and adolescence coupled with stereotypes of African women's perpetual victimization at the hands of African men only serve to discredit those services in the eyes of young women who might otherwise use them. Conversely, Djenebou's case illustrates that even when young women make the personal choice to marry later—a decision that is more consistent with Western values—educators are ill equipped to help young African immigrant women navigate the consequences of resisting their families. Although these young women spent significant time outside the school day receiving literacy and other academic help, they did not rely on their teachers as they planned their futures, whether or not they chose to get married.

The framing of early and forced marriage as solely generational and cultural conflict deflects attention from the "politics of exclusion and differentiation prevalent in immigrants' lives" (Ngo 2009) and limits the policy options that could improve the educational outcomes for this student population. Given the advanced age of most SIFE, they must be engaged as central actors in any intervention designed to better support them. These interventions should not only address their educational shortcomings but factor in their adult responsibilities of marriage, transnational financial obligations, and parenthood. Interventions should also provide them with educational and work opportunities, because financial independence was a key factor influencing the decisions of the women in this study. This approach would require a realistic assessment of the young women's educational prospects in the context of policies that promote alternative paths to graduation and post–high school careers. While tales of cultural conflict and parental conflict were also prevalent in the stories of these young women, more prevalent were structural challenges that limited their access to schooling and kept them from fulfilling their academic needs. For example, Fanta's college advisor may have best served Fanta by exploring other colleges in Ohio that may have been supportive of her educational goals. Djenebou's counselor may have been more effective if she had understood that family challenges and pressure to get married put her at risk for homelessness, and that Djenebou needed support finding alternative housing and employment opportunities that would help her become independent enough to make her own decisions while supporting her mother.

Finally, poverty was the overwhelming reason that the young women left school or never attended school in their countries of origin. By extension, economic insecurity was an undercurrent in many of our conversations about marriage. Based on reports from the young women, parents advocating or imposing marriage made the case to their daughters that their husbands would ensure they would be provided for, as was the case for both Bintou and Djenebou. In this way, they were not only trying to secure their daughters' futures in a religious or cultural sense, but also in this context of low-income urban communities in the US. The young women in the most precarious academic situations planned to get married sooner. Those who were doing well tended to play with the idea of postponing marriage. The lack of realistic talk about the post–high school economic prospects of youth with limited to no formal schooling undermines any effort to address early marriage. Furthermore, as financial distress becomes more widespread, particularly among women and children of color, the US should implement more effective poverty alleviation strategies targeted at low-income immigrant populations.

The findings in this chapter also demonstrate the resilience and adaptability of immigrant women and girls in the face of policies created with little or no acknowledgment of the reality of students' lives. Rather than accept the boundaries of their worlds, the women in this chapter used the tools at their disposal—in this case, marriage—to remake and expand their access to education. Such negotiations often go unnoticed because of the intersection of these women's identities: as mentioned above, as low-income women of color from the Global South, the participants in this study are often dismissed as passive victims of their circumstances (Suárez-Orozco 1999; Subramanian this volume; Baolian Qin 2009). Additionally, the agency they exercise in their decisions often goes unnoticed, particularly when associated with culturally influenced practices like marriage. This chapter demonstrates that, in fact, the opposite is true. The creative negotiation of restricted spaces is an essential element of the story of African women's immigration experiences in the US.

Although the stories of Bintou, Fanta, and Djenebou are not likely to make the covers of American women's magazines, they present a version of the modern woman's dilemma. The young women who participated in this study are trying to figure out how to have it all—family, education, career, children, and social credibility. This chapter offers insight into the negotiations, obstacles, and achievements inherent in this struggle, which is punctuated by the social inequities faced by immigrant young women of color in America's cities. A deeper understanding of the process of early and forced marriage can inform more effective and culturally specific policies that protect children impacted by this practice and empower young women to make choices that benefit themselves, their families, and their communities.

NOTES

1. I learned from my work that many of the young women referred to their father's other wives in polygamous families as their "stepmothers." This use of the term was confirmed by both Bintou and Djenebou.
2. Again, I assume these women are her grandfather's wives.

REFERENCES

Baolian Qin, Desiree. 2009. "Being 'Good' or Being 'Popular': Gender and Ethnic Identity Negotiations of Chinese Immigrant Adolescents." *Journal of Adolescent Research* 24 (1): 37–66.

Capps, Randy, Michael Fix, Julie Murray, Jason Ost, and Jeffrey S. Passel. 2005. *The New Demography of America's Schools: Immigration and the No Child Left Behind Education Act.* New York: Urban Institute.

Capps, Randy, Kristen McCabe, and Michael Fix. 2011. *New Streams: Black African Migration to the United States.* Washington, DC: Migration Policy Institute.

Fine, M., R. Jaffe-Walter, P. Pedraza, V. Futch, and B. Stoudt. 2007. "Swimming: On Oxygen, Resistance, and Possibility for Immigrant Youth under Siege." *Anthropology and Education Quarterly* 38 (1): 76–96.

Klein, Elaine C., and Gita Martohardjono. 2006. *Understanding the Student with Interrupted Formal Education (SIFE): A Study of SIFE Skills, Needs and Achievement.* New York: Research Institute for the Study of Language in Urban Society, CUNY Graduate Center (RISLUS).

LeCompte, Margaret D. 2000. "Analyzing Qualitative Data." *Theory into Practice* 39(3): 146–154.

Lee, Stacy J. 2005. *Up against Whiteness: Race, School, and Immigrant Youth.* New York: Teachers College Press.

Monekosso, Ticky. 2001. "Africa's Forced Marriages." BBC World. http://news.bbc.co.uk/2/hi/africa/1209099.stm.

Narayan, Uma. 1997. *Dislocating Cultures: Identities, Traditions, and Third World Feminism.* New York: Routledge.

Ngo, Bic. 2009. "Ambivalent Urban, Immigrant Identities: The Incompleteness of Lao American Student Identities." *International Journal of Qualitative Studies in Education* 22 (2): 201–220.

Office of English Language Learners. 2009. *Diverse Learners on the Road to Success: The Performance of New York City's English Language Learners.* New York: City of New York Department of Education.

Olsen, Laurie. 1997. "Love and Marriage: How Young Immigrant Women Negotiate the Terrain between Cultures." In *Made in America: Immigrant Students in Our Public Schools*, 121–149. New York: New Press.

Qin-Hilliard, Desireé. 2003. "Gendered expectations and gendered experiences: Immigrant students' adaptation in schools. *New Directions for Youth Development* 100: 91–109.

Shabaya, Judith and Kwadwo Konadu-Agyemangba. 2004. "Unequal access, unequal participation: some spatial and socio-economic dimensions of the gender gap in education in Africa with special reference to Ghana, Zimbabwe and Kenya." *Compare* 34(4): 395–424.

Suárez-Orozco, Marcelo M. 1999. "Immigrant Children: What Do We Know? What Do Schools Need to Do?" Keynote Address. All Means All Conference. The School District of Philadelphia. March 13, 1999.

UNESCO and UNICEF. 2005. *Children out of School: Measuring Exclusion from Primary Education.* Montreal: UNESCO Institute for Statistics.

Wilson, Jill. 2003. "African Immigrants in Metropolitan Washington: A Demographic Overview." Paper presented at the African Immigrants and Refugees Foundation Conference, Washington, DC, November 18.

"Youth Voices Stand Up against Child Marriage at the White House." 2011. *United Nations Foundation.* July 18. Accessed October 23, 2011. http://www.girlup.org/newsroom/press-releases/youth-voices-stand-out.html.

13 (Counter)Storytelling for Social Change

Pathways for Youth Participation in Policymaking

Mathangi Subramanian

From education to the criminal justice system, from reproductive rights to immigration, some of today's most visible and controversial reform movements directly and intimately impact young men and women of color. Despite the potentially dramatic effects these reforms have on their lives, institutionalized structures limit or exclude youth from policy conversations (Delgado and Staples 2006; Ginwright, Cammarota, and Noguera 2005). These exclusionary practices range from a voting age that bars young people from the ballot box; to scheduling hearings, rallies, and policy-related conversations and actions during the school day; to valuing data generated by advanced degree holders and quantitative approaches more than personal experience; to No Child Left Behind–era curricula that emphasize rote learning over critical thinking skills. As a result, young people have few opportunities to participate in the policymaking process, and policies created without input from the populations they are meant to serve reproduce and reinforce existing power structures that oppress young people of color.

Despite their exclusion from the political process, historically, youth have led movements that have resulted in widespread social change (Delgado and Staples 2006; Ginwright and James 2002; Ginwright, Cammarota, and Noguera 2005). From the Civil Rights movement of the 1960s, to educational reform efforts spearheaded by the Urban Youth Collaborative in New York City, to the Books Not Bars campaign in the Bay Area, youth have successfully organized and advocated for racial and educational justice for themselves and their communities.

Ginwright, Cammarota, and Noguera (2005) have identified a set of practices common to successful youth organizing movements. These include building social capital through connecting with community-based organizations, nurturing positive relationships with adults, and being exposed to "broad networks of informational exchange about political issues, ideas, and events" (33). Additionally, youth development experts claim that leadership development for youth organizers is most effective when youth can engage in identity work that allows them to personally understand how power functions in social structures, organize collective action involving disparate groups that share common interests and goals, and take advantage of popular culture to structure message campaigns and to recruit other youth to their cause (Delgado and Staples 2006; Ginwright and James 2002; Roth and Brooks-Gunn 2003). Youth development scholars culled these patterns from commonalities between successful social change movements led by young people.

Unfortunately, today's era of standardized testing and accountability-driven classrooms leaves educators, administrators, and youth workers with little room to build these skills and relationships. In addition to limiting space for conversations about politics and advocacy during the school day, No Child Left Behind rewards schools that use their after-school dollars to engage in test preparation and tutoring rather than youth development programs, where organizing may have occurred in the past; this is particularly true of low-performing schools designated as "schools in need of improvement," which are required to set aside a certain percentage of their Title I funding for tutoring (Koyama 2010). Furthermore, schools increasingly focus on academic results rather than building relationships, valuing diversity, or embracing the assets students bring from their home cultures, all of which contribute to students' confidence in themselves and ability to advocate for the needs of their families and communities (Valenzuela 2005). For educators who lack the luxury of teaching outside of tightly monitored curricula during the day and test preparation after it, schools can feel like impossible places to foster the skills necessary to build the next generation of youth organizers.

OUT-OF-SCHOOL LITERACY PRACTICES AND THE POTENTIAL FOR CHANGEMAKING

As Varenne (2007) argues, some of the most effective education occurs outside schools. A growing body of literature has begun to document the range and variety of ways in which young people's out-of-school literacy practices build knowledge and skills that are often ignored or devalued in the classroom, but are essential for the navigation of the ever-evolving digital media landscape (Dimitriadis 2001; Dyson 2003; Mahiri 2006; Ranker 2006; Skilton-Sylvester 2002). Authors such as Lam (2000, 2006) focus on the ways in which immigrant youth use literacy practices to both educate themselves about their languages and ethnic backgrounds and contribute to the development of new languages, symbols, and hybrid identities, traditions, and practices associated with diaspora rather than home countries. Authors like Duncan-Andrade (2006), Flores-González, Rodríguez, and Rodríguez-Muñiz (2006) document how youth use media, hip-hop, and other forms of youth-based popular culture to engage in advocacy. These studies situate literacy within political contexts, arguing that such out-of-school practices represent youth's reactions to the world around them, and that out-of-school spaces provide youth with the freedom to critique their worlds in ways that are not afforded by schools.

In this chapter, I engage Ginwright, Cammarota, and Noguera's (2005) youth development framework to demonstrate how specific out-of-school literacy practices provide opportunities for young people to learn how to successfully advocate for policy change. Specifically, I focus on a practice that is a promising way to build the skills, spaces, and structures youth need to organize: counterstorytelling.

STORYTELLING FOR SOCIAL CHANGE

In today's data-driven education policy landscape, quantifiable results drive everything from teacher evaluations to student achievement to school closings. Stone (2002) notes that quantifiable evidence (which Stone calls "numbers") is "the premier language for stories of decline and decay," and is often invoked to make a claim that systems need changing (172). This accurately illustrates the discourse surrounding public schools, where plummeting test scores, graduation rates, and dropout rates are used to paint a picture of a crisis. Stone (2002) argues that "numbers" are often privileged in policy debates because they are falsely considered objective evidence.In reality, numbers can be manipulated and do not tell the whole story. This is evident from work of researchers such as Koyama (2010), who study the effects of policy from an ethnographic perspective. Furthermore, the almost exclusive use of quantitative data limits policy conversations to participants who can produce, analyze, and understand statistical techniques that are rarely covered in public schools or universities, thereby severely narrowing the field of supposed experts capable of knowledge production (Chowdhury 2011; Nagar 2006). Those who choose to question the primacy of numbers by telling their own stories may be silenced or devalued. In reality their perspectives are essential for understanding how policy plays out on the ground. In a landscape where numbers are privileged, using personal stories as evidence is a radical act, challenging established norms of knowledge production and dissemination as well as the definition of expertise in the policy arena.

Critical race theorists use narratives called counterstories to frame the experiences of marginalized groups as data that is just as valid as that generated from quantitative studies (Ladson-Billings and Tate 2006; Rousseau and Dixson 2006; Yosso 2006). These counterstories do not always accurately recount actual events, although they are often based on rigorous research or personal experience. In Yosso's (2006) *Critical Race Counterstories along the Chicana/Chicano Educational Pipeline* and Rousseau and Dixson's (2006) *The First Day of School*, the authors communicate the results of years of rigorous research through fictional stories that combine personal experience with statistical trends to illustrate conflict and imagine a more just, alternative reality. They chose this avenue for communicating their research because they recognized that counterstorytelling is a powerful tool for analyzing the realities that marginalized individuals experience in their communities which existing documentation practices cannot properly articulate.

Counterstories are also valuable because counterstorytelling is not limited to scholars. Bell's (2003) work examines how teachers and youth workers who are outside of the academy use the power of personal storytelling to convey factual, lived experiences with the goal of reshaping cultural and social norms as well as the power structures that give rise to the dominant narrative. Bell claims that analyzing the disparities between personal narratives and the dominant narratives can raise awareness for both the oppressed and the oppressor, which in turn can build solidarity and lead to widespread change. In the current numbers-driven policy landscape, only those who have the ability to collect and analyze large sets of statistical data are respected by policymakers. The inclusion of counterstories as a valuable form of evidence opens discussions to others—particularly, for the purposes of this chapter, youth.

Solinger, Fox, and Irani (2008) assert that storytelling about personal truths is transformational for the narrator because it establishes him/her as an expert, a holder of authentic knowledge, and someone who has the prerogative to claim something that is his/her own—respect, rights, or property. In this sense, storytelling is particularly exciting as a tool for mobilizing youth, because youth are rarely granted any of these commodities. Ginwright, Cammarota, and Noguera (2005) argue that youth are routinely left out of policy decisions because they lack the social capital necessary to make their voices heard; the authors claim that one way to reverse this trend is to ensure that youth have "ongoing exposure to information [and] ideas" (35). While the authors illustrate this necessity with an example of youth organizing that involved youth "armed with statistics, reports, and financial forecasts," youth must also be made aware of the information they hold, and their ability to claim expertise in their own lives (35). As I will show, storytelling builds the relationships and spaces these authors claim are ideal for empowering emerging youth leaders.

One characteristic of counterstorytelling is that tellers challenge a dominant narrative, or what Yosso (2006) calls majoritarian storytelling. Dominant narratives are stories told by those in power. They often perpetuate stereotypes about race, class, and gender that erase both the institutionalized oppression that creates inequalities and the variety of experiences within broad categories such as "black," "poor," "female," or "queer." Dominant narratives are what we see in mainstream media and in academia, and they tend to "silence or dismiss people who offer evidence contradicting these racially unbalanced portrayals" (Yosso 2006, 9). Dominant narratives are tools for what Das Gupta (2006) calls space-taking, or practices that restrict the abilities of members of a community to question the oppressive boundaries defining their range of possible identities and actions. Counterstorytelling seeks to upend these narratives by unearthing different but equally valid truths, making space for possibilities that may otherwise be restricted by those in positions of power.

Examining the dominant narrative also helps us understand the limitations of the categories we use to describe the experiences of young people. While literature about youth activism and counterstorytelling addresses issues of race, it rarely takes into account the intersection of race, age, and gender. For young immigrant women of color, the mere act of counterstorytelling—regardless of the story—undermines existing narratives. Transnational feminist scholars like Chowdhury (2011), Nagar (2006), Mohanty (2003), and Narayan (1997) have documented how the academy and mainstream media reinforce the false notions that all women from developing nations—and, in particular, women from working-class communities—come from cultures that systematically devalue them as human beings and, as a result, silence their voices. Furthermore, the theory ignores the fact that women have agency, and are able to (and do) resist oppression alongside men. Indeed, in this volume, Bangura demonstrates how such assumptions undermine the ways in which institutional actors perceive the decisions of African young women, positioning them as victims even when they strategically negotiate institutions and policies that restrict their educational opportunities.

Transnational feminist scholars provide a useful framework for understanding how women of color are prevented from telling stories that could contribute to revolutionary dialogue and radical change. Mohanty (2003) describes, at times through autobiographical details, how third-world women's voices and experiences are silenced or erased unless they conform to a dominant narrative that positions them as submissive and pliable. Saldivar-Hull (2000) documents how women's stories and concerns are pushed to the sidelines even in the context of radical movements, a trend that persists today: even as women in Egypt fought side by side with men in Tahrir Square, their voices were excluded from the process of building a new government (Hosea 2011). As Mohanty (2003) documents, women's stories are erased when it is convenient to omit them and included when they conform to existing dominant storylines.

In this paper, I examine the experiences of two young women who use storytelling to create change and question the boundaries of the spaces delineated by policies that are blind to the needs of their communities. These young women produce and respond to digital stories that question the dominant narrative and imagine alternative realities for them and their communities. Through the data I present, I will outline a theory of the skills and concepts young people need to tell stories for social change. I will also elucidate how the practice of counterstorytelling contributes to the redefinition of educational policies via both the lessons learned through telling stories and the act of making these stories heard.

METHODOLOGY

The findings presented here came from a larger mixed methods study of South Asian American young women between the ages of eighteen and nineteen. The study began with fifty-seven anonymous surveys, which I triangulated with data from thirty in-depth, semistructured, ethnographic interviews with a subset of survey respondents. I collected the data over the course of one calendar year (2008). Surveys were anonymous, so there was no way to verify where respondents were based geographically. Because I recruited through snowball sampling, the majority of the young women I interviewed (specifically 25 out of 30 women) attended college in New York City. However, participants grew up in a variety of states and geographical regions, including California, Florida, Ohio, and New Jersey.

Although the definition of "South Asian" includes an ever-shifting list of nations, the women in this study traced their ancestry primarily to India, Bangladesh, or Pakistan. The mix of countries in the study reflected the immigrant populations which I had access to through snowball sampling.

I rooted my research in a feminist technique based on Fine's (1994) concept of "working the hyphens," which questions the existence of scientific neutrality, attempts to include (rather than "occlude") the researcher, and (re)defines qualitative research as a tool for action and change rather than domination, all with the objective of ending the destructive practice of "othering" the marginalized populations that are so often the subjects of ethnographic studies (135). In keeping with this approach, my goal during the research process was to equalize the relationship between interviewer and interviewee as much as possible, while admitting that a complete equalization is impossible. To this end, I sent all participants copies of their interviews for edits before writing about them, and sent them copies of my completed dissertation. I friended them on Facebook originally for the purpose of the study, but have since found that this connection has allowed me to engage in reciprocity with many of them, and to remain in touch with far more participants than I would have otherwise. I met with Neesha as recently as this summer, and helped her find an internship soon after our interview. She and I continue to be in touch, particularly because she has just graduated and is now teaching in a public school, which was also my first job out of college. Zainab and I do not meet in person, but she does communicate with me on Facebook. I have not been able to engage in the same level of reciprocity with her as I have with Neesha, but she occasionally comments on my Facebook page, usually in response to photos and links I post.

Perhaps most importantly, I believe the purpose of my research is to create social change. This informs everything from the way I analyze my work and the way I write about it to my agenda for publication. I hope this spirit is reflected in the findings that follow.

NEESHA, ZAINAB, AND THE DOMINANT NARRATIVE

The two women I profile here identify as South Asian American Muslims, although they come from different national backgrounds. Zainab is Bangladeshi American, and is a practicing Muslim who wears the traditional head covering known as *hijab*. Neesha is an Indian American Muslim whose parents were born and raised in East Africa but moved to the US for economic opportunities. Both live in working-class neighborhoods in an urban center.

Story #1: Neesha

Neesha engaged in counterstorytelling while participating in an after-school program where professional journalists teach youth how to make radio shows that are then aired on local stations and posted as podcasts on these stations' Web sites. In her first year in this program, Neesha collaborated with a fellow South Asian American young woman to create a short piece on intraracial gangs in low-income South Asian American communities. Neesha realized that although she and her peers were aware of these gangs, their existence was absent from the dominant narrative. She explained, "I know that a lot of the older generation don't know about it, but I know kids who know kids. And I see the beef or whatever between Punjabis and [Pakistanis] and stuff like that. I didn't know it was a big deal but we found this article online that a lady had written about how it was becoming a phenomenon, South Asian gangs was becoming a big thing" (Interview, September 21, 2008). Neesha's piece responded to the idea that her everyday reality was either nonexistent (because only youth knew about it) or sensationalized (as it was portrayed in the media), thereby disrupting the dominant narratives of both her own community and the outside world.

I counted myself in the "older generation" who did not know about gang violence between ethnic groups, despite the fact that at the time I conducted this research, I had been a teacher and youth worker in Neesha's community for several years. When I sent her a copy of her interview for her to do a member check, I asked her if she had anything to add. She wrote,

> i guess i would just add that when you were asking me about south asian gangs . . . my mind kind of went blank. but in [Neesha's school] there was a "gang" called the Caribbean Mafia which was a group of mostly guyanese-indian and trini-indian guys, some were muslim and some were hindu. they used to tag up the walls with their graffiti. and they used to walk around with knives and other weapons and get into fights and get arrested. and i knew these kids so that's *[sic]* why the whole desi gangs thing was nothing new to me. (Personal communication, September 25, 2008)

Neesha here again reveals her awareness that gangs are not part of the dominant narrative. This was the only edit Neesha made to her interview, which was almost two hours long and covered a wide range of issues beyond gangs, attesting to the importance of this clarification.

After she graduated from (meaning completed one year with) the radio production program, Neesha remained involved as a peer trainer. In this capacity, she did a report on a hate crime that occurred in the South Asian American community where both the perpetrator and the victim were South Asian American. Neesha said her group was drawn to the story specifically because they were skeptical of the dominant narrative presented in the press. As Neesha explained, "The whole point of the documentary was to question whether or not it was a hate crime or whether the media was just trying to sensationalize the story so like brown on brown crime" (Interview, September 21, 2008). In the production process, Neesha and her group interviewed the parties involved as well as a local council member to understand what was being done to address the situation. The following year—her last in the program—she did a project on East Asian refugees who were being denied health care, allowing her to work with ethnic communities that she would not ordinarily engage with, and building solidarity between these communities, an exercise that often leads to empowerment and an enhanced ability to fight for social justice (Mohanty 2003).

The stories that Neesha created problematized the dominant narrative in and about race in Asian American communities, known as the model minority myth. According to this false narrative, Asian Americans are uniformly economically and academically successful, unlike their "non-model" black and Latino immigrant peers who are described as problematically dependent on social services and experiencing high rates of poverty (Das Gupta 2006; Maira 2002; Prashad 2001; Teranishi 2002). In reality, the success of some of these South and East Asian populations is the result of xenophobic policies that facilitate legal immigration from Asian countries only for individuals who are wealthy, highly educated, and (often) fluent in English (Das Gupta 2006; Maira 2002; Prashad 2001). However, there is a growing number of East and South Asian Americans living at or below the poverty line; although they remain largely invisible, they are fast becoming the majority within the Asian American community (SAALT 2005; Maira 2002). These working-class communities are the ones that experience gang violence and hate crimes and lack access to health care—exactly the stories that Neesha chose to tell.

The model minority myth is inherently dangerous because it creates a false racial hierarchy and therefore creates divisions between oppressed racial groups that could otherwise join together to agitate for social change and an end to race-based injustice (Prashad 2001). Additionally, it homogenizes a group that is extraordinarily diverse in terms of faith, language, and national origin, thereby erasing and subsuming the experiences of individuals and unique populations. Unfortunately, powerful members of the Asian

American community are invested in perpetuating the myth because they derive benefits from being considered "almost" white, including relatively little racially motivated violence and lesser daily discrimination compared to their black and Latino counterparts, at least in elite communities (Das Gupta 2006; Prashad 2001). Investment in this myth has led to the erasure of stories that might suggest that segments of the Asian American community are, in fact, in need of government intervention and social services; perhaps the most visible erasure is the constant battle that anti–domestic violence and queer groups fight in trying to be included in the India and Pakistan Day parades in New York City, battles that continue today (Das Gupta 2006). The shaming and erasure of stories of poverty and abuse within Asian American communities has real consequences: Asian Americans access public assistance at much lower rates than other populations, partially as a result of the shame associated with public assistance. For example, according to the Child Center of New York, in New York City, less than half of Asian Americans who qualify for public assistance actually access it, partially as a result of shame (Child Center of New York2012). Yet, because of the erasure of this story, policymakers may not be aware of the extent of the need for services in the Asian American community, or the barriers to accessing public assistance certain populations face as a result of community norms.

The stories Neesha created during her after-school program disrupted these dominant narratives by drawing on the experiences of members of her community. By presenting these stories on a public platform—the radio station where they aired—Neesha reshaped perceptions of South Asian American young people, questioning the underlying assumptions that drove policies based on the idea that Asians are immune to institutionalized racism and xenophobia or exempt from the negative effects of poverty. Making these stories heard opened up the possibility of solidarity with similarly affected immigrant groups, and undermined the notion that immigrant women of color—in particular, South Asian Muslim women—accept their circumstances without resistance. Furthermore, these stories highlighted a number of oppressive policies that negatively affect the lives of youth, a phenomenon evident in the experiences of the undocumented students in A. Chen's chapter in this volume.

However, the power of these stories is not limited to their telling. Neesha's description of her time in the program revealed that the storytelling process helped her develop skills and connections necessary to advocate for policy changes. During her time in the program, Neesha built relationships with community-based organizations and political figures that could be influential in creating change, thereby building social capital she could use for advocacy (Ginwright, Cammarota, and Noguera 2005). By focusing on issues in her own community, she was able to start with identity work that helped her understand her place in the power structures of her community (Ginwright and James 2002). She forged bonds of solidarity (in her case, between South and East Asian groups) that, according to Mohanty (2003), represent a key first step in feminist movement building. Perhaps most importantly, Neesha's work makes strides in rendering the issue of poverty in Asian American communities visible both within and outside of racial groups; not only were these pieces broadcasted nationally, they are also available to this day as podcasts. Neesha participated in a public exchange of information and ideas essential to building momentum for change (Ginwright and James 2002). All of these experiences armed her with the tools and capital necessary to understand how changemaking works, and to engage in advocacy.

Neesha was part of a highly structured program that functioned outside of the school building and explicitly focused on creating change. Her example is instructive in thinking about ways to design in- and out-of-school activities so that they integrate both literacy and advocacy skills while fitting into set curricula and/or standardized testing requirements. Not all participants built their advocacy skills in structured environments. Zainab, for example, began learning about digital storytelling in an after-school program, but developed advocacy skills on her own.

Story #2: Zainab

Zainab participated in an after-school program in which she and her peers created a video about being South Asian American. Zainab said that she and her friends made the piece as a counterpoint to the numerous existing videos that "the white man" has created about South Asian Americans (Interview, October 12, 2008). Zainab described the video as "women of color representing their own selves through their own media. . . . It was just stuff about us as Muslims" (Interview, October 12, 2008). Zainab said the video reflected young women's investment in Islam and the benefits they derived from it. Additionally, she said the video "had a lot of Arab and South Asian cultures mixed . . . it was cool that we mixed Arab and South Asian." Like Neesha's experience, Zainab's storytelling experience became a locus for building solidarity.

At the time of our interview, Zainab was independently working on another video that told a counterstory about a narrative that was constantly in the local news about a highly politicized decision to fire a Muslim principal of a high school who had helped students organize a political protest. Zainab had been at the protest, and felt that the principal had been treated unfairly. She was creating the video to present another side of the story using the skills she had learned in her after-school program.

While the video she had created about "culture" with her after-school program appeared on YouTube, Zainab did not support the decision, nor was she sure that she would post her next video there. She felt that videos about Islam on YouTube invariably received negative commentary that made viewers skeptical of the content. Zainab said that she often noticed that videos that have to do with South Asia or Islam receive negative feedback. She reported, "Anything Muslim you always see negative comments and debates . . . it's so circular. You keep fighting and fighting and it still comes back to the same point . . . you guys [Muslims] are messed up or whatever" (Interview, October 2, 2008). Zainab felt that the comments perpetuated false and destructive stereotypes about Islam rather than provoking thoughtful and productive debate.

However, rather than seeing this pattern as a defeat, Zainab viewed it as an opportunity for activism. Even before this video was posted on YouTube, Zainab was (as she continues to be) active on the Web site. Zainab searches for videos about Islam that she feels represent her religion accurately, and posts positive comments on these videos' pages. She explained, "If there's a good YouTube video I give it thumbs up and increase the good comments so people will feel less inclined to write their negative comments. . . . It increases the chances of people looking at the video as well. Sometimes people see a video and they don't know what to think and the comments help you decide" (Interview, October 2, 2008). Here Zainab demonstrates the importance of not only producing counterstories, but also using comments in order to question dominant narratives or to help others understand where the dominant narrative fails.

Since 9/11, Muslim young women like Zainab have experienced marginalization as a result of the dominant narrative that equates Islam with violence and renders Muslims undeserving of American citizenship. Scholars like Maira (2009), Zaal (2007), Fine (2007), and Ghaffar-Kucher (2009) show how gatekeepers like teachers and social workers explicitly and implicitly question whether young Muslims (or those who others say "look" Muslim through the false practice of racializing religion) deserve access to citizenship and protection from bias-based harassment and stereotype them as budding terrorists or having behavior problems. Zaal (2007), for example, documented how young Muslim women who wear *hijab* are routinely verbally assaulted; in my own study, at least two women reported that their female relatives had been physically attacked as a result of their faith—one for wearing *hijab* and one for wearing the traditional pantsuit called *salwar kameez*. Ghaffar-Kucher (2009) found that Muslim Pakistani students who participated in her study stopped feeling American after 9/11, and were routinely called "Osama" and "Saddam" by peers when they were being bullied. The underlying assumption of these claims and actions is that Islam is synonymous with fundamentalism, terrorism, and tyranny, and that those who follow the religion will necessarily be violent and untrustworthy.

Zainab's documentary about her experience as a South Asian American Muslim positions her and her peers as the experts, disrupting the dominant narrative created by non-Muslim gatekeepers interpreting stories they hear on the news. Her comments on YouTube videos that she did not produce help undermine the dominant narrative by validating narratives which conform to her understanding of Islam as a peaceful religion. Her comments are also a show of solidarity with filmmakers who, like her, find the dominant narrative false.

Like Neesha's stories, Zainab's stories question the assumptions inherent in both local and global policies designed to "save" Muslim women from oppression. Western countries such as France are increasingly considering outlawing *hijab* in the name of protecting Muslim women ("The War of French Dressing" 2010). Here, Islam is framed as inherently oppressive to women, a claim commonly made about cultures in the developing world (Narayan 1997). Additionally, the commentary is symptomatic of the idea presented by Zainab that "the white man" often deems himself responsible for telling the stories of women of color. By telling her own story with her fellow Muslim women, and by talking about the benefits they find in Islam, Zainab and her peers disrupt the narrative in which Islam is deemed inherently oppressive to women.

Zainab's storytelling and commenting methods allow her to develop skills essential for successful youth organizing. For example, by strategically using the structures available on YouTube, Zainab engages popular youth culture, a key element in Ginwright and James's (2002) framework for youth organizing. By using YouTube to both tell and react to stories, Zainab employs platforms and multimodal storytelling techniques that have the potential to "go viral" and to engage with tropes youth are familiar with and find relatable. In Zainab's case, both the medium and the messages align with popular culture, ensuring that they are easy for youth to both find and understand—and to potentially identify as inspiration for building solidarity and creating change. Utilizing a popular, open platform like YouTube also allows Zainab to contribute to and participate in exchanges of ideas that generate momentum for social change (Ginwright, Cammarota, and Noguera 2005). Zainab's videos begin with and expand upon identity work that has allowed her to place herself and her peers within power structures and understand inequalities that must be addressed in order for change to take place, another foundation of successful organizing (Ginwright and James 2002). Zainab's work is instructive from the standpoint of an educator committed both to creating spaces within classrooms where students can learn the skills to engage in advocacy and to understanding funds of knowledge students have cultivated independently.

Zainab's case shows that young people are already experimenting with creative forms of advocacy that, with the right support and opportunities, could be leveraged into campaigns to influence policies directly affecting youth. Future possibilities aside, though, Zainab's immediate actions shape the stories presented in media, thereby broadening the conversation that underlies policymaking. By disrupting narratives positioning Islam as the source of global problems, Zainab, in her way, is contributing to reshaping the way policies are perceived and acted upon in her online community.

IMPLICATIONS

Neesha's and Zainab's (counter)stories reflect a critical understanding of the dominant narratives that shape their lives coupled with a motivation to disrupt these narratives through the creation and dissemination of counternarratives using new and old media. These young women characterized their experiences with storytelling as transformational. In their interviews they identified several common themes. First, creating counterstories was a way to build solidarity with other marginalized individuals and communities that may share common political interests, making the prospect of collective action more tenable. Second, creating stories positioned the tellers as experts, which in turn made them feel empowered to question dominant narrative based on the power of personal stories. Finally, storytelling was intertwined with political action—in Zainab's case, it was a way to document struggle; in Neesha's case, it provided her with access to political officials and community-based organizations that could create the type of change she envisioned. Neesha and Zainab were both developing skills and acquiring social capital that Ginwright, Cammarota, and Noguera (2005) characterize as the first steps in developing youth leaders capable of participation in policy conversations and radical actions in order to overturn oppressive institutions and structures.

Unfortunately, Neesha and Zainab were not typical of the participants in this study. Many were hesitant to tell stories about their own oppression, particularly if this involved exposing classmates and community members as racist. Participants were often apologetic about their personal experiences, peppering their stories with phrases like "it wasn't so bad" and "it didn't really affect me," even as they described moving out of neighborhoods as a result of harassment about their religions, or being told by principals that they would never get into college because their parents would "marry them off" first. These stories contrasted with the ways in which many of these young women approached me: almost every interview contains an expression of relief, an admission that they had never thought about these stories before in the context of a larger community, or (most commonly) enthusiasm that someone— from an Ivy League institution—wanted to hear what they had to say. Such responses highlight the need for more outlets for young immigrant women of color to tell their stories and have these stories be heard rather than dismissed.

In this chapter, I have attempted to use Ginwright and James's (2002) and Ginwright, Cammarota, and Noguera's (2005) social justice youth development frameworks to identify the critical factors that helped both Neesha and Zainab acquire the skills and social capital that are foundational for engaging in successful advocacy. Several recommendations for reform can be made on the basis of their experiences. First, the art of storytelling— and, in particular, counterstorytelling—is a critical skill that should be incorporated into mainstream curriculum. The nationwide adoption of common core standards focused on nonfiction writing and literacy across content areas provides an opportunity for educators to design lessons that encourage young people to tell stories based on personal experience that disrupt dominant narratives. The process of creating these narratives can engage students in identity work, integrate popular culture, and build relationships with community based organizations and elected officials. Admittedly, testing pressure can make this suggestion difficult to implement for all but the most bold and experienced educators. Consequently, a second recommendation is to preserve after-school spaces that are designed to provide more than just academic tutoring. Both Neesha and Zainab began their storytelling practices in community-based organizations dedicated to youth development rather than test preparation. Funding streams should be directed to these types of programs, and schools should be encouraged to provide a variety of programming after hours. Finally, policymakers that work on issues that affect youth should integrate these stories into decision-making processes. Although students may be unable to attend hearings or deliberations that occur during the school day, by seeking out student-produced narratives, policymakers can form more nuanced views about the effects of their work. More public figures must insist that quantitative data is insufficient evidence for advocacy, and that numerical claims should be reinforced by qualitative data. Most importantly, legislators and politicians must value personal stories as vital contributions to research on the potential impact of proposed policies, and must insist on seeking out the opinions of the communities and populations that their initiatives may affect before engaging in potentially oppressive endeavors.

For these young people, storytelling was an avenue for reshaping the policies that affected them. As mentioned, the process of storytelling equipped them with the tools to remake policies at the legislative level. Additionally, counterstorytelling allowed these young women to publicly present the ways in which they believed policy should be reshaped, and to publicize how collective action within their communities contributes to the process of renegotiating the consequences of policy during the implementation process. Storytelling legitimated these activities for the young women, making them feel powerful and capable of change.

As Bell (2003) writes, "ultimately, we need to uncover and generate stories that inspire action and hope if we are to create the world we envision" (24). Clearly the South Asian American community is full of stories and budding storytellers; now it is up to us to find ways to integrate these stories into mainstream discussions about policy. Stories told by youth provide important insights into the policies that affect them, and it is time that we invited them into conversations about the ways in which we run school systems and higher education institutions. If we are to create the world we envision, we must include those who inhabit this world—no matter their age, gender, economic status, or ethnic background.

REFERENCES

Bell, Lee Anne. 2003. "Telling Tales: What Stories Can Teach Us about Racism." *Race Ethnicity and Education* 6 (1): 3–27.

Child Center of New York. 2012. "Asian Outreach Program." Accessed March 11, 2012. http://www.childcenterny.org/asianoutreachprogram.html.

Chowdhury, Elora. 2011. *Transnationalism Reversed: Women Organizing against Gendered Violence in Bangladesh*. Albany, NY: SUNY University Press.

Das Gupta, Monisha. 2006. *Unruly Immigrants: Rights, Activism, and Transnational South Asian Politics in the United States*. Durham, NC: Duke University Press.

Delgado, Melvin, and Lee Staples. 2008. *Youth-Led Community Organizing: Theory and Action*. Oxford: Oxford University Press.

Dimitriadis, Greg. 2001. "'In the Clique': Popular Culture, Constructions of Place, and the Everyday Lives of Urban Youth." *Anthropology and Education Quarterly* 32 (1): 29–51.

Duncan-Andrade, Jeffrey. 2006. "Urban Youth, Media Literacy, and Increased Critical Civic Participation." In *Beyond Resistance: Youth Activism and Community Change, New Democratic Possibilities for Practice and Policy for America's Youth*, edited by Shawn Ginwright, Pedro Noguera, and Julio Cammarota, 149–169. New York: Routledge.

Dyson, Ann H. 2003. *The Brothers and Sisters Learn to Write*. New York: Teachers College Press.

Fine, Michelle. 1994. "Working the Hyphens: Reinventing the Self and Other in Qualitative Research." In *Handbook of Qualitative Research*, edited by Norman Denzin and Yvonna Lincoln, 70–82. Newbury Park, CA: Sage.

Fine, Michelle, Reva Jaffe-Walter, Pedro Pedraza, Valerie Futch, and Brett Stoudt. 2007. "Swimming: On Oxygen, Resistance, and Possibility for Immigrant Youth Under Siege." *Anthropology and Education Quarterly* 38 (1): 76–96.

Flores-González, N., M. Rodríguez, and M. Rodríguez-Muñiz. 2006. "From Hip-Hop to Humanization: Batey Urbano as a Space for Latino Youth Culture and Community Action." In *Beyond Resistance: Youth Activism and Community Change, New Democratic Possibilities for Practice and Policy for America's Youth*, edited by Shawn Ginwright, Pedro Noguera, and Julio Cammarota, 175–196. New York: Routledge.

Gee, James P. 2006. *Social Linguistics and Literacies: Ideology in Discourses*. London: Falmer Press.

Ghaffar-Kucher, Ameena. 2009. "Citizenship and Belonging: Pakistani Immigrant Youth and the Politics of Identity." In *New Approaches to Comparative Education: Vertical Case Studies from Africa, Europe, the Middle East, and the Americas*, edited by Francis Vavrus and Lesley Bartlett, 163–180. New York: Palgrave MacMillan.

Ginwright, Shawn, Julio Cammarota, and Pedro Noguera. 2005. "Youth, Social Justice, and Communities: Toward a Theory of Urban Youth Policy." *Social Justice* 32 (3): 24–40.

Ginwright, Shawn, and Taj James. 2002. "From Assets to Agents: Social Justice, Organizing, and Youth Development." *New Directions in Youth Development* 96: 27–46.

Hosea, Leanna. 2011. "A Woman's Place in the New Egypt." *BBC News*, March 23. Accessed March 25, 2011. http://www.bbc.co.uk/news/world-middle-east-12819919.

Koyama, Jill. 2010. *Making Failure Pay*. Chicago: University of Chicago Press.

Ladson-Billings, Gloria, and W. F. Tate. 2006. "Toward a Critical Race Theory of Education." In *Critical Race Theory in Education: All God's Children Got a Song*, edited by Adrienne Dixson and Celia Rousseau, 11–30. New York: Routledge.

Lam, W .S. E. 2000. "L2 Literacy and the Design of the Self: A Case Study of a Teenager Writing on the Internet." *TESOL Quarterly* 34 (3): 457–482.

———. 2006. "Re-envisioning Language, Literacy, and the Immigrant Subject in New Mediascapes." *Pedagogies: An International Journal* 1 (3): 171–195.

Mahiri, Jabari. 2006. "Digital DJ-ing: Rhythms of Learning in an Urban School." *Language Arts* 84 (1): 55–62.

Maira, Sunaina. 2002. *Desis in the House: Indian American Youth Culture in New York City*. Philadelphia: Temple University Press.

———. 2009. *Missing: Youth, Citizenship, and Empire after 9/11*. Durham, NC: Duke University Press.

Mohanty, Chandra T. 2003. *Feminism without Borders: Decolonizing Theory, Practicing Solidarity*. Durham, NC: Duke University Press.

Nagar, Richa. 2006. *Playing with Fire: Feminist Thought and Activism through Seven Lives in India*. Minneapolis: University of Minnesota Press.

Narayan, Uma. 1997. *Dislocating Cultures: Identities, Traditions, and Third World Feminism*. New York: Routledge.

Prashad, Vijay. 2001. *The Karma of Brown Folk*. Minneapolis: University of Minnesota Press.

Ranker, Jabari. 2006. "'There's Fire Magic, Electric Magic, Ice Magic, or Poison Magic': The World of Video Games and Adrian's Compositions about *Gauntlet Legends*." *Language Arts* 84 (1): 21–33.

Roth, Jodie L., and Jeanne Brooks-Gunn. 2003. "What Exactly Is a Youth Development Program? Answers from Research and Practice." *Applied Developmental Science* 7 (2): 94–111.

Rousseau, Celia, and Adrienne Dixson. 2006. "And We Are Still Not Saved: Critical Race Theory in Education Ten Years Later." In *Critical Race Theory in Education: All God's Children Got a Song*, edited by Adrienne Dixson and Celia Rousseau, 11–30. New York: Routledge.

SAALT. 2005. *Who are South Asian Americans?* Accessed March 18, 2008 from http://www.saalt.org/pdfs/Who_are_South_Asians.pdf

Saldívar-Hull, Sonia. 2000. *Feminism on the Border: Chicana Gender Politics and Literature*. Berkeley: University of California Press.

Scott, James C. 1990. *Domination and the Arts of Resistance: Hidden Transcripts*. New Haven, CT: Yale University Press.

Skilton-Sylvester, Ellen. 2002. "Literate at Home but Not at School: A Cambodian Girl's Journey from Playwright to Struggling Writer." In *School's Out! Bridging Out-of-School Literacies with Classroom Practices*, edited by Glynda Hull and Kathy Schultz, 61–89. New York: Teachers College Press.

Solinger, Rickie, Madeline Fox, and Kayhan Irani, eds. 2008. *Telling stories to change the world*. New York: Routledge.

Stone, Deborah. 2002. *Policy Paradox: The Art of Political Decision Making*. Rev. ed. New York: Norton and Company.

"The War of French Dressing: A Plan to Ban the Wearing of the Burqa in Public Stokes New Controversy." 2010. *The Economist*, January 14. Accessed March 7, 2010. http://www.economist.com/world/europe/displayStory.cfm?story_id=15270861.

Varenne, Herve. 2007. "Difficult Collective Deliberations: Anthropological Notes towards a Theory of Education." *Teachers College Record* 107 (7): 1559–1588.

Yosso, Tara. 2006. *Critical Race Counterstories along the Chicana/Chicano Educational Pipeline.* New York: Routledge.
Zaal, Mayida, Tahani Salah, and Michelle Fine. 2007. "The Weight of the Hyphen: Freedom, Fusion, and Responsibility Embodied by Young Muslim-American Women during a Time of Surveillance." *Applied Development Science* 3 (11): 164–177.

14 Navigating Institutional Structures
The Politics of Supporting Undocumented Students in Higher Education

Angela Chuan-Ru Chen

> Everybody is kind of scared to touch this issue. And you still wonder why. Because it's the site, this political debate at the institutional level. We are the site of political debates. . . . So, on the one hand, we have the real tragedy of students: the real precarious existence of undocumented students, the sheer numbers, and really how little institutional support there is. On the other hand, we have this political debate that has colored the so-called "access" to scarce resources. (Interview, Gabriel, May 26, 2010)

In this statement, "Gabriel," a professor at "Sunny Research University" (SRU),[1] captures both the challenges and consequences that confront the effort to build institutional support for undocumented students in higher education. Discrimination rooted in xenophobia and racism shapes the boundaries of citizenship and, consequently, determines entry points into higher education, resulting in the reluctance of colleges and universities to fully embrace undocumented students as members of the institution. Contrary to an idealized notion of education as the great equalizer, educational systems "may in fact contribute to the creation and maintenance of a division between 'us' and 'them'" (Hjerm 2001). Practices that exclude undocumented students in higher education are legitimized by laws that not only deny these students financial aid but also help "sustain a climate of antipathy and suspicion toward undocumented students and immigrants of color" (Rincón 2008, 62). Colleges and universities operate in a legal context that criminalize those who hire, house, aid, transport, or educate undocumented immigrants (Rincón 2008; Vargas 2012), which magnifies the actual or perceived constraints of providing the undocumented with postsecondary educational benefits. Such interlocking policies are what Das Gupta (2006) would term space-taking practices, because they effectively exclude students from educational institutions based on identity categories—in this case, citizenship. However, as the findings from this chapter demonstrate, students and their allies in university administration work together to remake these policies, finding space around the margins.

LEGISLATIVE AND INSTITUTIONAL AMBIGUITIES

The debate over educational access has become increasingly central to preserving boundaries of citizenship—particularly because citizenship increasingly determines one's ability to "accumulate capital and social prestige in the global arena" (Ong 1999, 6). Although immigration is under federal jurisdiction, the debate over immigrant rights has steadily shifted from federal lawmakers to state and local actors, including the right to higher education (NFHEPG 2012). Without clarification of existing federal provisions or Congressional actions for comprehensive immigration reform, state lawmakers and institutional leaders use local discretion when enacting federal regulations. The actions of local leaders are often ambiguous as they juggle compliance with legal mandates and attempts to meet the needs of undocumented students under their authority.

This ambiguity was evident at SRU, where the campus president apparently held different positions on legislative reform and institutional change. The SRU president was sympathetic to the plight of undocumented students and joined fellow chancellors and university presidents in public support for the Development, Relief and Education for Alien Minors (DREAM) Act, a decade-old immigration bill expected to provide a pathway to citizenship for approximately 38% of undocumented youth.[2] But this enthusiasm did not clearly carry over to institutional practices. The SRU president was less outspoken and intent on making systemic changes at the institutional level. Although this political stance made the president a symbolic ally to those in the immigrant rights movement, he simultaneously demonstrated his reservations in taking the lead at his home institution to improve undocumented student success at SRU.

The consequences of such contradictions were evident in the precarious existence of undocumented students in higher education (Abrego 2006; Abrego and Gonzalez 2010; Albrecht 2007; Lopez 2011; Perez 2009). Although most institutions do not explicitly ban undocumented students from attendance, the lack of financial aid (Olivérez 2006), an overwhelming degree of psychological distress imposed by their status (Perez and Cortes 2011), and inadequate institutional resources (Albrecht 2007) prevent many from completing a college degree.

IMPACTS ON UNDOCUMENTED STUDENTS

Studies have shown that undocumented students have diminished opportunities for postsecondary education, both in enrollment numbers and in the quality of their experience (Abrego and Gonzalez 2010; Perez 2009; Perez and Cortes 2011; Lopez 2011). At the national level, 65,000 undocumented youth graduate from high school each year, but only approximately 26% of graduates matriculate into higher education (Fortuny, Capps, and

Passel 2007). Compared to the national average of 70% for US-born high school graduates who matriculate into college (US Department of Education 2009a), this rate is dismal. The undocumented students constitute less than 1% of the two million undergraduates enrolled nationally (US Department of Education 2009a), and those who matriculate are disproportionately enrolled in community colleges as a cost-saving strategy (Albrecht 2007; Olivérez 2006). However, while legislative and institutional structures may be oppressive, undocumented students are able to make space for themselves in universities. As this chapter shows, allies within institutions willing to remake policies are key to this renegotiation of space.

LEGAL MANDATES FOR FINANCIAL SUPPORT OF UNDOCUMENTED STUDENTS IN CALIFORNIA

Undocumented students' access to postsecondary educational benefits is highly regulated by federal and state mandates. They are eligible to apply for and enroll in public postsecondary institutions in California and may qualify for in-state tuition if they meet residency requirements outlined in Assembly Bill 540 (AB 540).[3] However, they have limited access to public aid, loans, and other forms of financial support.

These governmental policies work cumulatively to restrict undocumented students' access to financial resources. Given that 66% of all undergraduates in the US rely on some form of financial aid (US Department of Education, 2009b), the inability to receive aid makes it financially challenging for undocumented students to pursue higher education. This hardship was also the main challenge to students' persistence in higher education (Albrecht, 2007; Rincon 2008). To finance their educations, undocumented students relied on a small number of competitive private scholarships, money from friends and family, and income from unauthorized employment (Buenavista and Tran 2010). In many cases, they depended solely on their income to cover educational costs and, as a result, took frequent academic leaves to save money to pay for the next term (Buenavista and Tran 2010).

THE INSTITUTIONAL RESPONSE

High school and college personnel, although well intentioned, were unprepared to address complications associated with a lack of documentation during the college-choice and matriculation processes. Their support also proved to be the exception within institutions that were largely unaware of the experiences of undocumented students.

Olivérez's (2006) study of undocumented high school students demonstrates that undocumented high school students need additional academic preparation, well-informed school-based adults who can provide college-related guidance relevant to students' immigration status, and a college-going culture. Additionally, Albrecht (2007) concluded that university administrators had a limited understanding of the needs of undocumented students. Seven of the nine administrators in her study "had not previously thought about undocumented students in their professional capacity" (142), whereas students stressed the need for accessible information, designated personnel to help them navigate the institution, and legal services to counsel them on immigration status.

Feranchak's (2007) national study on the attitudes of higher education leaders regarding the appropriateness of providing educational benefits to undocumented students revealed significant discrepancies among the respondents. The varying levels of support provided by educational leaders may explain why it is difficult for higher education to work uniformly in the treatment of undocumented students. Taken together, there is significant inaction by institutions and limited evidence to suggest institutionalized support for undocumented students in higher education.

THEORETICAL BASIS FOR THE STUDY

While it is essential that institutional leaders and scholarship on undocumented immigrants continue to call attention to the need for legislative reform for more equitable access to education (Abrego and Gonzalez 2010; Perez 2009; Perez and Cortes 2011; Rincón 2008), it is also critical to investigate the impact of institutional policy and practice in perpetuating educational inequity. Related to this inequity is *reproduction theory*, a branch of critical pedagogy which argues that educational institutions are sites of social reproduction in which hegemonic agendas are inherently embedded in educational policy and practice (Giroux 2001). Using this theoretical framework, I posit that the marginalization of undocumented students in higher education is a reflection of general discrimination; thus, support for undocumented students is fundamentally political, even at the institutional level. This study aims to identify areas in which institutional policy could foster greater inclusion by examining the contentious relationships between citizenship and educational access, and between undocumented students and the campus community.

This study focuses on institutional allies at SRU who, as faculty members and administrators with managerial or instructional roles, had some awareness of undocumented students and demonstrated a history of advocacy on their behalf. Contrary to other change agents in the movement—students, community members, and legislators who called for institutional change from the periphery—these faculty and administrators were entrenched in shaping priorities and carrying out the vision of the institution. Central to my analysis of those allies' role as change agents is the principle that "any critical theory both defines and is defined by the problems posed by the contexts it attempts to address" (Giroux 2001, xx). This reciprocal relationship exists within a structure the allies helped create and sustain. The study's findings discuss allies' understanding of educational disparities and their sense of agency (Freire 2002) with respect to maintaining, resisting, and transforming institutional structures. Like the other chapters in this section, this study foregrounds the work of resistance and remaking, illustrating Subramanian and Koyama's claim (this volume) that immigrants participate in the policymaking process by renegotiating the consequences of policies at the level of implementation.

METHODOLOGY

This qualitative study was conducted at SRU, a public research university in California. I chose SRU as a research site because it has a history of institutional support for undocumented students and one of the highest enrollments[4] of undocumented students among public research universities. I conducted participant observation over four years (2007–2011), during which I attended undocumented student group events and activities (including group meetings, fundraisers, rallies, and meetings with university administrators), conducted interviews, and served as a community advocate for immigrant students. I recruited participants using snowball sampling, a process of asking key participants to refer others who met selection criteria to the study (Merriam 2009). I conducted in-depth interviews with twenty-three institutional allies who shared their experiences of working with undocumented students; I also interviewed twenty-one undocumented students, who shared their experiences of navigating the institution. The sample of institutional allies included nine from academic affairs, six from student affairs, five faculty members, and two from general administration. Student participants were working toward a degree from the institution and self-identified as undocumented. The student sample includes seven transfer students and fourteen first-year entrant students from Latina/o and Asian backgrounds; race was a factor for analysis but was not a sampling criterion.

FINDINGS

This study highlights overlooked institutional practices that are relatively independent from government regulations, as well as the clandestine subculture created by allies who support undocumented students. In order to distinguish the various levels of governance that impact these students, I first examined how SRU interprets and complies with federal and state mandates. Second, I examined SRU policies and practices, particularly those unregulated by the state, which nevertheless restrict students' access to postsecondary education. Third, I analyzed how allies formed a subculture in an attempt to create support for undocumented students. This third level of analysis highlights the agency exercised by immigrants and their allies in remaking oppressive policies and practices.

Federal and State Mandates on Affordability and Participation

Federal and state governments determine which students may attend public educational institutions and receive financial aid. Although the federal government does not bar enrollment of undocumented students, several pieces of legislation exclude them from receiving federal, state, and local benefits for postsecondary education: Title IV of the Higher Education Act, PRWORA,[5] and IIRIRA[6] (Drachman 2006).

The most explicit provision regarding higher education is Section 505 of IIRIRA, which states that undocumented immigrants "shall not be eligible on the basis of residence within a State for any postsecondary education benefit unless a citizen or national of the United States is eligible for such a benefit without regard to whether the citizen or national is such a resident" (IIRIRA 1996). Although explicit, the provision is also vague. One key point of contention is the definition of "a postsecondary educational benefit" awarded by the state and by individual campuses. The vagueness allowed for discretionary interpretations by university officials, and consequently local institutions interpreted these laws in a wide range of ways. In practice the term could refer to a number of things beyond federal financial aid; thus certain resources at SRU came into question, including scholarships collected from student tuition, scholarships funded by private donors, and even participation in federally funded academic programs. An administrator in the study noted the gradual enforcement of the residency requirement, making undocumented students ineligible for scholarship awards. These changes steadily evolved into an all-encompassing ban on any form of financial awards offered by SRU. This practice became one of the most pervasive constraints hampering allies in their work with undocumented students.

Financial Hardship

My data indicates that students were experiencing financial challenges— out of twenty-one student respondents, eighteen identified as lower or working class, with an annual family income ranging from $15,000 to $30,000, and eight students enrolled part-time or took leaves during their undergraduate experience.

Evelyn, an academic affairs administrator, described the impact of a 20% tuition hike on undocumented students she knew well. Evelyn explained the layers of systemic barriers that impact student performance:

It's very, very sad because as tuition [has gone] up, students are faced with the fact that they don't have money. They have to work, but it's "under the table." So they don't get benefits. They only get paid very minimum, and sometimes not even the minimum wage. They don't have enough money to pay their tuition. (Interview, May 6, 2010).

What Evelyn described were the layers of hardships students experienced. In addition to having to work "under the table," many students felt they had to choose between buying food and buying books. In fact, one student was happy and proud of the fact that he got decent grades even though he did not buy any of the required texts for the class.

Evelyn continued,

Most of the time, they are part [of] this fee reduction plan, which is two classes per quarter. They take fewer classes than the normal student. Therefore, it takes them longer to graduate. And at the same time most of them commute, and that affects their academic performance. Sometimes, the students are able to pay full tuition, and they stay here for the whole quarter. Or they take a quarter off to work. Or, they are able to raise funds, and then they come back the following quarter. (Interview, May 6, 2010)

In addition, she described the multiple strategies undocumented students used to pay for school: balancing work and school, taking alternating leaves to save money, living at home and spending many hours commuting on public transportation, and organizing personal fundraisers:

So we can see that their GPA is lower than the normal student, but it's not because they are not smart. They are very smart, but there are other factors that affect their academic performance. They commute, they have to work, and they don't get paid enough. They also have to help their families with the money that they make, so it does affect their performance. (Interview, May 6, 2010)

Thus, financial challenges took attention away from school and negatively impacted academic performance. This often manifested as a low grade point average and delayed time to complete degrees. Evelyn attributed students' lower academic performance to barriers unrelated to their academic ability, emphasizing factors out of students' control. She expressed the frustration she felt, not only as their counselor, but also as an immigrant and a parent with college-aged children. Through her tenure as an administrator, she developed personal relationships with students, inviting them and their families to her home. She was initially concerned with academic issues, but through time she developed a more holistic understanding of the impact of undocumented status on students' well-being, including mental and physical health, aspirations after college, family relationships, and living situations. Evelyn's positionality as an immigrant, a parent, and an administrator heightened her awareness and concern, thus influencing her holistic approach to guiding undocumented students.

Effect on Paid Employment and Extended Learning Opportunities

In addition to the impact undocumented status has on students' ability to gain admission, it affects their ability to participate in intellectual and research activities. As undocumented immigrants, most cannot obtain US government–issued documents, such as a social security card or driver's license, excluding them from a wide range of curricular and cocurricular activities (Albrecht 2007). Without money and travel documents, such as a passport or identification card, they are unable to participate in distant conferences, field trips, and study-abroad programs. Additionally, without the legal right to work, they are often excluded from paid internships, research positions, and even volunteer opportunities to gain professional experience. When students in this study were able to secure paid positions as interns, student leaders, and research and teaching assistants, they had to forgo salaries and stipends because of the Immigration Reform and Control Act, which prohibits employers from hiring undocumented workers.

Alice, a science major compelled to find research opportunities to be a competitive candidate for graduate programs and careers in science, faced this difficulty in gaining work experience:

> I talked to the professor in charge. Luckily he was a good, a nice professor, so I didn't explain. I just simply told him that I could not work in the country legally. He was nice enough to say, "You can be part of the program but we're not going to pay you for it. We simply cannot pay you for it." And that's why I was able to do that internship for the summer. (Interview, April 26, 2010)

The pretext for such exploitative circumstances is a mutually beneficial relationship, which allows students to gain useful social and intellectual capital but discounts the contributions they make. The power dynamic offers little room for students to advocate for compensation. Whereas exploitative labor practices endured by undocumented immigrants in the private sector have been documented (Bacon 2008), there is little to no discussion of employment practices used by colleges and universities with regard to undocumented students (see Thomas, this volume). Although one can argue that college students are likely to take internships without pay, the key distinction is that undocumented students must actively decline payment—even in otherwise paid jobs—in order to participate.

Impact of Deportation Programs and Homeland Security Measures

The Secure Communities program has become another federal barrier to academic engagement. In 2007, the Department of Homeland Security initiated Secure Communities, a deportation program, which shares fingerprints collected by local law enforcement with the Federal Bureau of Investigation and with Immigration and Customs Enforcement, a program that promised to prioritize the deportation of convicted felons and has snared thousands of minor offenders (Bennett, 2011). According to Vargas (2012), "students and mothers have been detained and deported alongside murderers and rapists" (42). This program, designed to deport dangerous criminals, also prevented students such as Yasmine from tutoring as part of a service-learning (Eyler and Giles 1999) course at SRU. Yasmine encountered complications at the local police station:

> I went [to the local police department] and the woman [working there] was pretty mean, she goes, "No school ID allowed. I need an official government ID. That's like a passport or a driver's license." That was it. So I ended up having to drop the internship. I couldn't continue. (Interview, April 21, 2010)

Although it was unfortunate that she had to drop the course, Yasmine could have encountered more serious consequences by completing the background check that could potentially expose her to immigration authorities. Such complications have deterred students from pursuing certain service-learning courses, majors, graduate programs, and even professions that required a criminal background check. Yasmine found it ironic that the community youth served by the program were likely to be "undocumented" like her and said, "It sucks that I can't even be an intern there." This protocol requires us to critically examine how educators might act as an extension to immigration enforcement by inadvertently shuffling students into deportation channels. Further, it highlights the interconnectedness of immigration policy, such that even policies that were not intended to be education related can directly affect the lived educational experiences of undocumented youth.

Impact of Institutional Norms on Undocumented Students

As the examples above have shown, it is not only the interpretations of government policies that define the scope of support offered at the institutional level. Perhaps equally as detrimental as the laws and the institution's compliance with them was the lack of institutional recognition of the exclusionary impact on undocumented students. While all participants cited governmental barriers as the primary challenge, they also stressed a number of institutional policies that compromised undocumented students' academic pursuits. These institutional practices might appear trivial to those with legal status, such as entering a social security number into the online admissions application or having to show government-issued identification prior to receiving services at the student health center. However, these deeply embedded uses of red tape made it excessively difficult for undocumented students to navigate and participate as full members of SRU.

Institutional norms at SRU were partly sustained through the invisibility of undocumented students. The larger SRU community often assumed there were no undocumented students on campus. Despite continuous efforts by undocumented students to educate the SRU community about their presence, they consistently encountered campus personnel unaware that undocumented people could even attend college. Furthermore, commitment to long-standing institutional policy stood in the way of necessary reform. For instance, undocumented students who could not afford to pay tuition on time faced restricted access to campus resources; nevertheless, they were required to pay for them. SRU established a deferred-payment plan, which allowed students to defer tuition payment and minimize the need to stop out. Students who were approved for this extension—by their counselor, professors, and department—could conditionally enroll in classes but were banned from using services requiring a campus identity card, such as borrowing a book from the library and using health-related services. As a result, although the university benefited from students' participation in courses and their eventual full payment of tuition fees, this policy deprived students of full access to university services. A student affairs administrator, Adam, said,

> Our students, essentially, pay fees for services they don't use. The school knows they're going to pay their fees: they've done it before. They pay fees every quarter. You can't give them an opportunity to use the services that they're paying for? . . . No, no, no. That's crap. The marginal cost of additional students going to a particular service is negligible. It's basic microeconomic theory. It's not a big deal. So I think the school can do better on that. (Interview, May 13, 2010)

SRU lacked policies to adequately address the financial distress of undocumented students; thus, students used other existing policy to meet their needs. The extension provided by the deferred-payment plan enabled students to accumulate the necessary funds for the quarter. This policy was intended for students who experienced financial aid delay that typically lasted a couple of weeks. Unfortunately for undocumented students, delays usually lasted the entire term and were experienced more regularly, leaving

248   *Angela Chuan-Ru Chen*

them without services for extended periods of time. Whereas other students might have had access to resources, such as family health insurance, undocumented students rarely had comparable alternatives (Passel and Cohn 2009). Furthermore, Adam believed that undocumented students were more likely to defer payment than the general population. At the time of this interview, SRU records indicated that there were fewer than one hundred AB 540 undocumented students enrolled: this represents less than 0.03% of the total student population. Thus, the marginal cost of providing these students full access to university services would have been negligible.

Faith, an undocumented student who used the late-payment plan, felt that the limitations on services occurred at the most inopportune time, when she "faced a lot of uncertainty, anxiety, and depression." She says,

> Could SRU have done more? Yes. Did they? Not really. Even though there were only a few dozen of us enrolled, or even if there were only five, it does not make us any less significant, any less of a contributor, or any less of a student in the university. The university should be proactive in its quest to ensure the full participation of all its members, not just reactive. (Interview, May 27, 2010)

Faith's account highlights the indignation of knowing that SRU prioritized her tuition payment over her contributions as a student and her physical and mental wellness. By maintaining this practice, SRU marked her as an outsider.

Political Considerations for Allies Regarding Immigration Issues

Institutional allies also encountered resistance, especially when they raised immigration issues in a public or institutional context. Gabriel, a professor, felt that the act of informing others about the benefits of AB 540 became "political terrain" because it conveyed personal and political positions in the debate over immigrant rights in the US. While certain departments offered training on these issues, there was no institutional commitment to make it a campus-wide standard. Thus, the burden of informing the campus rested upon students and institutional allies, who made it their personal responsibility to offer workshops and teach-ins.

Gabriel explained,

> We're embedded in a debate about immigration and, therefore, it's almost your position about AB 540 that reveals your colors. Are you pro- or anti-? What do you do here? I mean if you're a bureaucrat you have to help undocumented students—I don't think it's that easy. I think most of the challenge we have is that following and implementing basic provisions such as AB 540 has become political terrain, too. (Interview, May 26, 2010)

At SRU, few departments mandated staff training on this issue, and whenever training was offered, the attendance was generally voluntary. To encourage greater awareness of AB 540, students and allies emphasized educators' responsibility to enact and report AB 540 as an educational issue rather than a political stance. Consequently, an active and engaged network of allies has been essential to disseminating information to undocumented immigrant communities in order to keep the gateway to higher education ajar.

Summary of Problems Created by Institutional Attitude

The problems outlined in this section are attributed to institutional commitment to established policies and cultural norms. These norms are derived from a web of policies shaping economic opportunities, security, and deportation. The collective challenges experienced by undocumented students and allies proved institutional culture had a damaging impact on their ability to receive relevant resources and increase awareness and acceptance. Rather than accepting these policies, which Das Gupta (2006) terms space-taking practices, consciousness of these challenges pushed some institutional actors to question the efficacy of existing policies and to make attempts to transform those regulations, or at least find means to resist them.

Undocumented Student Activism

The passage of AB 540 in 2001 opened a pathway for a new wave of undocumented students into public postsecondary institutions. The bill made college more accessible by allowing qualified undocumented students to pay in-state tuition. But the bill provided more than monetary benefits; to a degree, it also established the rightful presence of undocumented students in higher education.

By fall 2002, SRU had admitted its first cohort of AB 540 undocumented students, a handful of whom spoke privately with allies to explain the challenges they had experienced because of their status. These institutional allies realized they were working with seven or eight undocumented students on a one-on-one basis and had wanted to put these students in touch with one another. This initial gesture was the beginning of the partnership between undocumented students and institutional allies.

Their partnership formally began with an open meeting between the program staff at the student diversity program and undocumented students to talk about how administrators might better support student experiences at SRU. Alejandro, one of the coordinating administrators, recalled the event:

> We were shocked when the day of the meeting came and the time and instead of the eight to ten people about forty people came in. They just

kept coming and coming and coming. And we were actually pleased and shocked because we realized that there were a lot more students than we thought there might be. (Interview, May 2, 2010)

As the meeting progressed, Alejandro realized the extent of student challenges:

It was when we were going around the room and talking about who they were and what their challenges were that we realized that this was huge. This was something that we needed to do something about. That it was not just a fact that students needed a little support. It really was about that students needed a place to go to, a place to talk, people to talk to. And we had to figure out whatever we could do to support students, knowing that our hands were tied when it came to the financial aid piece of it. But realizing that there was so much more that we could do to help their experiences. (Interview, May 2, 2011)

After this first initial meeting, Alejandro and other administrators involved realized how "deep" some of the issues were at SRU and decided to organize a follow-up discussion with students and top administrators. "We had to make sure that the people who could make those changes would hear the stories of the students" and "that they had to actually hear from the students what it was like." They brought in the heads of student affairs, residential life, and academic affairs to meet with three to four student representatives. The goal of the meeting was to introduce the students and the newly established student group, DREAMERS, to key administrators on campus. Alejandro continued,

It was probably one of the most powerful meetings ever. Because the students told their own stories but also the stories of other students and talked about how they were treated as students here, how staff treated them, how some people made them feel like second- and third-class citizens, how people would out them and say "You're an illegal alien" in front of others, or how at the [student health center] they were required to show a driver's license when they don't have one and when nobody else was asked to do the same. (Interview, May 2, 2011)

Although this meeting took place seven years prior to my data collection, those who participated considered it a catalyst for campus administrators to start developing an awareness of and advocating for undocumented students. Faith, a longtime undocumented student activist who was present at the meeting, described it as a seminal point in the partnership between undocumented students and institutional allies:

We read a list of our needs out loud to them . . . that was the first meeting where administrators came into the picture officially. Because I'm sure there was administrative support before then but not an official proclamation of an alliance or something. (Interview, May 27, 2010)

For Faith, it was a turning point in which students were formally acknowledged by the institution. Julia, who oversaw the academic affairs division, also recalled her impression of that meeting with students:

Clearly, they had identified a series of issues that they felt needed to be addressed. So what we did was we went around the room and they kind of told their story. Which, to me, was just amazing because they really did have fascinating stories. And then they talked about some of the challenges. . . . They related to what they considered to be, in many ways, mistreatment and felt that if the campus understood that they were undocumented students and that if we could do some things that would make it easier for them, then at least they would have a slightly easier time. (Interview, May 5, 2011)

This initial meeting resonated with Julia because it was her first opportunity to learn about the challenges facing undocumented students.

At the time of my data collection, the working relationship between undocumented students and institutional allies had been ongoing for seven years. While it started modestly with students listing a number of challenges and needs to well-intentioned administrators, their partnership has evolved into a much more complex set of interactions due to the political, structural, and organizational challenges they have faced in their attempts to institutionalize support for such a controversial student population. In the years between the first meeting and the time of my data collection, both students and allies learned that issues of access and equity are difficult to achieve for a student population outside the law. To clarify the problems at hand, the following section provides a discussion of the challenges faced by undocumented students at SRU, from both student and ally perspectives.

Ally Network and Subculture Dynamic

In response to these legal and cultural constraints at SRU, supportive faculty members and administrators began to foster an ally subculture. According to Museus and Jayakumar (2012), institutional subcultures are "created and perpetuated by a group on campus" which has "distinct values, assumptions, and perspectives that guide behavior of its group members" in a manner that challenges monocultural norms (7). At SRU, the subculture consisted of fifty or so allies who formed a network of advocates through a collective concern about equitable outcomes for undocumented students. These allies, with varying levels of commitment, leveraged their professional roles and networks to create pockets of resources that could provide educational alternatives to validate student experiences and offer more meaningful participation. Whereas students displayed more overt forms of resistance through protest and rallies, allies used more subversive behaviors that "foster the impression of compliance, agreement, [and] deference" (Scott 1990, 90) when it came to their professional roles in public higher education.

Assembled in the network were faculty members from various disciplines and representatives of academic affairs, counseling, health services, community outreach, scholarships support, legal counsel, governmental relations, financial aid, career counseling, general administration, faith-based groups, and DREAMERS. Institutional allies gathered every two to three months to update the group on resources available to undocumented students through their respective department (such as meal coupons and book-lending programs) and to work collaboratively to address institutional challenges (such as restricted access to support services and funding). This seemingly hodgepodge group made up the official "unofficial" task force working for undocumented students at the university. Jane, a faculty member, described the composition and goals of this network:

> We've built this strong network of administrators and faculty and it's a handful who are advocates. Between a few latter faculty and administrators, there's a core group of us here on the campus who sort of see eye to eye about how we need to move an agenda forward around undocumented students. Whether we're teaching a class, or we're focusing on raising scholarship funds—it's making those links to key allies that we know can work together. (Interview, October 5, 2010)

A key function of this network was to foster a culture of inclusion, and to that end Jane and her colleagues developed several courses that centered on the narratives of undocumented immigrants. The network also allowed allies and undocumented students to become more visible to one another. The group dynamic allowed for increased communication among members, which led to more opportunities for collaboration and reduced redundancy in the services provided. While this space often mirrored the power dynamic between students, faculty, and administrators and although its segregation from official campus operations reinforced the marginality of the group, it nonetheless represented resistance.

Students from DREAMERS played a central role in the network. One ally described students as "the ones that are really leading this campaign and it's us trying to catch up with them." Students often used the space to urge allies to address institutional challenges experienced by members of DREAMERS and to garner ally support for events benefiting undocumented students and immigrant communities. This network became a task-oriented space where students could address a collective of campus professionals on a regular basis.

The collaboration between students and allies created a body of advocates that helped the issue gain momentum. The group used both top-down and bottom-up approaches. Samuel, an administrator, described the pieces that came together to foster activism:

> I think, you have people who had key positions in the university. In the academic side you have the vice provost. On the student affairs side you have the vice chancellor. . . . And you had the students who took ownership of their situation and that just created the right environment for activism. I think it first began as a support group to talk about our issues and then from there it has grown into this movement. (Interview, April 30, 2010)

The Institutional Response to DREAMERS

As a result of student activism working in partnership with institutional allies, SRU began to institutionalize programs for undocumented students. SRU assigned an advisor to offer guidance to undocumented students regarding educational strategies, financial opportunities, and tools to navigate the institution. Differing from previous efforts, these resources explicitly targeted undocumented students, and resources were more transparent and accessible on the campus website. There were conscious efforts to include undocumented students uninvolved in DREAMERS and to foster both academic and personal well-being for the entire student population. In addition to workshops on private scholarships, SRU also held programs on suicide prevention and stress management.

An example of institutional change at SRU that aimed to improve undocumented student experiences was the creation of the tuition payment plan. When allies overseeing student finances learned that students could not access campus resources if their tuition was not paid in full at the beginning of the term, that department began to explore ways to implement a tuition payment plan that would allow students to make three payments throughout the term, maintain good financial standing with SRU, and maintain full access to campus resources. Ellen, a student affairs administrator, discussed her rationale to put forth an installment plan:

> The university is trying to move to a differed payment plan, or installment plan. . . . Because of the fee hikes, we thought we needed to do something more immediate for undocumented students or students in general . . . with the hope that this option will be available to every student. (Interview, May 25, 2010)

In the pilot stages of the payment plan, individual administrators had to manually override the accounting system to test out the plan. It took several years before the institution formally developed a payment plan that was available to all students. In order to create buy-in for this overhaul of existing accounting infrastructure, institutional allies would emphasize that the resources developed for undocumented students would also benefit the campus as a whole. In this case, a program created to address the needs of undocumented students was promoted to the larger campus as a benefit for all students facing financial challenges. Paradoxically, the needs of undocumented students were rendered invisible in the process of institutionalizing resources that were most relevant to their experiences.

Because allies could not easily change financial aid policies, some began to fundraise with local community partners to award private scholarships to undocumented students attending SRU. Ellen, a student affairs administrator, explained the benefits of this partnership: "We are looking to community organizations that's not tied by all the rules and regulations that a state institution has to worry about." As nonprofit organizations, groups of community partners operated under a different set of laws and could give scholarships to undocumented students. A few allies took the extra step and established their own nonprofit organizations.

However, because many of these efforts remained camouflaged, certain allies felt compelled to support undocumented students in the "shadows" of SRU. According to Lena, an academic affairs administrator, there was a code between allies:

> I'll attempt to speak with other allies—and the conversations will end very quickly. It's kind of this eyewink, "I know you're an ally, you know I'm an ally but let's not talk about it because I get more done when nobody knows what I'm doing." (Interview, May 18, 2010)

She noted that the conversation "will end very quickly," suggesting that communication was limited and perhaps surreptitious, even among allies. Invitation into the network was based on referrals; allies would invite other allies to join. Through the network, they learned of each other's identities, but some remained relatively private about the details of their support for undocumented students. According to Lena, a formalized process at the institution may be less effective because it would require greater consensus from the institution. "Because public opinion is volatile, their decisions are sometimes deliberately made without publicity" (NFHEPG 2012, 5).

Another reason for the clandestine operation was uncertainty about institutional support. Samuel expressed his concern:

> I want to say it's so precarious this environment of support is always very precarious, always fragile. I'm always afraid that someone is going to pull the rug out from under us. The reason why it is the way it is, is

because of the people who are here. But that means it's not permanent. There's no permanency. And just right now, it is in many ways support-ive. It's not institutional at this point. I would say, in the sense that it is not embedded in the institution. It is embedded in the institution at this point because of the people who are there. But that could change. (Interview, April 30, 2010)

Samuel emphasized the fragility of a support system that was contingent upon individuals who "volunteered" to serve as allies—indicating that their work as allies was independent from their professional responsibilities. As a result, institutional allies were rarely rewarded for their efforts and they lacked accountability regarding their support to undocumented students. In this context, one student mockingly described these efforts as "side work" done out of the "kindness of their [allies'] hearts." This student's critique denotes the deficit thinking under which "heroic" allies "rescue" undocumented students who are disempowered by their status. Without more meaningful forms of inclusion, these random acts of kindness will continue to create unstable, undemocratic, and dehumanizing forms of sup-port, which reinforce the marginality of being undocumented.

CONCLUSION

The existing legal strictures require SRU officials to publicly comply with legal mandates, yet there was evidence to suggest that there was also room for institutional actors to cultivate a culture of resistance to exclu-sionary practices, thereby renegotiating a web of interlocking policies within the confines of an educational institution. This chapter calls for institutional actors to use greater discretion in creating a more inclusive environment for undocumented students in postsecondary education. The examples in this chapter offer some guidelines to consider in work-ing toward this goal.

First, this chapter calls upon institutional leaders to distinguish the various levels of governance, specifically to ascertain which institutional policies have been formed independently from government mandates. A narrow emphasis on legislation reform is overly reliant on long-drawn-out debate over immigrant rights and reduces the institution's accountability in serving its undocumented student population at the institutional level. In addition to questioning these assumptions, institu-tions can compensate for the time-consuming legislative reform process by responding to the immediate needs of local students. As evidenced in Bangura's chapter (this volume), a lack of understanding and flexibility among administrators can leave students isolated when they make cal-culated (albeit risky) decisions to challenge restrictive policies, expecta-tions, and legislation. As the administrators in this chapter demonstrate, collectively renegotiating these spaces, rather than questioning students' decisions, can be a more productive way to help young people access educational opportunities.

Second, because the educational experiences of undocumented students often mirror the needs of first-generation, working-class students of color (Perez 2009), programs developed to address their needs can often benefit the larger student body. However, the needs of undocumented students should not be rendered invisible in the process of institutionalizing resources that are most relevant to their experiences. Instead, counselors or others who advise students should be informed about resources that can greatly assist this population of students. For example, a tuition payment plan that allows students to pay tuition in installments can be particularly helpful to undocumented students who are systemically banned from financial aid, but it can also benefit all students with financial difficulties.

Third, building on Albrecht's (2007) study, I also conclude that there is a need for designated personnel to help students navigate the institution. However, I caution against tokenized initiatives that aim to pacify the protest of undocumented students. Designated personnel should be available to serve as a reference for students, and students should be able to consult all departments so that the campus can share the responsibility of fostering greater inclusion. This study shows that isolated efforts will overwhelm individuals or units and reinforce the marginalization of undocumented students.

Finally, institutional response needs to be proactive. To achieve democratic outcomes, practitioners and educators need to consider all marginalized experiences when developing a set of requirements for participation. As much as institutions reflect broader social agendas, colleges and universities play a reciprocal role in informing and shaping society. This reciprocal relationship allows postsecondary institutions to redefine the boundaries of citizenship so that they more actually reflect the shift from finite nation-state boundaries to more global standards.

One of the most important implications of this chapter is the need to recognize that undocumented immigrants—and, indeed, immigrants with a variety of citizenship statuses—must confront a series of policies both within and outside educational institutions that restrict their ability to access educational opportunities. As the other chapters in this section demonstrate, immigrant young people are adept at creatively confronting these and other restrictions, exerting their agency to reshape the boundaries established by restrictive policies. However, this chapter illustrates the potential for institutional allies to contribute to these struggles, resulting in greater potential for resistance and renegotiation through collective action. While students of all ages can, and do, remake their worlds, solidarity opens a realm of possibilities for creating space for the hopes, dreams, and futures of immigrant youth.

NOTES

1. Pseudonyms are used throughout the chapter.. Identifiers such as gender, major, and department may also be switched in the reporting of this data.
2. The DREAM Act is a bipartisan bill that would provide undocumented youths a path to citizenship on the condition that they entered the US before the age of sixteen, complete two years of college or serve in the US military, and maintain good moral character. However, due to its stringent requirements "roughly 38 percent of potential beneficiaries—825,000 people—would likely obtain permanent legal status through the DREAM Act's education and military routes while as many as 62 percent would likely fail to do so" (Batalova and McHugh 2010, 1). Thus, educational access is expected to greatly determine the efficacy of the DREAM Act in providing a realistic path to citizenship for undocumented youth.
3. California's AB 540 passed on October 12, 2001, under Governor Gray Davis. The bill allows undocumented students to qualify for in-state tuition in the state's public higher education institutions if they (1) attended a California high school for three or more academic years; (2) received a GED or an equivalent; (3) registered or are currently enrolled at an accredited public institution of higher education in California; and (4) filed an affidavit with the individual institutions stating that they have filed an application to legalize their immigration status or will file an application as soon as they are eligible to do so.
4. The central office of SRU issues an annual report on the enrollment figure of AB 540 recipients within the university system. To maintain the anonymity of the institution, the name of the report cannot be revealed.
5. Personal Responsibility and Work Opportunity Reconciliation Act of 1996 (PRWORA).
6. Illegal Immigration Reform and Immigrant Responsibility Act of 1996 (IIRIRA).

REFERENCES

Abrego, Leisy. 2006. "'I Can't Go to College because I Don't Have Papers': Incorporation Patterns of Undocumented of Latino Undocumented Youth." *Latino Studies* 4: 212–231.
Abrego, Leisy, and Roberto Gonzalez. 2010. "Blocked Paths, Uncertain Futures: The Postsecondary Education and Labor Market Prospects of Undocumented Latino Youth." *Journal of Education for Students Placed at Risk* 15 (1): 144–157.
Albrecht, Teri. 2007. "Challenges and Service Needs of Undocumented Mexican Undergraduate Students: Students' Voices and Administrators' Perspectives." PhD diss., University of Texas.
Bacon, David. 2008. *Illegal People: How Globalization Creates Migration and Criminalizes Immigrants.* Boston: Beacon Press.
Batalova, Jeanne, and Margie McHugh. 2010. *DREAM vs. Reality: An Analysis of Potential DREAM Act Beneficiaries.* Washington, DC: Migration Policy Institute.
Bennett, Brian. 2011."States Can't Opt Out of Secure Communities Program." *Los Angeles Times*, August 6.
Buenavista, Tracy, and Tam Tran. 2010. "Asian American Undocumented Immigrant Students." In *Encyclopedia of Contemporary Asian American Issues*,

edited by Edith Chen and Grace Yoo, 253–257. Westport, CT: Greenwood Press.

Drachman, Edward. 2006. "Access to Higher Education for Undocumented Students." *Peace Review* 18 (1): 91–100.

Eyler, Janet, and Dwight Giles. 1999. *Where's the Learning in Service-Learning?* San Francisco: Jossey-Bass Publishers.

Feranchak, Elizabeth. 2007. "An Analysis of the Attitudes of Higher Education Leaders in 18 High-Immigration States about the Appropriateness of Providing Education Benefits to Undocumented Immigrants." EdD diss., East Tennessee State University.

Fortuny, Karina, Randy Capps, and Jeffrey Passel. 2007. *The Characteristics of Unauthorized Immigrants in California, Los Angeles County, and the United States*. Washington, DC: The Urban Institute.

Freire, Paulo. 2002. *Pedagogy of the Oppressed*. 30th anniversary ed. New York: Continuum International Publishing Group Inc.

Giroux, Henry. 2001. *Theory and Resistance in Education: Towards a Pedagogy for the Opposition*. Westport, CT: Bergin & Garvey.

Harlan, Kosta. 2011. "8 Undocumented Youth Arrested in Georgia as Hundreds March to Protest Educational Ban." *Fight Back News*, April 7.

Hebel, Sara. 2010. "Georgia Regents Ban Illegal Immigrants from Selective Public Colleges." *Chronicle of Higher Education*, October 13.

Hjerm, Mikael. 2001. "Education, Xenophobia and Nationalism: A Comparative Analysis." *Journal of Ethnic and Migration Studies* 27 (1): 37–60.

Hoefer, Michael, Nancy Rytina, and Bryan Baker. 2009. *Estimates of the Unauthorized Immigrant Population Residing in the United States: January 2008*. Washington, DC: US Dept. of Homeland Security, Office of Immigration Statistics.

Illegal Immigration Reform and Immigrant Responsibility Act of 1996 (IIRIRA). 1996. Pub. L. No. 104–208, 110 Stat. 3009–660.

Lopez, Janet. 2010. *Undocumented Students and the Policies of Wasted Potential*. El Paso, TX: LFB Scholarly Pub.

Merriam, Sharan. 2009. *Qualitative Research: A Guide to Design and Implementation*. Hoboken, NJ: John Wiley & Sons, Inc.

Museus, Samuel, and Uma Jayakumar. 2012. *Creating Campus Cultures: Fostering Success among Racially Diverse Student Populations*. New York: Routledge.

National Forum on Higher Education for the Public Good (NFHEPG). 2012. *Reconciling Federal, State, and Institutional Policies Determining Educational Access for Undocumented Students: Implications for Professional Practice*. Ann Arbor, MI: NFHEPG.

Olivas, Michael. 2005. "Plyer v. Doe, the Education of Undocumented Children, and the Polity." In *Immigrant Stories 2005*, edited by David Martin and Peter Schuck, 197–220. New York: Foundation Press.

Olivérez, Paz. 2006. "Ready but Restricted: An Examination of the Challenges of College Access and Financial Aid for College-Ready Undocumented Students in the United States." PhD diss., University of Southern California.

Ong, Aihwa. 1999. *Flexible Citizenship: The Cultural Logics of Transnationality*. Durham, NC: Duke University Press Books.

Passel, Jeffrey. 2006. *Further Demographic Information Relating to the DREAM Act*. Washington, DC: The Urban Institute.

Passel, Jeffrey, and D'Vera Cohn. 2009. *A Portrait of Unauthorized Immigrants in the United States*. Washington, DC: Pew Hispanic Center.

Perez, William. 2009. *We Are Americans: Undocumented Students Pursuing the American Dream*. Sterling, VA: Stylus Publishing.

Perez, William, and Richard Cortes. 2011. *Undocumented Latino College Students: Their Socioemotional and Academic Experience*. El Paso, TX: LFB Scholarly Publishing.

Rincón, Alejandra. 2008. *Undocumented Immigrant and Higher Education: Sí Se Puede!* New York: LFB Scholarly Publishing. New Haven, CT: Yale University Press.

Scott, James. 1990. *Domination and the Arts of Resistance: Hidden Transcripts.*

US Department of Education, National Center for Education Statistics. 2009a. *Table 208, Recent High School Completers and Their Enrollment in College, by Sex: 1960 through 2009. Digest of Education Statistics.* Retrieved May 1, 2013. http://nces.ed.gov/programs/digest/d10/tables/dt10_208.asp

US Department of Education, National Center for Education Statistics. 2009b. *2007–08, National Postsecondary Student Aid Study (NPSAS:08) Student Financial Aid Estimates for 2007–08.* Washington, DC: US Department of Education, National Center for Education Statistics.

Vargas, Jose. 2012. "Shadow Americans." *Times Magazine*, June.

Contributors

Ramatu T. Bangura is program director of the Sauti Yetu Center for African Women, a community-based organization in New York City. She has dedicated her career to educational programming and direct advocacy in support of women and girls in vulnerable circumstances, including survivors of sexual violence, immigrant and refugee women, and youth involved in the commercial sex trade. Her dissertation, titled *In Pursuit of Success: The Educational Identities and Decision-Making of African Girls with Limited Formal Schooling*, utilized African feminism to examine how immigrant girls with limited formal schooling navigate American schools and make decisions about college and marriage. She coauthored an article in the November 2012 issue of *Global Studies Journal* entitled "(Re)Framing African Immigrant Women's Civic Leadership: A Case Study of the Role of Families, Schooling and Transnationalism." Dr. Bangura earned her EdD and EdM in international and transcultural studies from Teachers College, Columbia University.

Avary Carhill-Poza is assistant professor of applied linguistics at the University of Massachusetts, Boston. She is an emerging scholar who has conducted extensive interdisciplinary research examining the ways peer groups and classroom contexts shape language learning experiences and outcomes for language minority students in public schools. She has authored and coauthored several articles and chapters on the schooling experiences of immigrant youth and the sociocultural contexts of English language learning. Her current scholarship, based in New York City public high schools, focuses on the conditions that foster variable opportunities for adolescent English learners to engage their multilingual repertoires in learning academic English.

Qiongqiong Chen is a PhD candidate in the Department of Educational Leadership and Policy at the State University of New York at Buffalo. She received her master's degree in higher education from East China Normal University, China, and also studied in the higher education program in Nagoya University, Japan, as an exchange graduate student. Her research interests include international and comparative higher education, transnational academic mobility, and cultural studies of globalization. Her latest work explores the relations between academic mobility, transnational identities, and higher education internationalization in the context of China, with a focus on the Chinese knowledge diaspora and academic returnees.

Angela Chuan-Ru Chen is an Undocumented Student Program Coordinator and lecturer at University of California, Los Angeles. Her research interests include higher education policies and practices and immigrant student experiences.

Anita Chikkatur is assistant professor in the Department of Educational Studies at Carleton College, in Minnesota. Her research and teaching interests include student and teacher perspectives on race, gender, and sexuality and issues of diversity and difference in educational institutions. Her recent publications include "Difference Matters: Embodiment of and Discourse on Difference at an Urban Public High School," published in *Anthropology & Educational Quarterly* in 2012 and "The Influence of Researcher Identities in Ethnographies of Multiracial Schools," published in *International Journal of Qualitative Studies in Education* in 2012 and coauthored with Cheryl Jones-Walker.

Neriko Musha Doerr received a PhD in cultural anthropology from Cornell University. Her research interests include language and power, the politics of difference, and education in Japan, Aotearoa/New Zealand, and the US, as well as study abroad and alternative break abroad experiences. Her publications include *Meaningful Inconsistencies: Bicultural Nationhood, the Free Market, and Schooling in Aotearoa/New Zealand* (Berghahn Books) and, as an editor, *The Native Speaker Concept: Ethnographic Investigations of "Native Speaker Effects"* (Mouton de Gruyter) and *Heritage, Nationhood, and Language* (Routledge). She also coauthored *Constructing the Heritage Language Learner: Knowledge, Power, and New Subjectivities* with Kiri Lee (Mouton de Gruyter). Her articles have appeared in various journals, such as *Anthropology and Education Quarterly, Compare, Critical Asian Studies, Critical Discourse Studies, Critical Studies in Education, Ethnos, International Multilingual Research Journal, Language and Education, Journal of Language, Identity, and Education*, and *Learning, Media, and Technologies*. She currently teaches at Ramapo College in New Jersey.

Ronald Fuentes is assistant professor in the Department of English at the University of Memphis. His research interests include language policy in education, language ideology and socialization, and immigration and transnationalism. He is particularly interested in how different social,

political, familial, and educational decisions position individuals in multilingual and multicultural environments. He examines how these decisions affect individuals' language attitudes and practices and how these
decisions are shaped by immigration and transnationalism.

Omar Kamara received an MA from DePaul University and has been a high
school teacher of mathematics and physics since 1986, initially in Sierra
Leone and the Gambia; he was then recruited to teach in the US in the
program examined in his chapter. His master's thesis, the main source
of data for this chapter, examined the same program.

Jill Koyama is Assistant Professor in Educational Policy Studies and Practice at the University of Arizona. Her publications include her 2010
book, *Making Failure Pay: For-Profit Tutoring, High-Stakes Testing,
and Public Schools* and articles in Anthropology and Education Quarterly, British Journal of Sociology of Education, Journal of Education
Policy, and Educational Researcher.

Kiri Lee is associate professor of Japanese in the Department of Modern
Languages and Literatures, Lehigh University (Bethlehem, Pennsylvania).
She received her PhD in linguistics from Harvard University in 1993. Her
research areas are pragmatics and heritage language education. She is the
coauthor (with Neriko M. Doerr) of the book *Constructing the Heritage
Language Learner: Knowledge, Power, and New Subjectivities* (Mouton
de Gruyter, 2013), and a journal article, "'Drop-Outs' or 'Heritage Learners'? Competing Mentalities of Governmentality and Invested Meanings
at a Weekend Japanese Language School in the United States" (*Discourse:
Studies in the Cultural Politics of Education* 34, 2012). She also coauthored "Beyond 'Power and Solidarity'": Indexing Intimacy in Korean
and Japanese terms of address" with Young-mee Yu Cho (*Korean
Linguistics* 15, 2013).

Karen Monkman received a PhD from the University of Southern California and is professor at DePaul University. Her research focuses on issues
related to migration, transnationalism, and globalization in relation to
education, along with gender and education policy. She has led study
abroad programs with high school and graduate students to Guatemala
and Mexico, lived and taught in West Africa, and done research in various African countries. She was recently a visiting professor at Stellenbosch
University in South Africa.

Ana Luisa Muñoz-García is a PhD student at the State University of New
York at Buffalo, teaches history and geography, and holds a master's
in curriculum studies. Her areas of work are educational research and
practice in poverty areas in Chile. Various ethnographies of teacher
practices in these areas, conducted for UNICEF, shape her chapters in

the book *Escuelas Efectivas en Sectores de Pobreza: ¿Quién dijo que no se puede?* (Effective schools in marginal communities: Who says it can't be done?) and her coedited book *Good Practices for Effective Pedagogy: Guide of Support for Teachers and for Principals*, both published by UNICEF. Her most recent work engages studies of gender policies in higher education and the process of internationalization in the Chilean higher education system, investigating issues related to the process of knowledge construction in academia, such as curriculum reform and academic mobility.

Krystal A. Smalls is a PhD candidate in educational linguistics and Africana studies at the University of Pennsylvania. Her research examines processes of race-making among black youth in the US, Caribbean, and Africa, focusing on discursive and semiotic strategies young people deploy in attempts at forging viable selves and productive futures out of past and present tragedy. She has conducted ethnographic research on youth registers and race-making in and around Philadelphia; Monrovia, Liberia; Nairobi, Kenya; and the low country and sea islands of South Carolina. Some of her work on education and Gullah/Geechee personhood has appeared in *Language and Communication*.

Mathangi Subramanian is a writer, educator, and activist. A former Fulbright Scholar, her work has appeared in academic and mainstream publications including Gender and Education, Current Issues in Comparative Education, The Hindu Sunday Magazine, and the anthology *Click!: The Moment We Knew We Were Feminists*. Her book, *Bullying: The Ultimate Teen Guide*, will be published in 2014.

Susan Thomas received her PhD from the University of Pennsylvania in 2013 and is currently serving as an adjunct faculty member in New School's Education Studies program. She coauthored a chapter titled "In Whose Interest? A Cross-Case Analysis of Universities' Role in Gentrification" for the volume *Critical Race Theory Applied to Education Policy and Practice* (in press) and reviewed Vanessa Fong's *Paradise Redefined: Transnational Chinese Students and the Quest for Flexible Citizenship in the Developed World* for *Anthropology and Education Quarterly*. She is currently in the process of turning her dissertation into a book manuscript, an ethnography that further examines the lives of middle-class overseas students from South Asia studying in the US. Her areas of expertise include transnationalism, the neoliberalization of higher education, the South Asian diaspora, post-9/11 racialization, and the national security state.

Rebecca Torres is assistant professor in geography and the environment at the University of Texas at Austin. Her research interests include international and internal migration, US Latino communities, agricultural transformation, and rural and community development. She has worked in Mexico, Peru, Cuba, and the US South. She has collaborated with a rural North Carolina school system to establish the first rural dual language immersion program in the state, along with a related research agenda. Dr. Torres has received numerous grants for academic research, curriculum development, and community engagement from sources such as the National Science Foundation, the Z. Smith Reynolds Foundation, the Golden LEAF Foundation, and the University of Texas Harrington Faculty Fellows Program, among various others. She has published in a wide range of journals, including *Annals of the Association of American Geographers, Geoforum, Professional Geographer,* and *Transactions of the Institute of British Geographers.*

Melissa Wicks-Asbun is an adjunct instructor at Wayne Community College in Goldsboro, North Carolina. Her research interests are international migration and children's geographies. She was a Latin American Fellow at East Carolina University and continues to conduct research on foreign-born students in rural North Carolina. She became interested in immigrant youth and their educational aspirations ten years ago while working as an ESL instructor for incarcerated immigrant youth in a close-custody prison in western North Carolina. Her most recent publication appeared in *Professional Geographer.*

Index

For Product Safety Concerns and Information please contact our EU
representative GPSR@taylorandfrancis.com
Taylor & Francis Verlag GmbH, Kaufingerstraße 24, 80331 München, Germany

9 781138 286719